Global Shell Games

Shell companies that cannot be traced back to their real owners are crucial for enabling crimes like grand corruption, sanctions-busting, tax evasion, and the illegal trade in drugs and weapons. In investigating this shadowy, illicit world, *Global Shell Games* adopts a unique, experimental methodology based on posing as twenty-one different international consultants and making over 7,000 solicitations for prohibited untraceable shell companies from firms in more than 180 countries. Combining rigorous quantitative analysis, qualitative investigation of responses, and lurid news reports, this book makes a major contribution to research on compliance with key global rules, while also offering a novel approach to political science research. *Global Shell Games* is an invaluable resource for scholars of international relations, and a fascinating, accessible read for anyone interested in learning about worldwide criminal finance.

MICHAEL G. FINDLEY is Assistant Professor in the Department of Government at the University of Texas at Austin.

DANIEL L. NIELSON is Associate Professor in the Department of Political Science at Brigham Young University.

J. C. SHARMAN is Professor at the Centre for Governance and Public Policy at Griffith University.

CAMBRIDGE STUDIES IN INTERNATIONAL RELATIONS: 128

Global Shell Games

Cambridge Studies in International Relations is a joint initiative of Cambridge University Press and the British International Studies Association (BISA). The series will include a wide range of material, from undergraduate textbooks and surveys to research-based monographs and collaborative volumes. The aim of the series is to publish the best new scholarship in International Studies from Europe, North America and the rest of the world.

CAMBRIDGE STUDIES IN INTERNATIONAL RELATIONS

Series list continues after index

GLOBAL SHELL GAMES

Experiments in Transnational Relations, Crime, and Terrorism

MICHAEL G. FINDLEY
University of Texas at Austin

DANIEL L. NIELSON
Brigham Young University

J. C. SHARMAN
Griffith University

CAMBRIDGE
UNIVERSITY PRESS

CAMBRIDGE
UNIVERSITY PRESS

University Printing House, Cambridge CB2 8BS, United Kingdom

One Liberty Plaza, 20th Floor, New York, NY 10006, USA

477 Williamstown Road, Port Melbourne, VIC 3207, Australia

4843/24, 2nd Floor, Ansari Road, Daryaganj, Delhi - 110002, India

79 Anson Road, #06-04/06, Singapore 079906

Cambridge University Press is part of the University of Cambridge.

It furthers the University's mission by disseminating knowledge in the pursuit of education, learning and research at the highest international levels of excellence.

www.cambridge.org
Information on this title: www.cambridge.org/9781107638839

© Findley, Nielson & Sharman 2014

First published 2014

A catalogue record for this publication is available from the British Library

Library of Congress Cataloging in Publication data
Findley, Michael G., 1976–
Global shell games : experiments in transnational relations, crime, and terrorism / Michael G. Findley, University of Texas at Austin, Daniel L. Nielson, Brigham Young University, J. C. Sharman, Griffith University.
  pages   cm. – (Cambridge studies in international relations ; 128)
Includes bibliographical references and index.
ISBN 978-1-107-04314-5 (hardback) – ISBN 978-1-107-63883-9 (pbk.)
1. Transnational crime–History–21st century.   2. Terrorism–History–21st century.   3. International economic relations–History–21st century.   4. Political science–Research–Methodology.   5. International finance.   I. Title.
HV6252.F53   2013
364.1–dc23
2013029431

ISBN   978-1-107-63883-9   Paperback

Michael Findley: For Heather, and Andrea, David, Joshua, and Spencer
Daniel Nielson: For Jenn, Catie, Abi, and Rob
J.C. Sharman: To my family and Bilyana

Contents

Figures

Tables

Preface

A critic of the scientific approach to international relations might wonder how much "knowledge" has accumulated in half a century. In the pages of *World Politics* in 1966, Morton Kaplan defended the scientific method as the best means of studying international relations. Taking issue with E. H. Carr's assault on science in *The Twenty Years' Crisis*, Kaplan noted that the "traditionalist asserts that those who aspire to a 'science' of politics insist upon precision, rigor, quantification, and general theory. The traditionalist further claims that the complexity of international politics is such that these goals cannot be attained nor the important questions of international politics be investigated by these means" (Kaplan 1966: 7). Our sense is that this basic debate still seethes today with little resolution. This book is an attempt to move the discussion forward.

Advocates of science as a means to understanding international politics face at least two significant challenges. First, transnational relations is, in effect, infinitely complex – many millions of individuals, firms, organizations, and agencies from different countries and international organizations interact daily. Second, progress in the science of international relations requires the identification of causal effects, and observational scientific methods can only suggest correlations. The target is thus much too big, the instrument much too limited. In this book we argue that the first problem contains the answer to the second: the sheer number of transnational actors can serve as subjects in field experiments capable of revealing causal effects in international relations. The vastness of transnational interactions thus offers the means for precisely testing important theories of international relations.

We hope the book will be pathbreaking in several respects. First, it offers the most systematic and detailed evidence to date on the availability of anonymous shell corporations globally. We draw a detailed map of cross-national transparency in company formation practices derived from more than 7,400 contacts made to roughly 3,800 corporate service providers (CSPs) in 181 countries. Because the data are based on realistic requests for assistance with incorporation, they provide information gleaned from the relevant units of analysis behaving in their normal day-to-day routines. The data in this book therefore provide the most accurate picture of the issue area available.

Further, as far as we can learn, this is the first field experiment conducted on a global scale, where subjects reside in almost every country, treatment conditions involve more than a score of national jurisdictions, and the salience of international law is explicitly tested in a way that can reveal causal effects. It is also the first of what we hope will be many studies that fit what we call the experimental science of transnational relations, or Experimental TR. This broader research program probes the effects of international factors on the behavior of individuals, firms, and organizations. As noted above, these units of analysis exist in relatively large numbers, they can be practically and ethically assigned randomly to conditions, and outcomes of interest for them can be effectively measured – all of which makes them ideal as research subjects in field experiments. Experimental TR thus holds out the promise of a science of international relations research based on precise estimates of causal effects.

It is also the first published political science study of which we are aware to register the experimental research design prior to collecting the data and performing the data analysis. Registration of the research design pre-commits authors to follow through on precisely the planned experiment without massaging of the data analysis after the data are collected. We registered the planned experiment before we began collecting data, and the details of the registration procedure we followed can be found in the Chapter 2 Appendix at the end of the book.

As with any book-length endeavor, many more people contributed to the project than just the authors. We wonder if this has ever been more the case than for this study. First, our colleague Shima Baradaran was involved in the discussions of the research design and gave helpful direction especially where the study intersected her specializations in international and criminal law. With Shima as lead author we prepared two law review articles based on the research for the legal audience (Baradaran et al. 2013, 2014). Many scholars saw various presentations of the experiment and results, asked probing questions, and offered helpful suggestions. We therefore express gratitude to the Yale, Columbia, Cornell, George Washington, Northwestern, Vanderbilt,

William & Mary, Adelaide, Griffith, Miami, Wisconsin, and BYU law and political science faculties. We also thank the Experiments in Governance and Politics Network, the Asian Development Bank, and the Norwegian Institute of International Affairs for their feedback.

Individuals in private practice and at several governmental institutions, non-governmental organizations, and international organizations sat for interviews and otherwise offered guidance, including personnel at the US Department of Justice, the Internal Revenue Service, the Financial Action Task Force (FATF), the World Bank, the International Monetary Fund (IMF), the US Senate Permanent Subcommittee on Investigations, and the United Nations Office on Drugs and Crime for their assistance in this project. Their perspectives on the issue area proved especially helpful. In particular, we are grateful to individuals from the private sector including Richard Hay, Bruce Zagaris, Ross Delston, Steve Flynn, David Spencer, David Harvey, Nigel Bristow, Glenn Cherepovich, and the Society for Trust and Estate Practitioners. From Global Witness we thank Robert Palmer, Anthea Lawson, and Rosie Sharpe. And from the World Bank we are especially grateful to Emile van der Does de Willebois, Rick Messick, and Larissa Gray.

Many scholars read and commented on various iterations of the research design and its manuscript incarnations. We express heartfelt gratitude to Karen Alter, Anne Cameron, Scott Cooper, Paul Diehl, Peter Gourevitch, Josh Gubler, Don Green, Guy Grossman, Darren Hawkins, Macartan Humphreys, Susan Hyde, Wade Jacoby, Chris Karpowitz, Robert Keohane, Daniel Kono, Jim Kuklinski, Ashley Leeds, Helen Milner, Quin Monson, Bob Pahre, Kelly Patterson, Jeremy Pope, Jessica Preece, Ernesto Reuben, Stephanie Rickard, Toby Rider, Jay Seawright, Joel Selway, Mike Tierney, Dustin Tingley, Mike Tomz, Jeremy Weinstein, Nick Wheeler, and Scott Wolford for providing very helpful comments. Our unhelpful critics remain nameless, but they are almost certainly responsible for all of the flaws in the book. Lamentably, their identities are hidden by anonymous shell universities.

A virtual army of talented research assistants did much of the hard work involved in the book by compiling the subject pool, contacting corporate service providers, and coding responses. We therefore thank Allyson Adams, Jessica Allred, Lauren Barden, Peter Carroll, Drew Chapman, Zach Christensen, Stephanie Dowdle, Madeleine Gleave, Dano Gunderson, Matt Hadley, Ben Haymond, Dustin Homer, James

Juchau, Diana Kunakaeva, Brock Laney, Rob Morello, Catie Nielson, Henry Pascoe, Brian Reed, Wayne Sandholtz, Tara Simmons, Megan Spencer, Deborah Sutton, Brittany Thorley, Dane Thorley, and Danny Walker for remarkable research assistance. We offer special thanks to Dustin Homer and Brock Laney for so ably leading the data collection.

Finally, we are grateful for funding provided by the Australian Research Council grants DP0771521 and DP0986608 and the Norwegian Research Council "Systems of Tax Evasion and Laundering" grant. Also generous in their financial support were the Department of Political Science; the College of Family, Home, and Social Sciences; and the David M. Kennedy Center for International Studies at Brigham Young University. Richard and Judy Finch have been especially generous supporters of the Political Economy and Development Lab at BYU both financially and by way of moral support and intellectual engagement. We could not ask for more gracious and helpful benefactors. Replication data are available at http://michael-findley.com.

1 | *Introduction*

The notorious Lu Zhang

In December 2009 Thai special forces seized a cargo plane at Bangkok Airport. The manifest claimed the airplane carried drilling equipment intended for oil exploration. Instead, 35 tons of weapons crammed the hold – arms that included rocket launchers and anti-aircraft missiles. The weapons originated in North Korea and were bound for Iran, mocking the United Nations arms embargo that targeted two of the three "Axes of Evil" (Michaels and Coker 2009).

Law enforcement officials traced the arms shipment to an obscure Chinese national, Lu Zhang, who was a recent immigrant to New Zealand. The 28-year-old woman served as the sole director of SP Trading, the company that hired the plane and apparently engineered this arms trade. In fact, Lu directed scores of other companies.

But, apparently, Lu Zhang had no idea that she was a notorious arms trader and international financial criminal until officials contacted her. Rather, she had worked as a short-order cook at a Burger King in Auckland. Representatives of the GT Group, a shady incorporation service specializing in setting up companies for others, had hired Lu as a patsy. To supplement her income, for fifteen dollars each she signed the documents they placed in front of her.

The genius of the scheme meant that any corporations set up by the GT Group could not be traced beyond Lu Zhang. New Zealand law requires that only a single "nominee" director of a company be named; the actual owners can remain completely anonymous. To this day the perpetrators of the North-Korea-to-Iran arms deal remain unknown and at large, their identities protected by the anonymous shell corporation set up by the GT Group. (We will return to the GT Group in Chapter 2 since it is associated with a series of other criminal schemes enabled by shell companies.)

A New Zealand court convicted Lu Zhang of 74 counts of giving a false address but quickly discharged her from custody when it was clear she had no knowledge of any other crimes. Astoundingly, the rest of the GT Group's actions were perfectly legal according to New Zealand law (Francis 2010; Field 2011; Ryle 2011). Despite the fact that the GT Group also formed shell companies used to launder money for the Mexican Sinaloa drug cartels, and others employed to perpetrate a $230 million tax fraud against the Russian government, the firm remains in business today under a different name (Preasca et al. 2012).

It is not supposed to work this way. Indeed, international organizations and the governments of the world have jointly propagated a list of rules intended to prevent money laundering, terrorist financing, and other financial crimes like those linked to the GT Group's shell companies and to thousands of other untraceable anonymous corporations around the world. Governments have also empowered an international institution, the Financial Action Task Force (FATF), to implement the standards. Nearly every country in the world has agreed to abide by the FATF rules.

The FATF aggressively exposes and blacklists countries that fail to incorporate its international standards into domestic law. First published in 2000, the inaugural blacklist mostly targeted tax havens such as the Bahamas, the Cayman Islands, Liechtenstein, and Panama, but later targets included Israel, the Philippines, and Russia – signaling that states with significant resources could also come under censure. Governments worked hard to remove themselves from the blacklist and, tellingly, by 2007 no countries remained listed by the FATF as having failed to commit to the transparency standards. By conventional international relations (IR) measures, the case would be mostly closed: a global problem was identified, an international institution was empowered to enforce new standards, and countries relatively quickly came into statutory compliance with the rules. Problem largely solved.

Compliance, experiments, and transnational relations

Or is it? It turns out that governments are not the main locus of compliance with international financial transparency standards. Rather, firms such as the GT Group, which provide incorporation services for clients seeking to set up new businesses, are the primary points where international standards mandating that shell companies can be traced back to their real owners are either followed or violated. Is GT Group the rule or the exception? What makes some of those selling shell companies abide by rules while others routinely defy them?

This book is based on an experiment soliciting offers for prohibited untraceable or anonymous shell corporations. Our research team posed as a variety of low- and high-risk customers, including would-be money launderers, corrupt officials, and terrorist financiers when requesting the anonymous companies. We made more than 7,400 email solicitations to nearly 3,800 corporate service providers (CSPs) that make and sell shell companies in 181 countries. The design of the experiment allows us to test whether international rules are actually effective when they mandate that CSPs must collect identity documents from their customers. Furthermore, the random assignment of different email approaches also provides unique insight into what causes those who sell shell companies to either comply with or violate international rules.

The significance of this issue is that shell companies that cannot be traced back to their real owners are widely held to be one of the most common means for laundering money, giving and receiving bribes, busting sanctions, evading taxes, and financing terrorism. Yet until now, no one has known the effectiveness of the requirements that authorities be able to look through the "corporate veil" to find the real individuals in control of shell companies. Our study goes a long way to remedying this fundamental ignorance. By identifying the serious weaknesses in the existing regime in this book and related work we hope to provoke governments to much greater efforts in enforcing corporate transparency (Baradaran et al. 2013, 2014; Findley et al. 2013).

In focusing on transnational actors, private firms, as the key locus of compliance, our results show that such actors routinely flout international standards, even while fully aware of the standards that should apply. Half of all responses to the thousands of inquiries described in this book failed to demand certified photo identification. And half of those required no photo identification at all. Untraceable shell companies like SP Trading are thus relatively easy to acquire in today's global economy.

Shell companies per se are usually legitimate devices in business practice, acting as holding companies, providing limited liability, and serving as neutral vehicles for joint ventures. But there are few if any legitimate business purposes employing *anonymous* shell companies. If organized crime depends on financial secrecy, untraceable shell companies are the most important means of providing it. Anonymous shells highlight the central challenges of global governance according to which governments struggle to manage burgeoning transnational interactions.

Many other questions involving international standards and practices share the same logic as the issue of financial transparency that is central to this book. Firms play key roles in trade agreements when they choose to dump products in competitors' markets overseas. Banks, brokerages, and private individuals invest and divest in response to exchange-rate pacts, or, alternatively, aggregated financial behavior by a plethora of actors provokes international monetary coordination. Private individuals and companies are the actors that decide whether or not to pollute the environment, destroy biodiversity, or poach endangered species in violation of international environmental conventions. And individual police officers, military personnel, and prison wardens choose to respect or violate the personal integrity of their prisoners and therefore comply or not with international human rights accords.

Examining inter-governmental actions in such cases illuminates only parts of the picture. And they may not be the most interesting or important parts. Uncovering actual patterns of behavior in each of these and many other vital areas requires a different focus, a new framework, and a better method. We take steps toward providing all three here in the Introduction, and in the remainder of the book we demonstrate the potential of this new approach through our global shell company experiment, the first of its kind in international relations.

We call our approach the experimental science of transnational relations (Experimental TR, hereafter).[1] Experimental TR has three main components: an empirical focus on non-state actors as the locus of behavior, a conceptual reorientation around transnational relations far less dependent on states, and a methodological commitment to field experimental methods.

First, this book calls for an empirical refocusing of international relations scholarship in a manner that would shine new light on

---

[1] We thank Robert Keohane for suggesting this label.

understudied, interesting, and vital areas of world politics. We urge a focus on the subjects that carry out most of the international activity in the world. In this study we target the actual locus of transnational action in our issue area: firm-by-firm compliance with international corporate transparency standards.

Second, we develop a conceptual approach that complements traditional international relations scholarship. We situate this study in a broader framework that encompasses all transnational activity including but also extending well beyond state-to-state relations. While states mediate many important international interactions, the vast majority of transnational activities occur at most within the shadow of government control. And many of those activities prove very important for world affairs, especially in the aggregate.

Third, we demonstrate how the most powerful method in science can be brought to bear on important questions that this new focus and framework provoke. We do this by executing the first randomized field experiment on a global scale. Field experiments provide for the accurate diagnosis of causal relationships (high internal validity), but also allow us to generalize to similar phenomena outside the particular study (high external validity). Just as the random assignment to control (placebo) and treatment groups in drug trials isolates the effect of a new medicine, so too the random assignment of low-risk "Placebo" emails and different high-risk "treatment" emails isolated the effects of different kinds of risk on the likelihood of (a) being offered a shell company and (b) being required to provide proof of identity. In expectation, randomization balances not only all of the observable factors that might confound results, but also neutralizes all unobservable confounds. The power of the method enables precise tests of the observable implications of many international relations theories. In particular, experiments allow for the resolution of an impasse that has stymied progress on one of the biggest questions in international relations scholarship: when and why actors comply with international rules.

In this book we are speaking to two broad audiences. First, we address international relations scholars interested in transnational relations, international law, and the potential of experiments to reveal causal effects in related issue areas. Second, we provide rich data for policy-makers and practitioners about the availability of anonymous shell corporations throughout the world and the factors that make their acquisition more or less difficult. Both audiences will benefit from the significant synergy among these topics, but IR scholars may especially gain from the remainder of this chapter along with close examination of Chapter 5 on laws and standards, Chapter 6 on penalties and norms, and Chapter 7 on ways forward for Experimental TR. Policy-makers and practitioners may wish to pay special attention to Chapter 2 providing background on financial transparency, Chapter 3 on descriptive patterns of global practice in the availability of anonymous shells, and Chapter 4 reporting the results of the Terrorism, Corruption, and Premium treatments, as well as Chapter 5 on laws and standards. Nevertheless, both audiences will likely benefit from understanding the context of international relations scholarship that motivated the study, which we describe in the remainder of this chapter.

The foundation of IR is that international politics occurs in an anarchical environment where there is no central enforcer, and thus compliance with international rules presents particular challenges. Despite this, many scholars of international law have observed that most states act in a manner consistent with most laws most of the time (Henkin 1979; Chayes and Chayes 1993). Yet this observation tells us relatively little about whether international rules actually cause compliance, with compliance understood as when "the actual behavior of a given subject conforms to prescribed behavior," as opposed to non-compliance, "when actual behavior departs significantly from prescribed behavior" (Young 1979).

Compliance with international standards might be high precisely because states agreed to those standards where compliance proves easiest (Raustiala and Slaughter 2002; Drezner 2007). If this is so, self-selection – and not the inherent constraining power of international law – explains compliance. Indeed, an authoritative review has noted, "Almost all studies of the influence of treaties on state behaviour encounter serious issues of endogeneity and selection" (Simmons 2010: 273), meaning that cause and effect cannot be disentangled. It is hard to see a way to resolve this problem using only observational data. Von Stein (2005: 612) laments the inability to use experiments to tease out causal effects in international relations. The implication: if only they could be employed, field experiments could break this impasse. In this book we argue that Experimental TR offers a way forward.

The shell game experiment

This study therefore provides a detailed illustration of Experimental TR. In it we focus on actors that undertake important transnational behavior by forming corporations for foreign customers. Corporate service providers comply with international rules when they demand notarized identification documents from their clients. Failure to require certified ID enables the formation of untraceable, anonymous shell corporations, which can be used for tax evasion, sanctions-busting, money laundering, terrorist financing, and many other criminal activities. Our central question probes the degree to which firms around the world are in compliance with international corporate transparency standards and, by extension, the degree to which the states that approve international standards effectively monitor and encourage compliance with the standards.

We are especially interested in whether different information in our various email "treatments" can increase or decrease the rate at which those selling shell companies require the identity documents that international rules mandate (the compliance rate). With university and Institutional Review Board clearance, we adopted alias identities and sent 7,456 emails in two to three rounds to 3,771 firms in 181 countries. All of the emails requested confidential incorporation, but we randomly assigned different conditions to learn if the target firms would exercise more or less vigilance when (1) informed specifically about international law, (2) warned about enforcement by a domestic government agency, (3) told about possible legal penalties, (4) prompted to behave appropriately, (5) offered a premium payment, (6) apprised of a voluntary private certification body and its standards, or (7) informed of standards jointly promoted by both the private body and an international organization.

We also assessed firms' sensitivity to changes in the identity of the requester, including (8) a United States citizen, (9) a citizen of a corruption-prone country working in government procurement, and (10) a citizen of a country associated with terrorism and claiming to work in Saudi Arabia for Islamic charities. We compare all of these experimental conditions to a "Placebo" condition where the requester claims to originate from a minor-power, low-corruption wealthy country.

The basic descriptive results contradict the conventional wisdom in international relations and policy circles. Firms in tax haven countries proved significantly more compliant with international law compared to both wealthy and developing countries. Services in poor countries sometimes followed international standards with significantly more diligence than rich countries. Overall, firms in wealthy countries were the least inclined to comply with international standards.

With the experiments we learned that prompting firms with information about international law had no significant effects on the compliance rate, but attributing the rules to a private standards body marginally increased compliance compared to the public standards. Associating the rules with the Internal Revenue Service (IRS) in the United States significantly decreased non-compliance, which is one of the few encouraging experimental results we encountered. Posing as a US citizen caused a significant decrease in compliance rates compared to the Placebo. Promising a premium payment also decreased compliance. Additionally, invoking norms of appropriateness caused lower compliance in a few analyses, though not robustly. And mentioning legal penalties decreased refusal rates and, in some specifications, compliance rates as well.

In the Corruption condition response rates fell but, against expectations, *so did compliance rates*. We suspect a collusion effect: firms inclined to comply drop out when the risk increases, but non-compliant services appear undeterred – and may even be encouraged – by corrupt customers. Finally, the Terrorism condition caused a decrease both in response rates and in non-compliance – a second encouraging result. But the Terrorism condition also caused a decrease in part-compliance, compliance and (in the US) refusal rates, which tempers our optimism.

In the chapters that follow we develop each of these results more fully and draw lessons about compliance in international relations. First, however, we now introduce the three components of Experimental TR – locus of behavior, transnational relations, and field experimental methods – by using illustrations drawn from the recent history of anonymous shell corporations. With its focus on international financial transparency, the study provides an extended example of how to undertake Experimental TR and the results it can produce.

Locus of behavior: firm compliance and the challenge of heterogeneity

A tiny home in sleepy Cheyenne, Wyoming, houses 2,000 companies. Mailboxes crowd the main room from floor to ceiling – and each box is the formal residence of a shell corporation. Shell companies do not employ workers, sell products, or conduct any other substantive business. But because corporations are "legal persons," they can shield owners from legal liability and hide identities while enabling people to move millions – or even billions – of dollars around the world in ways that are impossible to trace. The corporate service provider Wyoming Corporate Services Inc. (WCSI) excels at protecting its clients. And many of its customers are particularly unsavory. Transactions and assets can be traced back to shell companies established by this firm, but not to the real person in control.

A Reuters News Service special report by Kelly Carr and Brian Grow detailed some of the activities of shell companies formed by Wyoming Corporate Services Inc. (at the time of writing, more than two years after the Reuters report, Wyoming Corporate Services Inc. is still in business selling shell companies). One company shields earnings from illegal internet poker businesses. Another sold fake truck parts to the Pentagon. Others hawked controlled pharmaceuticals illegally and routed earnings from unlawful sub-prime credit cards. Still others have been sued for unpaid taxes, securities fraud, and trademark infringement. One company apparently shelters the still-considerable real estate assets of Pavlo Lazarenko, the former Prime Minister of Ukraine now serving an eight-year US federal prison term in California for wire fraud, extortion, and money laundering. Transparency International named Lazarenko the eighth most corrupt politician in the world.

WCSI's website touted the allure of shell companies and distilled the essence of the problem of shell company misuse: "A corporation is a legal person created by state statute that can be used as a fall guy, a servant, a good friend or a decoy. A person you control ... yet cannot be held accountable for its actions. Imagine the possibilities!" (Carr and Grow 2011). Of course, as the many nocuous activities of Wyoming Corporate Services Inc. shell companies illustrate, financial criminals have vivid imaginations. It is precisely these sorts of dangers that global corporate transparency standards are designed to prevent.

When analysts want to know about compliance with corporate transparency standards, they turn to the Financial Action Task Force, which issues comprehensive evaluation reports assessing its member states. Among other matters, the reports detail the degree to which the governments have issued national laws regulating incorporation services and business law firms as they form new companies for clients. But as we detail in Chapter 3, the official FATF reports on government-level statutory compliance with global standards correlate weakly with the actual incorporation behavior of the thousands of firms in our experiments (see also Baradaran et al. 2013). We suspect that this pattern extends well beyond the issue area of international financial transparency: governments may do one thing, but individuals and organizations are often likely to be doing something quite different.

The challenge for many areas of international relations is that states do not perform most of the actions central to compliance with international standards. Individuals, firms, and non-governmental organizations (NGOs) do. Yet international relations scholars interested in the effects of international regulations typically fail to investigate non-state actors. State-level statutory compliance is not unimportant, of course; indeed it is likely an important step towards achieving compliance by those targeted individuals and organizations. But a focus on states alone misses the most important part of the compliance story.

Of course, we are far from the first analysts to note that the locus of much international behavior occurs beneath and beyond the level of national governments (see Nye and Keohane 1971; Keohane and Nye 1972). Important contributions from realists, liberal institutionalists, and constructivists have all underscored the key roles that individual citizens and private organizations play in international affairs, particularly in relation to compliance (e.g. Keohane et al. 1993: 16; Drezner 2007: 13; Avant et al. 2010: 15; Simmons 2010: 273). Indeed, in their seminal work on compliance, Downs et al. (1996) highlight maritime regimes, where the maintenance of oil tankers features prominently. As important as oil tankers are in maritime regimes, however, their maintenance clearly falls outside the everyday actions of governments.

The transnational relations literature extends well beyond the realm of compliance with international law. Constructivists have argued that "norm entrepreneurs" have shifted the global environmental and human rights agendas (Risse-Kappen 1995; Keck and Sikkink 1998; Sikkink 2011). Neoliberal institutionalists have investigated the roles of multinational corporations in driving trade accords and foreign investment (Milner 1988; Jensen 2003), and they have also studied the effects of private standards-setting bodies on corporate behavior (Mattli and Büthe 2003, 2011; Mosley 2009). These important scholars all agree that non-state actors matter in international relations.

That said, we readily acknowledge that international laws, standards, and norms create the authoritative context in which all of these non-state actors act, even if this authority is flouted. Governments can heighten the relevance of international rules when they instantiate international agreements into domestic laws and apply them rigorously. We merely emphasize here that research should attempt to learn about actual transnational behavior, rather than just state agreements or formal law, by studying the agents who perform most of the relevant actions.

What is more, attention to the number of individuals and organizations acting internationally requires sensitivity to the heterogeneity among non-state actors, which contrasts with the received wisdom in rational choice scholarship treating preferences of actors as uniform (see Mayhew 1974; Waltz 1979). Specifically, individuals and organizations may differ widely in their tolerance to risk (see Kahneman and Tversky 1979; Slovic 1987).

This may be especially true of the incorporation services we contacted, a diverse collection of individual freelancers, specialized company formation outfits, and law and accounting firms spread across 181 countries. As in most large populations, various actors will likely weigh these risks differently, resulting in heterogeneity in risk tolerance among incorporation services. Similarly, different service providers may adhere more or less strongly to a particular norm, or perhaps different providers subscribe to different norms (Elster 1989: 133–134). In contrast to international law scholars who see global standards as being able to constrain actors generally (see Henkin 1979; Chayes and Chayes 1993; Simmons 2000), we expect that some actors will prove sensitive to the laws while others will ignore the rules in pursuit of financial gain.

Transnational relations

The case of Viktor Bout illustrates this point. Referred to as "The Merchant of Death," the former Soviet military officer darted about the globe for decades, selling weapons to anyone willing to pay. He violated UN arms embargoes to supply combatants in the brutal civil wars in Angola, Liberia, Sierra Leone, and the Congo in the 1990s, and he very likely delivered weapons to the Taliban and al-Qaeda in Afghanistan before 2001. In November 2011 Bout was convicted in a Manhattan US Federal Court of attempting to sell anti-aircraft missiles to terrorists. His exploits seem like fodder for a Hollywood action movie, and indeed the 2005 Nicolas Cage film *Lord of War* was allegedly based on his life.

A 2009 grand jury indictment clarifies that Bout financed his arms empire through an elaborate network of US and foreign anonymous shell corporations with names such as "RP Aviation Inc.," "Insured Aircraft Title Services," and "Aviation Aventura LLC"(United States District Court Southern District of New York 2009). The indictment indicates that his shell companies and bank accounts were created in places like Tajikistan, Kazakhstan, and Cyprus, but he also held others based in Germany, Florida, and New York. Without the anonymous shell companies, it is hard to imagine a criminal enterprise like Bout's succeeding for so long. His story illustrates just how transnational the convoluted world of anonymous incorporation has become. Bout managed to turn violence into wealth through surreptitious border crossings and transnational financial transactions shielded by the anonymous shells.

Numerous recent examples demonstrate the importance of non-state actors in transnational relations more generally. Non-state actors often provoke intergovernmental behavior in the first place. From 2010, for example, the economic fortunes of several European countries hinged on the collective judgment of international bond buyers regarding the countries' ability to tackle fiscal deficits and public debt. In response, the European Union and International Monetary Fund were forced to extend massive rescue packages to Greece, Ireland, and Portugal. Relatedly, during the 2008–2011 "Great Recession," the prospects for reviving global economic demand depended on the individual choices of millions of households in the United States and elsewhere. Would the moral stigma of dishonoring mortgage debt prove more acceptable than the cost of continuing to make payments on "underwater" properties?

The 2006–2010 China–US trade war began when Chinese tire companies undercut US manufacturers; the successive anti-dumping and countervailing actions spiraled to encompass US poultry, Chinese steel pipes, and US polymers and provoked a ruling from the World Trade Organization. Likewise, in the 2000s activists including members of Amnesty International and the Genocide Intervention Network sent tens of thousands of letters to members of the US Congress and to parliamentarians throughout Europe urging sanctions on Sudan to halt genocide in the country's Darfur region. The crusade culminated in national laws aimed at stopping the genocide and in related sanctions by the United Nations and the African Union, as well as the indictment of Sudanese leader Omar al-Bashir by the International Criminal Court for genocide in 2010.

Finally, in the most important international event since the end of the Cold War, in 2001 a set of particularly ruthless transnational activists illicitly financed a scheme to hijack passenger airliners and crash them into the Pentagon and the World Trade Center. Not only did nearly 3,000 people die in the attacks, the terrorist actions also provoked costly wars in Afghanistan and Iraq. Non-state actors clearly matter for international relations.

Likewise, problems with anonymous shells and related violations of financial transparency standards have caused governments to come together repeatedly to take action aimed at thwarting money laundering and terrorist financing. Beyond the creation of the Financial Action Task Force, whose standards are central to this book, governments also negotiated and enacted the United Nations Convention Against Illicit Traffic in Narcotic Drugs and Psychotropic Substances in 1988, the International Convention for the Suppression of the Financing of Terrorism in 1999, the United Nations Convention Against Transnational Organized Crime (the Palermo Convention) in 2000, and the United Nations Convention Against Corruption in 2003.

The causal sequence from the individual to the international also works in reverse. International laws, standards, and norms affect the ways people travel (International Civil Aviation Organization), talk on their phones and listen to the radio (International Telecommunication Union), and even check the weather (World Meteorological Organization). More fundamentally even, international agreements and their organizations also condition what we buy (World Trade Organization), what we eat (Food and Agriculture Organization), how we work (International Labour Organization), how healthy we are (World Health Organization), how confident we are in our investments (Bank for International Settlements, International Organization of Securities Commissions), and how secure we feel (Interpol, NATO, and countless other security agreements and alliances). Experimental TR provides a way to learn the precise real-world effects of each of these international regimes by focusing on the day-to-day behavior of individuals, firms, and NGOs.

We assert that too little is known about these effects of international agreements on citizens, firms, and NGOs. And critically, we perhaps grasp even less about how such transnational relations at the lower level of non-state actors, when aggregated, eventually impact intergovernmental affairs in the main. A major shift in IR scholars' attention to the actual locus of behavior is therefore overdue.

These examples raise the question of just how important governments are in a borderless world made small by transportation and communications technologies and where anonymous shell companies can move huge amounts of money without official notice. This problem raises disconcerting questions for conventional international relations theory.

Two seminal works of IR have perhaps distracted scholars from pursuing fully the implications of non-state actors in transnational relations. First, Kenneth Waltz's levels of analysis categorized IR into system, state, and individual strata with the state critically interposed between the system and the individual (1959, 1979). Second, Robert Putnam's Two-Level Games heightened the state's intermediary role by depicting a leader representing the state interceding between her international counterparts and her domestic constituents (1988). Both contributions were more frameworks than theories, and Putnam explicitly calls his idea a "metaphor." But both works nevertheless helped to calcify the idea that the government is the dominant gatekeeper of the international.

It appears that the influence of these seminal works countered a move toward a full examination of transnational relations that was initiated by Robert Keohane and Joseph Nye (Nye and Keohane 1971; Keohane and Nye 1972). The refreshing insights offered by the idea of transnational relations perhaps appeared too complicated in a field trying desperately to simplify theoretically an infinitely complex world. Yet the authors themselves underscore the dangers of a state-centric framework: "Knowing the policies and capabilities of a set of governments may not allow us accurately to predict outcomes or future characteristics of the system if significant transnational interactions or powerful transnational organizations are involved" (Nye and Keohane 1971: 345).

Yet in the decades following Keohane and Nye's insights, even when IR analysts focus explicitly on non-state actors as either independent or dependent variables in their models, they also appear to presume that national governments in theory and practice mediate most international interactions that ultimately matter. The assumption that states are the central actors in most meaningful international relations is conventional but, to our minds, it needs to be relaxed. As Nye and Keohane wrote, "A good deal of intersocietal intercourse, with significant political importance, takes place without government control" (Nye and Keohane 1971: 330). Assuming that states necessarily mediate international interactions makes state dominance in IR a theoretical *constant*.

In the realm of financial transparency this book provides a running example of the significant oversights caused by assuming that states dominate all international interactions that matter. Most prior work on money laundering, terrorist financing, and other illicit financial flows has either focused on statutory compliance with the rules at the level of national governments, speculated generally about the problem, or lamented governments' and intergovernmental organizations' unwillingness to gather serious data (Andreas and Nadelmann 2006; Levi and Reuter 2006; Drezner 2007; Friman 2009; Walker and Unger 2009; Andreas 2010; Palan et al. 2010; Reuter 2012). So long as governments are seen as the relevant actors, loci of compliance, and sole providers of data, meaningful progress in accumulating knowledge about the scope of the problem will be stymied. Anonymous shell corporations pose a problem of transnational violation of rules, and our study suggests that many national governments play relatively passive roles if they act at all.

Experimental TR thus sees state mediation as a *variable*, as depicted in Figure 1.1. We acknowledge that states, in the end, may dominate many and perhaps even most interactions that ultimately matter in world politics. But we caution that this conclusion should not be presupposed until it is established by careful scientific testing. We thus invoke Nye and Keohane (1971; Keohane and Nye 1972) and interject that states may not dominate all IR arenas. Indeed, in some realms – such as the private incorporation transactions central to this book – states may play a minor role. And in yet others the state may in effect not matter at all. Here, the many million transnational interactions that occur each day over the internet come to mind.

The variation in state influence is thus interesting and worthy of study. Experimental TR converts state influence over international dealings into a variable and asks, "How much do governments matter

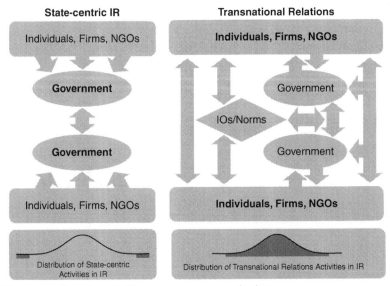

Figure 1.1 State-centric IR versus transnational relations.

for normal action in IR alongside other factors such as cultural norms, international organizations, or international law?" Experimental TR asks for theory that explicitly models why and how states will matter together with other influences – material, ideational, and organizational – in determining the behavior of individuals, firms, and NGOs that interact internationally.

These theoretical insights can then be put to rigorous empirical tests, preferably with field experiments that can establish causality. In our experiments we randomly assigned whether or not the financial transparency standards were attributed to an international organization (the FATF), a domestic agency (the IRS), or a private standards body (Association of Certified Anti-Money Laundering Specialists). We also tested, somewhat subtly, the effects of government enforcement in the treatment where we invoked the possibility of legal penalties for violation of the standards. Tests such as these relax the assumption that governments matter uniformly and convert the constant implied by the strong presumption of state centrism into a testable variable. We hope that other analysts will follow up on this possibility.

Theories employing the Experimental TR framework may also suggest conditions under which states may matter more than other factors. For example, governments may affect outcomes more in conventional issue areas than in new domains. Alternatively, in areas where non-state actor behavior is more measurable or monitorable, governments may exert more influence than when the behavior is less visible. Likewise, governments may dominate when there are few sites of interaction versus when there are many. More conventionally, governments may matter more in security affairs than economic concerns. And there may be many other such conjectures implied by the insight that government influence is a variable and not a constant.

In short, Experimental TR calls for a rigorous science of the international causes of individuals' and private organizations' international behavior and the effects that private actors – alongside state influence – have on international politics. States may play a leading role in much of this work, but the dominant role should be not be assumed. The effects of state or international organization influence on private international interactions, and vice versa, should be tested rigorously with methods that can establish causality.

Experimental TR stands in relief to what might be termed "state-centric," "elite," or even "outlier" international relations. We use the term outlier in the sense that formal relations among governments represent a very small, albeit influential, proportion of the actual international dealings that take place constantly in global society. In contrast, Experimental TR focuses on the "normal" behavior of transnational actors. By encouraging research in Experimental TR we by no means imply that state-centric international relations are somehow less than critical for making sense of global patterns. Nor do we mean that studies of individual international interactions somehow supersede studies of interstate relations. We merely suggest that a rich realm of potentially important international relations research remains largely unexplored.

Again the area of global financial transparency provides a useful example. While governments move substantial amounts of money transnationally, private flows dwarf intergovernmental transactions by orders of magnitude. While it is very difficult to count transnational exchanges, most of these private transactions occur between corporations, and shell corporations provide especially convenient vehicles for moving money globally. Of course, if particularly unsavory actors want to get their money across national borders, an anonymous shell company can shield them from scrutiny and liability. The volume of such exchanges – and the degree to which governments fundamentally lack knowledge of their scope – has prompted governmental and intergovernmental action to stymie the illicit activity. By focusing on private actors in the context of a field experiment, this book documents governments' rate of success and failure in curbing anonymous incorporation.

Figure 1.1 is complex, and we suspect that the natural tendency when viewing such a diagram is to dismiss it as a "kitchen-sink" model of the world. But given wide dissatisfaction with past attempts to create grand theories of world politics, we ask readers to indulge the complexity for a moment. We do not intend Figure 1.1 to be used as a rigorous theoretical model of international relations. No model with so many actors and omnidirectional causal arrows could ever be very helpful as an explanation of IR. Rather, we propose all of the nodes and arrows as places for analysts to look for sites where experiments might be designed to probe specific mid-level causal relationships and thus tame some of this complexity.

Field experiments

This brings us to the method. After learning about the shell-company-related anecdotes of Lu Zhang, the GT Group, Pavlo Lazarenko, Wyoming Corporate Services Inc., and Viktor Bout, readers might naturally wonder if these cases are representative of industry norms or are mere outliers. We had the same question. But only a systematic method employed globally can answer it with confidence.

The experimental method is the most powerful tool in science, but field experiments, which possess strong advantages in external validity, have been underutilized in the study of politics (Gerber and Green 2003). And among all of the positivist fields of political science, it appears that international relations has employed experiments the least. For example, until fall of 2012 the leading journal of the field, *International Organization*, listed 22 different methods that authors could select when they submitted manuscripts. Among more conventional quantitative and qualitative approaches, the methodological categories included cultural analysis, discourse analysis, ethnographic analysis, linguistic analysis, and genealogical analysis. But until September of 2012 the list still excluded the experimental method. A comprehensive update of the methods corrected the oversight in late

2012 and added several experimental categories to the list. Relatedly, the Teaching, Research, and International Policy survey, which tracks trends in international relations scholarship, reports that less than one percent of IR articles in the leading journals employ experiments as their method (Maliniak et al. 2012). Closer scrutiny reveals that most of those were computational models using simulated data.

Despite these patterns, pioneering IR scholars have used experiments for several decades to illuminate the topics of foreign policy-making, negotiation, and bargaining (see Etheredge 1978; Druckman et al. 1988; Druckman 1993; Mintz and Geva 1993; Mintz et al. 1997; Redd 2002; Tomz 2007; and McDermott et al. 2009). The studies have accumulated evidence reflecting on the conditions that lead to resolution of international conflict. Nearly all of the studies were lab experiments, however, and skeptics have charged that the results derived using undergraduate students as subjects cannot be credibly extrapolated to foreign policy decision-makers. While we feel this criticism is somewhat overblown and particularly unfair to the studies that recruited more relevant professionals (see Mintz et al. 1997), we note that most of the work focuses on official decision-making by elites, which moves it away from the non-state actors central to Experimental TR (for important exceptions, see Tomz 2007 and McDermott et al. 2009). Susan Hyde's pathbreaking field experimental work on international election observers provides the best model for what we envision (see Hyde 2007, 2010, 2011), as subjects are in their natural environment and exposed to international interventions.

Experiments offer many advantages over conventional observational research methods using case studies or statistical analysis. While the sequence of events in case studies can allow inferences about causal mechanisms, the conclusions are restricted to the cases themselves, making it hard to infer more general explanations (low external validity). Moreover, process tracing in case studies, which resembles historical analysis, often identifies multiple causes for a single event, so the related models are necessarily overdetermined.

Statistical analysis using large samples faces other challenges relating to the dependence on naturally occurring observational data rather than that produced by the experimental method of random assignment to treatment and control groups. While the large number of cases in studies relying on observational data appears to enhance external validity, analysts cannot be confident that the statistical models have taken into account all of the possible factors that might cause the outcome of interest, i.e. that the models are properly specified. Model misspecification thus raises grave doubts about whether causal relationships have been accurately identified (i.e. problematic internal validity). On the one hand, elaborate models with many variables often create ambiguous estimates of causal effects that fail to distinguish between different potential causes that co-vary with each other (multicollinearity). On the other, failing to include sufficient controls for other variables induces specification bias. Even if all of the observable potential causes are controlled for, statistical models necessarily omit all the variables that cannot be observed. So the problem is intractable, and, as a consequence of these internal validity problems, the resulting explanations of causality are inherently uncertain.

All these problems threaten even those studies with well-formulated models. The reliability of the method plummets when analysts add or omit control variables and swap estimation strategies on the fly in pursuit of the desired findings. The ubiquity of the statistical method in top political science journals suggests that individual scholars and the field collectively may underestimate the challenges of observational analysis and exaggerate the ability to accumulate knowledge from the results (see Gerber et al. 2004; Gerber and Green 2012).

The biggest problem is bias. Errors caused by the omission of unobserved potential causes in statistical research using observational data bias estimates of causal effects. What is more, these potential biases cannot be known before the fact and remain difficult to identify afterwards except when informed by experimental studies, which are by design unbiased in expectation. Of course, some types of studies based on observational data can prove quite informative, especially when randomization of the presumed cause occurs naturally – when the actors of interest are exposed to the cause or not in a near-random fashion.

An example is a study of the effect of receiving West German television on attitudes among East Germans toward their government during the Cold War (Kern and Hainmueller 2009). Thanks to various accidents of topography and atmospheric conditions, some areas of East Germany could receive West German television (equivalent to the treatment) while others could not (equivalent to the control). Against the conventional wisdom, those that received television from the West were actually more satisfied with the Communist government than those who did not. These observational designs are especially attractive where researchers cannot manipulate assignment to conditions (Gerber et al. 2004).

Well-designed experiments can overcome many of the problems that plague statistical research built on observational data. First, in expectation the randomization process balances all of the possible covariates across experimental conditions. This means that, if the analyst employs a large enough pool of subjects and executes the randomization properly, not only are all observable factors that might conceivably influence the outcome evenly distributed between treatment and control groups, all such *un*observable factors are also balanced. The only factor not common to the treatment and control groups is the treatment itself, so any subsequent differences in outcomes must have necessarily been caused by the treatment. Experiments have very high internal validity and can thus reveal actual causal effects, not just mere statistical correlations, even when those correlations are dressed up in regression form. Randomization eliminates the need for elaborate model specification with a penumbra of statistical controls and the corresponding need for extensive and often unrealistic assumptions.

Among many other successes, the power of randomized experiments has helped transform medicine from quackery to a science that has doubled human life expectancy, revealed very promising interventions to relieve global poverty, and even begun to map emotional responses in the human brain. A key step in the evolution of medical science involved the establishment of pre-research public registration for randomized controlled drug trials. Investigators were required to declare their plans publicly before the research; and, because the plans were public, they had to stick with them! Unfortunately, most social science research does not bind itself to such standards. Hoping to adopt the discipline of medicine, consistent with an initiative gaining some traction in political science (Findley et al. 2012a), we registered our experimental design in advance of the research. We describe the registration and our adherence to it in the Preface and in the Chapter 2 Appendix at the end of the book.

All methods are not equal in their ability to produce cumulative knowledge – on this score experiments are generally considered superior to qualitative case studies and observational statistics. As with any method, however, there are limitations. Randomization imbalances may occur naturally, and the results may not coincide exactly with the parameter of interest. It is important to remember, however, that experiments are technically unbiased, so larger subject pools and cell sizes will, in expectation, eliminate imbalances. Additionally, lab experiments, as noted, face questions about the ability to generalize the results beyond the lab: external validity may thus be limited. Critics have also raised similar concerns for some field experiments, particularly when peculiarities of specific cultures or geographies may confound results and prevent their generalization beyond their specific contexts (see Deaton 2007; Rodrik 2008).

The conventional wisdom in political science and other related fields seems to be that, while experiments are superior when it comes to accurately uncovering causal relationships, observational statistics are still better when it comes to generalizing to the world outside the laboratory. But let us return to the subject of international financial transparency. In this case observational analysis using cross-national statistics would likely quantify and analyze the Financial Action Task Force country reports (e.g. Ferwerda 2009). But it is possible – indeed our results indicate that it is very likely – that the assessments of national statutory compliance with FATF standards may fail to account for whether or not incorporation services, which are the actual locus of relevant behavior, actually comply with the rules. The available data do not reflect reality. Furthermore, especially in developing countries, available data in many realms may prove highly unreliable given their relatively limited capacity.

As an alternative source of data on financial transparency, surveys of incorporation services and business law firms would likely receive low response rates and selection effects would probably bias the results in a debilitating way. Indeed, we performed just such a survey and its results are wildly misleading: the firms that responded to the survey were significantly different than those replying in the field experiment, and many respondents claimed they would adhere to standards that our experiments showed they have obviously violated. When the subjects of study have reason to dissemble – as when they typically behave inappropriately by offering anonymous incorporation – none of the conventional methods in IR can generate credible results.

With field experiments, however, the data-generation process is built into the research design. Indeed, we have strong reason to believe – and interviews with officials at the Financial Action Task Force, the International Monetary Fund, the World Bank, the US Treasury

Department, the US Senate Permanent Subcommittee on Investigations, and major private financial institutions corroborate – that the results we present here on global patterns of firms' compliance with international financial standards are the best available information on the subject by a significant degree. Other methods fail to produce accurate data on the actual behavior of interest. And since rival methods are all observational, none of them can generate credible results showing how different information cues can cause changes in firms' compliance rates, whereas our field experiments can do just that.

Given the many acknowledged advantages of field experiments, some readers may be puzzled as to why they remain in such short supply in international relations. Several factors may account for the paucity of IR field experiments. First, field experiments are believed to be inherently impossible to the extent that states (or the international system of states) are the units of analysis, because scholars cannot assign states to control and treatment groups in the manner that is necessary to conduct experiments. Second, experiments may be regarded as unethical, especially when they involve deception. Finally, even where they are possible in practical and ethical terms, many analysts see them as overly complicated and economically unfeasible. We address each issue in turn.

The first objection, that scholars lack the power to assign states to control and treatment groups, does indeed mean that a whole class of issues in the field are not amenable to experimental study. To this extent, qualitative research and that based on observational data – particularly if the identification strategies are credible – represent the best ways forward. Yet as argued above, IR scholars have been too quick to dismiss the empirical and theoretical significance of non-state actors. Taking proper account of the full range of transnational relations brings a much wider range of actors into the frame. Many of these actors can in fact be assigned to experimental conditions in ways that allow scholars to make causal inferences on important questions in IR.[2]

Given that IR experiments are often practicable, are they ethical? Once more, there may be many situations where it is immoral to

---

[2] We hasten to add, however, that field experiments at the level of states and relevant government officials may even be possible. Indeed, two of us are in the middle of a field experiment on members of parliament regarding foreign aid. The experiment requires no deception and will occur in scores of countries globally.

perform experiments and thus where scholars must rely on the conventional repertoire of IR methods. But it is important to realize that deception may be ethically defensible under some circumstances, and that many experiments do not need to involve deception. The corporate transparency experiment at the heart of this book relies on the stratagem of posing as a variety of consultants in the market for a shell company. Removing the potential biases introduced by participants having to choose to participate in the experiment, and being able to observe participants' natural behavior, creates major methodological dividends, but how can this kind of deception be justified?

In this specific instance, the deception involved minor costs for the subjects; specifically firms might spend five to fifteen minutes responding to our email (for similar correspondence-based experiments, see Bertrand and Mullainathan 2004; Butler and Broockman 2011). Contrast this cost to the kind of medical trials that win ethical approval, in which doctors sometimes perform "sham" surgeries on patients – complete with anesthesia, incisions, sutures, and the nontrivial risk of infection, but no actual surgery – in order to differentiate the benefits of, say, arthroscopic knee surgery for osteoarthritis from placebo effects (see Moseley et al. 2002).

More positively, experiments such as ours may generate knowledge in relation to major policy problems that create large-scale human suffering – knowledge that simply could not be gained in any non-experimental fashion or in a conventional experiment with the fully informed consent of the subjects. Incorporation service employees would likely ignore our inquiries or dissemble if they knew they were being studied. This conjecture was vindicated by our conventional survey of the corporate service providers, which we conducted after the contacts from the aliases in the experiment had concluded. Response rates for the survey were dismal, and the results were wildly misleading. Thus, we – and scores of other scholars we consulted – simply could not conceive of another way to obtain unbiased findings on financial transparency except to use deception in the context of a field experiment. Despite the idiosyncrasies of anonymous incorporation, we stress here that most field experiments in IR, beyond the minimum requirement to not tell participants the exact details and aims of the experiment, do not require deception (we discuss a range of IR field experiments in Chapter 7, none of which involve active deception).

Finally, where experiments are possible and ethical, are they logistically and financially feasible for IR scholars? We admit that field experiments can sometimes prove expensive. However, with Susan Hyde's excellent work, her NGO partners paid most of the relevant expenses. This cost absorption by partners or governments has typically been the case for the hundreds of field experiments in development economics performed by scholars and affiliates at MIT's Jameel Poverty Action Lab (for examples, see Chattopadhyay and Duflo 2004; Banerjee et al. 2007). In one of our experiments at Brigham Young University's Political Economy and Development Lab (PEDL), we partnered with UNICEF-Uganda to test incentive mechanisms for motivating citizens to use their cellphones to SMS-text development information on their neighborhoods and villages to UNICEF's centralized system. Called UReport, the system cost UNICEF significant resources to develop and maintain, but they sought expertise from an academic partner to design the experiment and analyze the data. The partnership thus cost PEDL very little in terms of cash outlays, with most costs paid through personnel involved in project management.

The present study on anonymous incorporation is the most elaborate that we have undertaken, requiring individualized management of thousands of pieces of correspondence. A sizable team of research assistants was occupied for more than a year with the tasks of compiling, sending, receiving, following up on, and coding the correspondence with incorporation services. Even so, we estimate that the costs were something on the order of three to four dollars per observation, which is considerably less expensive than most laboratory experiments and, even with more than 3,700 subjects over 7,400 total observations, within many political science research budgets.

PEDL has now completed a dozen or so IR field experiments, and most cost pennies per observation rather than dollars. With creative use of the internet and sufficient research assistance, many IR field experiments reflecting on important transnational patterns can be performed from a single location. Field experiments do bring with them logistical challenges, but they are not inherently complicated. Rather, to be effective experiments need to be simple in conception. Examples of additional Experimental TR studies are listed in Chapter 7.

Plan of the book

The rest of the book demonstrates the potential of the idea of Experimental TR by way of a global field experiment in anonymous incorporation. Chapter 2 explains the substantive focus of the study: shell corporations and the firms that create and sell them. Here we also describe the basis of global financial transparency standards with a discussion of how state and non-state compliance should occur in this particular context. After providing the necessary substantive background, we discuss the methodology briefly, with technical details relegated to the Appendix. We provide the context of the field experiments in which we used email aliases to request anonymous shell corporations from businesses that specialize in setting up new companies for clients (corporate service providers). The aliases all sought "confidentiality" – incorporation with less identifying information than is stipulated by international standards. Our expected outcomes from this exercise included recording whether such businesses responded to our inquiries, and if so whether their responses were compliant with international standards.

Chapter 3 provides an extensive descriptive overview of patterns in global compliance. The patterns highlight comparisons among tax havens, Organisation for Economic Co-operation and Development (OECD) members, and developing countries internationally along with a detailed sub-national account of compliance across US states. We find that firms in tax havens obey international law significantly more often than companies based in OECD countries. Firms in poor countries are just as compliant as OECD services in most instances, in some cases more so. Incorporation services in the United States are particularly delinquent, but US law firms are more inclined than US incorporation services to refuse service. Services in "business-friendly" Delaware, Nevada, and Wyoming are particularly prone to violate international standards.

With the concepts and overall descriptive patterns established, we turn to the first of three chapters describing the results from the randomized field experiments. In Chapter 4 we address whether perceived connections to corruption and terrorism discourage providers from offering anonymous incorporation. We also test the effects of an offer to make an extra "premium" payment for anonymity on compliance. This chapter provides some encouragement to offset the somewhat troubling results about the global lack of compliance, but it still indicates that there is a sizeable minority of providers willing to establish shell companies even for the riskiest customers. The Premium, Corruption and Terrorism treatments caused significantly lower response rates compared to the baseline or to the other treatments, suggesting that some service providers distance themselves from potentially nefarious activities of their customers. Among those that did respond, however, compliance rates were often significantly lower than the Placebo. In the pursuit of profits, many firms appear indifferent to customer risk and willing to provide anonymous shell companies to any and all comers, even blatant corruption risks. However, the Terrorism treatment caused a significant decrease in the non-compliance rate, an encouraging result that is partially offset by the simultaneous decrease in compliance rates. Alarmingly, willingness to provide an additional money premium to service providers encouraged them to break international law: compliance rates dropped significantly.

Chapter 5 asks whether providing information about international standards motivates greater levels of compliance. In these experiments we varied information about public and private standards for incorporation practices. The emails with public standards explicitly reference the Financial Action Task Force, the inter-governmental rule-making body in this area, whereas the private standards reference the Association of Certified Anti-Money Laundering Specialists, a for-profit US multinational business. In the domestic enforcement experiment deployed for US service providers, we attributed the standards to the US Internal Revenue Service. The results of these analyses show that reference to the FATF's international standards did not cause greater compliance. Mention of the private standards endorsed by the Association of Certified Anti-Money Laundering Specialists only marginally improved compliance compared to some of the other treatment conditions. Explicit reference to enforcement by the IRS, however, significantly decreased the non-compliance rate for US firms, suggesting that domestic standards might prove more effective.

In Chapter 6 we examine what the experiments reveal about the effect of prospective penalties versus normative suasion on compliance. In our emails to service providers, we contrasted information about likely legal penalties associated with failure to follow international standards with normative appeals to probity and reputation to see whether these interventions changed the incidence of compliant or non-compliant behavior. The evidence is both surprising and revealing. Providers responding to the Penalties treatment were *less* likely to refuse service or, in some specifications, to comply with international standards. We interpret this as a collusion effect, where revealing information about international law may signal to firms a knowledge of the rules and a disinterest in reporting violations. Firms assigned to the Norms condition were similarly likely to reply as in the Placebo condition, but in some specifications they were significantly *less inclined* to require notarized identifying documents and be found in compliance with international law. Reference to appropriate behavior may reassure firms that the customer is lower risk or once again be taken as a signal for collusion (or both, remembering the issue of heterogeneous effects).

The concluding chapter brings together the lessons learned from the different treatments for the experimental science of transnational relations. The results show that compliance with international law is often weak. Yet there is evidence that some incorporation businesses may be sensitive to the risks posed by corruption and terrorism. But many other services prove indifferent to risk. More generally, we contend that a greater emphasis on studying non-state actors with greater precision (e.g. experiments) holds significant promise for the study of international relations, and we present several more examples of how such experiments can be conducted. In demonstrating the potential of a novel method, the book thus combines valuable lessons for scholars in IR and international law, as well as policy-makers.

2 | *Explaining the global shell game*

The mainstay of this book is a global field experiment based on soliciting thousands of offers for shell companies. But what are shell companies? Why are they important? And what are the challenges in regulating their use? This chapter is devoted to answering each of these questions.

The antics of the American comic Stephen Colbert illustrate some of the challenges associated with shell companies. In the lead-up to the 2012 US Presidential election, Colbert satirized the artifice and conceits involved in election fundraising by creating both a Super-PAC and an anonymous shell corporation to hide its donors. His lampoon gets to the heart of the separation between legal form and substantive reality that provides the rationale for shell companies.

Colbert's spoof began with a Super-PAC (Political Action Committee), i.e. a group that may receive unlimited funds for election campaigns, but must stay ostensibly independent of any candidate or political party. While Super-PACs maintain a legal fiction of independence, in reality they appear to coordinate with a candidate, such as Mitt Romney's Restore Our Future Super-PAC or President Barack Obama's Priorities USA Action. Mocking this pretense of independence coupled with the reality of close control, Colbert set up his own Super-PAC called "Definitely Not Coordinating with Stephen Colbert."

But the tragicomedy deepens. Super-PACs must reveal the identity of their donors, some of whom may prefer to keep their affiliation with a particular candidate secret (and the feeling may be mutual). To get around this problem, former President George W. Bush's Svengali Karl Rove registered a dedicated shell company with the sole purpose of receiving donations to then pass the money on to Bush's Super-PAC, American Crossroads. Because corporations do not have to reveal the identity of their financial backers in the way a Super-PAC does, the real purpose of the company here is to veil the identity of donors by inter-posing itself between the contributors and the Super-PAC. Referring to this kind of shell company by its legal title, Colbert observed, "Clearly, these (c)(4)s have created an unprecedented, unaccountable, untraceable cash tsunami that will infect every corner of the next election … And I feel like an idiot for not having one."

In response, Colbert got John McCain's former campaign advisor, Trevor Potter, to set up a similar company registered in Delaware under the legal name of "Anonymous Shell Corporation." Colbert asked Potter how this sort of process was different from money laundering. After pausing for a moment, Potter replied wearing a smirk, "it's hard to say." Colbert's ruse gets to the heart of the shell company issue: an ostensibly independent legal person that is in practical terms very much a controlled instrument used to separate, screen, and conceal the true identity of those engaged in financial activities they would like to keep secret.

The first half of this chapter explains the nature of shell companies and how they are used for legitimate and illegitimate purposes, including examples of tax evasion, corruption, and sanctions-busting. It provides a brief overview of the corporate service provider industry that exists to create shell companies. It also discusses the international regulatory standards that mandate corporate transparency by ensuring that authorities are able to "look through" the corporate veil to determine a company's real owner.

The second half of the chapter explains how we designed and conducted the experiment to test the effectiveness of these standards by impersonating a range of more or less risky consultants and soliciting offers for shell companies from thousands of corporate service providers around the world. This meant first designing a standard email approach template, based on a cover story of who the consultants were and why they wanted a shell company, which comprised the Placebo in the experiment. All of these Placebo emails originated from aliases based in rich, innocuous, low-corruption, minor-power countries. The rate at which providers responded to the Placebo email and complied with international standards in doing so set a baseline or yardstick against which to compare response rates to ten treatment emails, which varied the information in the email and/or the risk profile of the would-be clients. Dispatching the emails meant both building a comprehensive list of thousands of corporate service providers and taking precautions to obscure the real source and purpose of the email approaches. The final section discusses the procedure for coding the responses received and for deciding what counts as compliant and non-compliant; it also provides some examples of our email inquiries and actual (anonymized) replies.

Shell companies

When we think of companies, the natural association is to imagine workers and bosses, a headquarters, a production line or service offered, profit, loss, and employee benefits, such as a pension scheme. When stripped down to its essentials, however, a company is simply a legal person, an actor summoned into existence by law. Shell corporations are thus companies with nothing more than their basic legal essence, and as such lack all of the marks of substance listed above. In this sense, companies or corporations (we use the two terms interchangeably) may be described as "legal fictions" (Picciotto 2011). Yet the idea of legal fictions should not give the impression of inconsequentiality; these are powerful and important fictions, as the intense interest by governments, the UN, and FATF demonstrate. In some sense institutions like money and states are legal fictions too. Shell companies can hold bank accounts, own assets, and engage in transactions. Companies may start as a shell and then acquire substantial business operations, or (more rarely) go the opposite way by maintaining legal existence after substantive business has ceased.

Shell companies are cheap to establish, ranging from a couple of hundred to a few thousand dollars to set up. In dozens of jurisdictions they can be formed very quickly online; in some cases the process takes as little as 10 minutes. Rich OECD countries, especially English-speaking nations, have deliberately made it easy to incorporate as part of reforms to help small businesses, and in line with broader efforts at deregulation. This philosophy is also reflected in the World Bank's closely watched *Doing Business Survey*, which gives high marks to those countries that facilitate fast incorporation. However, it is worth noting here that the World Bank's *Ease of Doing Business* rankings are not significantly correlated with the compliance rates we find in our experiments, neither for the overall rankings nor for the rankings assessing the ease of starting a business. And this is true both for all countries in the study and for the OECD members considered separately.[1] This lack of correlation suggests that non-compliance with international transparency standards involves more than merely facilitating the ease of doing business.

The tendency to lower barriers to incorporation has also been accentuated by a competitive dynamic that has seen jurisdictions competing for greater incorporation numbers. This form of regulatory competition (sometimes characterized as a "race to the bottom") has been in evidence both internationally and between the states in the United States. In developing countries, in contrast, forming a company is often more expensive, much slower, and may involve many more bureaucratic hurdles, in keeping with the common challenges of engaging with the state apparatus in such countries (de Soto 2000; World Bank 2011).

Shell companies are often conflated with companies formed in tax havens, also known as offshore financial centers (OFCs). Very roughly, tax havens are jurisdictions that design their financial, tax, and corporate laws with the primary aim of attracting foreign customers (Economist Intelligence Unit 2002; Palan 2003; Palan et al. 2010; Shaxson 2011). In the popular imagination they are associated with especially lax regulation, strong secrecy provisions, low or no taxes, and exotic tropical islands. While each of these characterizations contains important kernels of truth, they are also wrong in key ways, as we discuss in Chapter 3. Shell companies can be formed in "offshore" tax havens or "onshore" jurisdictions (a distinction that is to a large extent in the eye of the beholder). While most companies formed offshore are shell companies, the majority of shell companies overall are probably formed in *on*shore jurisdictions. The leading offshore shell company jurisdictions are the British Virgin Islands and Panama, in which between 40,000 and 70,000 shell companies are formed each year. This compares with about 300,000 companies of all

---

[1] We checked for statistical association between the compliance rates found in the experiment and several World Bank *Ease of Doing Business* categories, including the overall *Ease of Doing Business* ranking, the category rank for starting a business, the number of procedures required for licensing a business, the time for business startup in number of days, and the cost of business startup as a percentage of GDP per capita. None of these categories was significantly related to actual compliance rates among OECD members. Among all countries, only cost was significantly and negatively related to compliance rates ($p = 0.006$, $r = -0.23$), with higher costs associated with lower compliance rates.

kinds formed in Britain annually, and roughly 2 million formed in the United States (StAR 2011).

A subtype of shell companies are shelf corporations. Sometimes referred to as "aged" or "pre-formed companies," shelf corporations are formed and then kept "on the shelf" for sale later on. Not only may shelf companies reduce the time clients have to wait to acquire a company compared to forming one from scratch, but their appearance of longevity and their corporate track record may prove useful in dealing with counterparts. For example, some banks only extend loans to companies that have been in existence for a specified minimum time, while other firms may be reluctant to deal with a partner that has only been summoned into existence the week before. For criminals, shelf companies can be useful in confusing investigators, given the transfer in control from those who originally formed the company to the new owners. In general, the longer the company has been aged, the higher the price of the shelf corporation, and there is a market for "second-hand" shell companies, which are then sold as shelf companies.

This book is primarily concerned with the illicit uses of shell companies in facilitating crimes like money laundering, corruption, tax evasion, and the financing of terrorism, but it is important to point out that most shell companies are used for legitimate business purposes. When the Walt Disney Corporation purchased the land that is now Disney World in Orlando, Florida, it used an array of shell companies with names such as Tomahawk Properties and Reedy Creek Ranch – names that are still visible in the second-floor windows of Disney World's Main Street USA – to hide its identity as a monopsony buyer. The shells prevented price gouging by local landholders; the sellers, believing they were dealing with smaller real-estate firms, were more inclined to offer a fair market price (Sullivan 2011). Likewise, Chinese nationals commonly use foreign shell companies to list and raise capital on US, British, and Hong Kong stock markets. The process of forming a company in China takes more than a month, as opposed to days elsewhere, and Chinese firms are in any case barred from listing on most foreign stock exchanges. The foreign shell is thus set up to list in the United States (for example) and own the original Chinese company as an operating subsidiary. Capital raised in the United States by those buying the shares of the shell company is then funneled back to the operating company in China (Sharman 2012).

For another legitimate example, imagine the situation of two partners from the United States and Canada looking to start a joint venture in a corruption-prone developing country. Both partners are aware that differences may arise between them in the future, and they are reluctant to see any future problems solved by the courts in the developing country, which may lack expertise and impartiality. Each partner, however, is also reluctant to concede the home ground advantage that would come from any dispute being heard in the other's court system. Instead, the solution may be for each partner to set up a shell company in England or another British law jurisdiction (perhaps Hong Kong or the Channel Islands), which then jointly owns the third company that actually conducts the joint venture. This way, both partners can be confident that any future dispute between them will be held on neutral ground in a familiar, reliable court system with considerable expertise in corporate law. Aside from acting as a listing vehicle or shoring up joint ventures in this manner, shell companies are also commonly used to hold assets, whether it is real estate, capital equipment, share portfolios, or intellectual property including trademarks and patents (Burns and McConvill 2011).

Finally, in more of a borderline example, imagine the case of a Russian NGO devoted to monitoring elections to ensure their free and fair conduct, which receives funding from foreign philanthropic foundations. From November 2012 all such organizations receiving outside funding had to register as "foreign agents," a move widely interpreted as a means to clamp down on opposition to Russia's authoritarian government. But by copying the strategy of Karl Rove and Colbert, establishing a Russian shell company to receive foreign donations, which then passes them on to the NGO, the organization can escape the law and preserve its independence. Foreign money filtered through a Russian shell company becomes Russian money.

Although the majority of shell companies are used in a legitimate fashion, they are nevertheless a crucial means by which malefactors obscure their illicit financial affairs. To bolster the examples noted in the previous chapter, this section considers further instances of the more nefarious uses of shell companies relating to tax evasion, corruption, and sanctions-busting. A relatively simple example of shell company-enabled tax evasion is detailed in the US Department of Justice's indictment of the Swiss banks UBS and Wegelin.

UBS had assisted thousands of American clients to escape their duty to pay taxes on their worldwide income, including income in the form of interest on foreign accounts. In some cases this was simply a matter of individuals not declaring their accounts and the associated interest income to the IRS, confident that Swiss bank secrecy laws would protect them. In other cases, however, UBS assisted their US customers to hold their accounts through foreign shell companies. Although the customers maintained control of the account, the legal fiction suggested that they were held by an unconnected shell company of no relevance to US tax authorities. After promising never to reveal the details of these schemes to the US authorities, UBS reneged by handing over the details of 4,450 clients in August 2009 in the face of severe pressure from Washington (Sheppard 2009).

Stepping into the breach in 2008 and 2009, Wegelin decided to move into the market niche for tax-shy American clients after UBS capitulated. By 2010 Wegelin held $1.2 billion in deposits for US clients (Department of Justice 2011: 6–7). Wegelin reasoned that because it did not have a presence in the United States (unlike UBS), it would not be vulnerable to the sort of pressure that had felled its compatriot. However, the success of the scheme depended on keeping it secret from the US government, and once again shell companies were an important mechanism in achieving this secrecy.

Wegelin took extensive measures to hide its relationship with American clients from the US authorities. New clients were given code names (like "Elvis"), and bank staff were told to communicate with clients via text messages, on the grounds that US authorities could not monitor such messages in the same way they could track phone and email communication (Department of Justice 2011: 20 and 37). Wegelin's means of transferring money in and out of the United States were unorthodox to say the least, as the story of Wegelin employee FREI and client GG illustrates:

On or about August 21, 2007, Client GG carried ... $16,000 in cash with him to a lunch meeting in Manhattan with FREI, again at FREI's request. At the lunch, Client GG handed FREI an unmarked envelope containing the $16,000. During the lunch, the head waiter informed FREI that someone else at the restaurant wished to speak with him. FREI then excused himself from Client GG, walked to the other side of the restaurant, and met with FREI's Other Client for approximately 10 minutes. At or about that time, FREI gave the Other Client the cash-filled unmarked envelope that Client GG had given to FREI moments earlier. FREI then returned to Client GG and noted that it was becoming increasingly difficult to move funds out of

Switzerland, and that, to do so, he employed this technique of transferring cash directly between his clients. Thereafter, FREI credited approximately $16,000 to Client GG's undeclared account at WEGELIN. (Department of Justice 2011: 48)

Cash-filled envelopes to one side, however, shell companies provided a far more reliable means of hiding clients' identities (at least until voluntary disclosures to the IRS by some of the clients in question gave the game away). A typical example is that of one married couple, described in the indictment as clients J and K, who had possessed an undeclared UBS account since the 1980s. After the UBS settlement, the couple was advised by a Los Angeles attorney to first establish a company in the Caribbean island of Nevis (White Tower Holdings LLC), and then open an account for White Tower with Wegelin to receive their money from UBS. Wegelin conspired with the fiction that White Tower was the final owner of the account, even though the bank knew the company's only function was to conceal the fact that J and K were really in control of the funds. As long as White Tower could not be traced back to J and K, as long as the corporate veil remained intact, they could successfully evade their tax obligations.

Shell companies are also one of the most common devices used in major corruption offenses, as the case of Sergei Magnitsky tragically illustrates. Magnitsky was a Russian lawyer who discovered a $230 million tax fraud perpetrated by corrupt Russian tax officials and Interior Ministry personnel. Upon learning of the fraud, Magnitsky revealed key information to the Russian government. Officials promptly arrested Magnitsky and handed him over to the very same corrupt officials he had exposed. They accused him of the tax fraud, held him without trial, moved him to increasingly foul prison cells, tortured him, and then ruthlessly withheld medical treatment until he died on November 16, 2009 – conveniently, for the corrupt officials, just before the one-year maximum was reached for holding prisoners without a trial (Nocera 2012).

The means by which the leading corrupt tax official, Olga Stepanova, obtained her share of the misappropriated funds again illustrates the screening function of shell companies. Stepanova approved a fraudulent tax refund of $230 million on December 24, 2008, which was wired from the Russian central bank to Universal Savings Bank in Moscow. Shortly afterwards the bank was liquidated, its owner fell to his death from his balcony and, at least according to the Russian government, all of the bank's records were destroyed when the truck carrying them exploded and burned. The money, however, had been wired via Austria's Raiffeisen Bank, from where several transactions of $12.6 million were made by a shell company, Bristoll Exports of New Zealand, to the corporate accounts of two other shell companies with Credit Suisse in Zurich: Arivust Holdings (Cyprus) and Aikate Properties Inc. (British Virgin Islands). Very little information was publicly available on either company, but identity documents taken and kept on file by the firms that incorporated Arivust and Aikate later revealed that the owner of both shell companies was one Vladlen Stepanov, husband of none other than Olga Stepanova. Bristoll Exports had been formed by the ubiquitous GT Group in New Zealand (employer of Lu Zhang, whose story opened Chapter 1), which – true to form – had not collected any material on the real person in control of the company. Thus, while authorities strongly suspected that Bristoll Exports was an instrument of Stepanova or one of her confederates, this cannot be proven either way. The trail ends with the untraceable shell company (Alpert 2011; Russian Untouchables 2012). In an incredible postscript to the Magnitsky case, in February 2012 the Russian police laid new tax evasion charges – against Sergei Magnitsky, more than two years after his death at the hands of the Russian authorities.

The final example shows how shell companies can be used to evade international sanctions. In Chapter 1 we referenced the case of the GT Group's supplying a shell company to lease the cargo plane full of weapons shipped from North Korea to Iran and gun-runner Viktor Bout. But the case of the state-owned Islamic Republic of Iran Shipping Lines (IRISL) is also illustrative (Becker 2010).

In 2008, the US government blacklisted the shipping line as a confederate in Iran's nuclear program as part of sanctions that were later broadened and deepened under the auspices of the UN Security Council. The sanctions are specifically targeted at named entities like IRISL and its ships. These ships have been used by Iran to transport various pieces of military hardware, as well as assisting Syria to evade US and EU sanctions imposed in 2011 in response to the massive human rights violations the Syrian government committed against its own people (Saigol 2012). But in 2010 IRISL's fleet of 123 ships appeared to dwindle, with 73 being renamed (in one case the new name was actually "Alias"), and then re-flagged and "sold" or otherwise transferred to ostensibly independent third-party shell companies based in Germany, Malta, Cyprus, Hong Kong, and the Isle of Man set up by a British corporate service provider (Becker 2010). As such, because companies from friendly countries owned them, the ships were no longer on the sanctions list and were thus free to go about their business. Yet digging deeper led to strong indications that IRISL maintained control of the ships through shell companies.

One telling feature was that five ships launched in 2009–2010 were valued at $145 million, yet they were sold to their new Maltese shell company owners for only $8,200. Although many of the shell companies owning the ships had other shell companies as owners or directors, in most cases it was possible to trace past owners or office holders back to IRISL, one of its Iranian subsidiaries, or to individual office holders in the company. But because the ownership could be transferred quickly from one shell company to another, the sanctions list remained at least one step behind. Once again, the shell companies were a legal fiction acting to hide IRISL's practical control of the ships.

Corporate service providers and the shell company industry

In the examples above, those in control of shell companies like White Tower, Arivust, Aikate, Bristoll Exports, and those used by IRISL all employed professional intermediaries to set up the companies. Although it is possible in some countries for an individual to set up a company directly with the corporate registry, it is more common to go through an intermediary firm. These intermediaries, which we refer to as corporate service providers (CSPs), play a central role in the shell company industry and are a key focus of this book. This section of the chapter explains who they are and what they do. These firms are the entities whose business it is to establish, sell, and maintain shell companies, like the GT Group or Wyoming Corporate Services Inc. as discussed in the previous chapter. Service providers are the crucial locus of enforcement and compliance for rules mandating corporate transparency; if these intermediaries are not collecting information on the real owner of a company and thus ensuring transparency, no one else will. Corporate service providers may be large firms with offices in a dozen or more countries, or a single person selling companies via a website. They may be law or accounting firms for whom company formation is one among many functions, or they may be wholly devoted to this line of business.

Given that shell companies are incorporeal legal fictions, what do corporate service providers actually do? Because a company only exists as a legal person through some sort of government recognition, at minimum some documents must be filed with an official registry, either electronically or in hard copy. The type of information required varies widely, but at the very least it must include the name of the company, and almost always an address, sometimes information on the type of shares issued, and perhaps the shareholders. The address requirement means that a vast number of shell companies may officially have the same residence, such as the 138,000 companies registered at Suite 2, 23–24 Great James Street in London, or the Wyoming house referred to in Chapter 1. A fee must be paid for registration, often a few hundred dollars or more, and then paid again annually to maintain the company in good standing.

Corporate service providers lodge the documentation and pay the government fees for their clients, and they serve as the official contact address for the company. In addition there are a wide range of auxiliary services that they may provide. These range from phone- and mail-forwarding services to secretarial assistance and legal or tax advice. Importantly with regard to transparency, they also act as stand-ins for customers in important corporate positions. The provider may act as the director or shareholder of record, i.e. act as the nominee, as did Lu Zhang for scores of companies set up by the GT Group. The significance of these nominee services is that, to the extent that such details as director or shareholder are recorded, these documents lead only to the corporate service provider and not to the customer. Thus advertising material from the GT Group suggests that owner Geoffrey Taylor "can act as Director and Shareholder for clients without arousing suspicion that he is a nominee only. In this way he can act as your front man and attract attention away from you" (Global Witness 2012: 39). In line with the general theme of shell companies providing a combination of legal separation with practical control, however, in practice the customer steers the company through a legal agreement with the provider.

As with most other industries, corporate service providers specialize to fit various roles. For example, there are a small number of large wholesalers who form and then sell companies in bulk to a much larger number of retailers. The main wholesalers of offshore companies are firms like Offshore Incorporation Limited (OIL, Hong Kong), Mossack Fonseca (Panama), Morgan & Morgan (Panama), Offshore Company Registration Agents (OCRA, Isle of Man), and ILS Fiduciaries.[2] In the United States the biggest players are CT Corp and Corporation Service Company (CSC). In Britain, @UKplc claims to have set up 200,000 companies (Global Witness 2012). These wholesalers form and maintain thousands or even tens of thousands of shell companies, and may be worth several hundred million dollars in their own right. At their headquarters there are whole floors of staff in glass cubicles forming shell companies day in, day out.

Although these wholesalers sometimes sell shell companies on a bespoke basis to individual clients, it is much more common for them to sell companies to hundreds of retail corporate service providers. These retailers might be banks, law firms, or sole traders, which might order companies from wholesalers one-by-one or by the dozen. Thus, for example, a US government report described how the CSP Euro-American, based in New York, formed 2,000 Delaware shell companies – many of which were then sold for $350 each to somewhere between 30 and 50 brokers in Moscow, sometimes in blocks of 10 to 20 companies at a time. The Russian brokers then in turn sold them to end-users, who were unknown to both Euro-American and the US government (GAO 2000). A smaller five-person business in Hong Kong specializing in selling Caribbean shell companies to Chinese clients forms 200–300 companies a month (Isle of Man).[3] Many such companies are set up only for a single deal and then left dormant, but from the service provider's point of view it is preferable for clients to keep their shell companies active, which generates a steady revenue stream,

---

[2] Author interviews: George Town, Cayman Islands, April 19–20, 2004; Road Town, British Virgin Islands, January 20–21, 2005; Douglas, Isle of Man, January 31–February 2, 2005; Victoria, Seychelles, May 30, 2005; Port Louis, Mauritius, May 25 and June 1–2, 2005; Bridgetown, Barbados, June 29, 2005; London, UK, September 19, 2005; Port Vila, Vanuatu, March 10, 2006; Road Town, British Virgin Islands, May 21–22, 2007; Panama City, Panama, April 2–4, 2008; Fort Lauderdale, United States, February 19, 2009; Willemstad, Netherlands Antilles, February 23–26, 2009; Apia, Samoa, June 30–1 July 2009; Singapore, October 20, 2009; Avarua, Cook Islands, December 2–4, 2009; Hong Kong, November 9, 2010; London, UK, September 7, 2011; Hong Kong, September 17–18, 2011; Miami, United States, April 30–May 1, 2012; London, UK, May 17–18, 2012; Gold Coast, Australia, November 7, 2012.
[3] Author interview: Hong Kong, October 18, 2011.

thanks to the annual fee and paperwork requirements for keeping the company in good standing. About 50 to 80 percent of companies are renewed each year.

The largest corporate service providers may be able to create new variations on the basic shell company concept by inducing governments to pass legislation composed by the provider, as in the case of the Seychelles where Offshore Corporation Registration Agents (OCRA) contacted the government with its preferred legislation. Or small, impoverished countries looking for extra revenue may approach a provider to set up a shell company business for them. Thus the Pacific island of Niue (population: 1,200) sought out Panamanian law firm Mossack Fonseca to set up a Niuean shell company business. Mossack Fonseca wrote the legislation for the Niuean parliament, and then marketed the new product and ran the business from Panama City, remitting a share of the proceeds to the government of Niue. When international pressure forced Niue out of the shell company business in 2005, Mossack Fonseca reincorporated the companies faced with deregistration in the neighboring Pacific island of Samoa.[4]

Service providers themselves often know surprisingly little about the market they sell to or the industry in general. One trend seems to be a move towards consolidation in the industry, as there is a greater premium on providers being "supermarkets" that can quickly offer shell companies from a variety of different jurisdictions, and if necessary stitch them together into more complex corporate structures (e.g. where shell companies act as the director and/or shareholders of another such company). From what is tentatively known, competition occurs on price, as well as according to the slightly different legal characteristics and prerogatives of shell companies from different jurisdictions.[5]

But again mirroring other industries, fads and fashions matter too. Explaining the popularity of British Virgin Islands (BVI) companies

---

[4] Author interviews: Victoria, Seychelles, May 30, 2005; Panama City, Panama, April 2, 2008; Apia, Samoa, July 1, 2009; Hong Kong, November 9, 2010.

[5] Author interviews: Basseterre, St. Kitts, January 22, 2004; Vaduz, Liechtenstein, January 29, 2004; Road Town, British Virgin Islands, January 20–21, 2005 and May 21–22, 2007; Port Louis, Mauritius, May 25 and June 1, 2005; Douglas, Isle of Man, January 31–February 2, 2005; Panama City, Panama, April 2–4, 2008; Avarua, Cook Islands, December 4, 2009; Hong Kong, November 9, 2010 and October 18, 2011; Washington, DC, United States, March 21–22, 2011 and April 24–25, 2012.

relative to other jurisdictions that have copied the BVI legislation almost word for word to produce identical shell companies, one provider reasoned by analogy that "there are lots of colas out there, but people prefer Coke."[6] Because companies are corporate citizens of a particular country (or sometimes sub-national jurisdiction like Delaware), the standing, reputation, or "brand" of the country may affect the desirability of the shell company. US or British shell companies may be seen as solid, reliable, and well regulated, while those from obscure tax havens may be seen to carry an air of exoticism, disrepute, or even criminality (Sharman 2011: chapter 3; Economist Intelligence Unit 2002).

The global corporate transparency standards

Because shell companies are so prone to misuse in order to disguise criminal schemes, international standards have been formulated to try to regulate their use. Measuring the effectiveness of these standards is one of the key aims of the book, and thus it is important to explain these rules. The ability to "look through" the corporate veil to find the person or people in control is key. A series of reports by governments, international organizations, and NGOs have again and again returned to the centrality of shell companies in combating a wide range of serious crimes (OECD 2001; GAO 2006; FATF 2006a; Financial Crimes Enforcement Network 2006; Global Witness 2009, 2012; StAR 2011).

Although many bodies are relevant in the regulation of shell companies, none is more important that the Financial Action Task Force (FATF) (Gilmore 2011; Sharman 2011). The FATF was set up in the wake of the G7 heads of state summit in July 1989. Its original mandate was to counter money laundering associated with the international drug trade, in the waning days of the Cold War regarded as a major threat to US national security, and which also afflicted other G7 members. Because drug traffickers (much like other organized crime groups) are motivated by profit, to the extent that authorities could follow the money trail to apprehend criminals and take the profit out of crime, the drug trade would be greatly reduced. Or so the logic went.

Starting with a membership of rich OECD countries, the FATF has since expanded to take in other "strategically important" countries,

---

[6] Author interview: Brades, Montserrat, January 25, 2006.

including Russia, China, India, Brazil, and South Africa. Its small secretariat of around 20 staff is housed within the OECD headquarters in Paris, though the FATF is an independent body. As a Task Force, the FATF is not a formal treaty organization, and thus it produces "soft" rather than formally binding "hard" international law. The FATF has come to be recognized as the authoritative standard-setter and enforcer of anti-money laundering regulations, garnering endorsements from the UN Security Council among many others, and having its rules incorporated within the suite of World Bank and International Monetary Fund financial standards and codes (Gordon 2010). It presides over eight regional satellite organizations devoted to diffusing FATF rules among their member states, and nearly all countries not in the FATF belong to one of these regional FATF satellites and thus subscribe to FATF standards.

The FATF rules were first codified as the 40 Recommendations, later augmented by 9 Special Recommendations to combat the financing of terrorism. In 2012 these were redrafted as the International Standards on Combating Money Laundering and the Financing of Terrorism and Proliferation. Despite their soft law status and the term "recommendation," the FATF has been remarkably successful in persuading or coercing more than 180 states to sign up and implement its preferred measures. Part of this success can be attributed to periodic public blacklisting campaigns waged against those countries judged to be derelict in their duty to fight money laundering. Being named on one of these blacklists has tended to constrict targeted countries' access to international financial networks (Drezner 2007: 142–143). The FATF monitors adherence to the rules more systematically with rolling Mutual Evaluation Reports, often conducted in conjunction with the World Bank or IMF, in which all members are publicly graded on their compliance with each Recommendation.

Just because the rules have been adopted, however, does not necessarily mean that they have been effective, which is a key uncertainty that provides much of the motivation for writing this book. The Recommendations first specify that countries must criminalize the practice of money laundering, while also setting out the requirements on how governments should regulate financial firms to ensure transparency and screen out the proceeds of crime. The essence of the Recommendations is to collect much more information on those using the financial system.

In practice, however, direct action by governments to counter money laundering is only the tip of the iceberg; the bulk of implementation is delegated to private firms, especially banks, but also to corporate service providers. Rather than just following set, detailed procedures, these private firms are legally required to evaluate all of their customers and transactions for money laundering risk; this "risk-based approach" is referred to as the "essential foundation" of the regulatory regime (FATF 2012: 11). The interpretive notes list risk factors as "countries or geographic areas; and products, services, transactions or delivery channels."

The most relevant section of the FATF rules on shell companies states: "Countries should take measures to prevent the misuse of legal persons for money laundering or terrorist financing. Countries should ensure that there is adequate, accurate and timely information on the beneficial ownership and control of legal persons that can be obtained or accessed in a timely fashion by competent authorities" (Recommendation 24). It is difficult to come up with a watertight definition of beneficial ownership in law, but substantively it refers to the real person or people in control of the company (StAR 2011). Beneficial ownership is distinct from the concept of legal ownership. This difference can be appreciated with reference to the earlier quote from the GT Group where Geoffrey Taylor offered to act as the nominee shareholder for the client. According to this arrangement, Taylor would be the company's legal owner, while the client would retain control as the beneficial owner.

Other relevant sections of the Recommendations impose extensive customer due diligence and record-keeping responsibilities on corporate service providers when establishing a business relationship (Recommendation 22). Specifically, this entails "identifying the customer and verifying that customer's identity using reliable, independent source documents, data or information" (Recommendation 10), later identified as comprising passports, national identity cards, or drivers' licenses.

Other international standards tend to echo this same priority of corporate transparency, including the United Nations Convention Against Corruption (Article 12 (c)), the United Nations Convention on Transnational Organized Crime (Article 31 d (I)), the United Nations International Convention for the Suppression of the Financing of Terrorism (Article 18, 1 (b) (ii)), and many other regional agreements on similar topics. The G20 has identified establishing beneficial ownership as a priority area for international action, requesting that the FATF "help detect and deter the proceeds of corruption by prioritizing work to strengthen standards on customer due diligence, beneficial ownership and transparency" (FATF 2011: 11).

The clarion calls of international organizations notwithstanding, what does or should the proper procedure look like when it comes to shell companies? Recognizing the importance of being able to look through shell companies to find the real owner, a report by the OECD suggests three approaches: strong investigative powers for law enforcement, looking at the corporate registry, or regulating corporate service providers (OECD 2001). In fact, however, it is argued here that the first two suggestions are not feasible, and that in practice corporate service providers afford the only reliable (though certainly not infallible) route to the real owner.

The first approach, relying on law enforcement agencies with strong investigative powers, is epitomized by the United States. For example, US law enforcement bodies are able to mount undercover sting operations in foreign countries (like that in Thailand, which proved to be Viktor Bout's undoing) and strike plea bargains in a way that is forbidden to counterparts in most European countries. The US government has also been willing to take an extremely robust position vis-à-vis foreign firms and governments in a way that has often been successful in ripping aside the corporate veil, as with the Swiss banks discussed earlier.

Yet relying on tough coercive powers has distinct limitations, especially when it comes to foreign nationals using US shell companies. These are encapsulated in the disarmingly straightforward reply of one US provider in response to a solicitation that was part of an earlier audit study: "Regarding confidentiality, no information is taken so none can be given – it is that simple!" (Sharman 2011). Rather than a one-off, this reply mirrors many others we received from US providers, as discussed in the following chapters. As the international organizations recognize, no amount of coercive pressure applied to corporate service providers will produce information that was never collected (OECD 2001; FATF 2006b). Thus one of the most active legislative critics of the status quo in the United States, Senator Carl Levin, has referred to the way the United States has repeatedly been caught "red-faced and empty handed" when presented with foreign requests for information on the real owners of US shell companies (Levin 2006).

The second approach, relying on the company registry, has increasingly been pushed by NGOs such as Global Witness. As discussed earlier, companies only exist as legal persons thanks to the official recognition that comes from being listed on the corporate registry, which in turn requires a minimum of documentation to be lodged. The registry, then, would seem to be the place from which to establish the ownership of companies. In practice, however, things are not so simple. According to a World Bank study (StAR 2011), only one registry in the world, the Channel Island of Jersey, has a requirement that beneficial ownership information be supplied for each company registered. Almost everywhere else registries function as archives that receive documents but do not have a role in verifying these documents. The information contained is generally sparse. For example, the UK registry has the following information on one UK shell company, Sorento Resources Ltd, that has been linked with $32 million of suspected corruption funds from Kyrgyzstan (Global Witness 2012) (the "consulting" and "management" duties of its corporate shareholder and secretary are notable given that this is also the cover story for our approach emails).

Name: Sorento Resources Ltd
Registered 6 November 2007.
Address: 6A Vulcan House, Calleva Park, Reading
Agent: @UKplc Client Director Ltd, 5 Jupiter House, Calleva Park, Reading.
Shareholder and Initial Director: Mita Consulting Ltd, British Virgin Islands.
Secretary: Rainmore Management Co, Marshall Islands.
Dormant Accounts for 2008 & 2009.
Director was changed on 3 October 2008 to Mario Castillo, Panama.
Dissolved 12 October 2010

The address listed plays host to 15,000 other shell companies, while the only real person named, Mario Castillo, was director of at least 275 other companies, and thus almost certainly a nominee.

With reference to Aikate Properties Inc., mentioned earlier in connection with the Magnitsky case, the information held by the British Virgin Islands registry is similarly sparse:

Company Name: Aikate Properties Inc.
Company Number: 1382955
Date of Incorporation / Registration: 29 January, 2007
Maximum Number of Shares Company is Authorised to Issue: 50,000
Company Status: Struck off Dissolved
Company Status Date: 30 July, 2010
First Registered Agent: COMMONWEALTH TRUST LIMITED
First Registered Office: 1st Floor Yamraj Bldg, P.O. Box 3321, Road Town,
Tortola VG1110, British Virgin Islands
Tel#: 1–284–494–4541 Fax#: 1–284–494–3016
Current Registered Agent: COMMONWEALTH TRUST LIMITED
Current Registered Office: 1st Floor Yamraj Bldg, P.O. Box 3321, Road
Town, Tortola VG1110, British Virgin Islands
Tel#: 1–284–494–4541 Fax#: 1–284–494–3016

In private, those working in registries admit that even the records they do have are often incomplete and out of date. They are aghast at the suggestion that they should be charged with the responsibility of establishing beneficial ownership, regarding this as far beyond their capacities. So while registries may provide a valuable first point of contact for those looking to pierce the corporate veil, they do not contain the information necessary to trace the identity of those behind shell companies, nor does this situation look likely to change in the foreseeable future.

This leaves the third option for tracing shell company owners, which relies on the crucial intermediating role of corporate service providers. In line with the FATF Recommendations quoted earlier, and the more general tendency to delegate implementation to private firms, here the approach is to require these agents to collect and verify identity documentation for customers looking to purchase a company. Specifically, this imposes a duty on providers requiring them to collect certified or notarized copies of official documents like a national identity card or the picture page of a passport, usually augmented by utility bills as proof of current address. Service providers must keep these documents on file (usually for five years), and produce them on request to local law enforcement agencies and regulators, who may in turn be acting on requests from foreign counterparts. The British Virgin Islands provides an example of this system. Those incorporating BVI companies must be licensed with the local Financial Services Commission and abide by the rules on customer identification. Every year the Commission picks companies at random from the registry and contacts the relevant service provider to request the documents on beneficial ownership. Any provider that cannot produce the documentation within a few days has its license revoked, and thus can no longer form BVI companies.[7] Other countries with this requirement include the Cayman Islands and Jersey.

Of course, imposing Know Your Customer duties on providers is not a panacea. The identity documents they hold on the real owner are not public, and they are only revealed on request to duly authorized agencies. Where information requests are coming from foreign authorities there may be delays and paperwork in having the request processed. In countries such as the United States and Britain, individuals can go online to register companies directly without using the services of an intermediary. Even when service providers are required, they may be negligent, willfully blind, or actively in cahoots with criminals. When asked by one of the authors of this study about their customer due diligence practices, one provider representative laughingly mimed the proverbial three monkeys – see no evil, hear no evil, speak no evil.

A prominent example of collusion between a criminal and a CSP is the case of Teodorin Obiang, forestry minister and heir-apparent of the oil-rich West African nation of Equatorial Guinea, and his American lawyer Michael Jay Berger. Reacting to strong evidence of major corruption offenses, in October 2011 the US government sought to freeze over $70 million of Obiang's assets, including a private jet, a Malibu mansion, and $1.8 million in Michael Jackson memorabilia (including a crystal-studded glove) (Ferran and Ryan 2011). For a retainer of $5,000 a month over the period 2004–2008, Berger had established Californian shell companies Beautiful Vision and Unlimited Horizons, and then opened multiple accounts for both. Berger did so in his own name, so as to obscure Obiang's controlling role (US Senate Permanent Subcommittee on Investigations 2010: 27–30). Intermediaries like Berger (who remains in business) and other corporate service providers are unregulated in the United States, the consequences of which are discussed in Chapter 3.

In general, the international standards relating to shell companies endorsed by more than 180 countries are quite clear: authorities must be able to "see through" the shell company to find the real individual or individuals in control: the beneficial owner. In practice, ensuring

---

[7] Author interviews: London, UK, September 7, 2011; Miami, United States, April 30–May 1, 2012.

this corporate transparency requires corporate service providers to demand and hold certified copies of identity documents on their clients. If providers do not do so, this information is simply not available. Registries do not hold beneficial ownership information, and law enforcement cannot extract information from providers where it was never collected. To this point, however, it has been unclear just how often providers fulfill these obligations to demand appropriate documentation. Our study provides significant data on this question through a randomized field experiment.

Experimental design

This chapter so far has explained what shell companies are and why they are important, provided a brief sketch of the global incorporation industry, and summarized the relevant international rules. This section explains the design and conduct of the experiments whereby we posed as a variety of more or less risky would-be customers to test the effectiveness of these standards. This task is broken down into sections describing how we assembled the subject pool of more than 3,700 corporate service providers and designed the basic approach email, as well as covering the measures taken to conceal the true purpose of the experiments, the play-book for responding to CSPs, and the coding scheme according to which their replies were classified. This chapter is deliberately light on the details of the experiments, opting to convey the essence through a discussion of major components. The Appendix provides much more detail on the experiments' design and process.

The first challenge was to be as comprehensive as possible in compiling a list of corporate service providers. Yet CSPs are not like banks; in many countries (such as the United States) there is no official licensing or registration requirement, so anyone can form and sell shell companies. The upshot is that there can be no definitive worldwide list of corporate service providers, which means we cannot begin with an established sampling frame. Instead we used a series of internet searches for every country in the world using key terms like "company formation," "shell company," and "offshore company." This resulted in a list of more than 3,700 firms in 181 countries, including 1,700 in the United States.

Although this is the most comprehensive list ever compiled, it cannot be complete; what about those omitted from the list? Those we missed seem likely to be very small concerns without a Web presence in non-tax haven, developing countries catering to the local market. These sorts of businesses are unlikely to form many companies, and they are even less likely to cater to the sort of international clientele linked with the serious financial crimes covered earlier. Given this fact, the figures on non-compliance presented in Chapters 4–6 may actually understate the degree to which untraceable shell companies are available. But although we cannot be absolutely certain, it seems probable that the study has captured those firms responsible for creating the large majority of shell companies worldwide, as well as those most likely to be involved in cross-border business patronized by the sort of risky individuals we impersonate. Where possible we collected information on the nature of the corporate service provider, including their countries of operation and whether or not they were law firms.

At the center of the experiment were the email approaches. First, the standard Placebo email constituted the benchmark for both the rate at which CSPs replied to emails and the frequency with which they complied with international standards by requiring proper identity documentation. Next, the ten treatment emails included crucial variations in information to see what difference, if any, this made to the rates of response and compliance. Each corporate service provider was randomly assigned at least two different emails, either the Placebo and a treatment or two different treatments, with the first and second emails spaced at least nine months apart. A minority of firms received three emails spaced four months apart. The intervals of several months were intended to further minimize the possibility of detection.

At its most basic, each email gave a brief rationale for requesting a shell company and asked what identity documents the provider required in order to form the company. An example of a Placebo email, the template from which each of the treatments are derived and against which they are measured, reads as follows:

Dear [name/company]
I am an international consultant living in [Norstralia]. My associates and I have been based in [Norstralia] for some time and we have done extensive international work, especially in your area.

After looking at the specific needs of our growing company, we were feeling that it would make sense for us to expand and to set up an international company. We especially hope to limit taxes and reduce liability.

We were wondering what you require us to give in order to do this. We would like to form this corporation as privately as possible. What identifying documents will you need from us? We would also like to know what your usual prices are. We appreciate the help.

I travel a lot for my work, so I communicate best via email.

I hope to hear from you soon.

Yours,
[Alias]

The "Norstralia" term refers to the fact that these emails purportedly came from individuals residing in one of eight countries assigned randomly: Australia, Austria, Denmark, Finland, the Netherlands, New Zealand, Norway, and Sweden. These developed countries share important similarities in their being relatively minor powers conventionally perceived as having low levels of corruption and posing a low terrorism risk.

Using a basket of countries rather than just one insured against the risk that some vital country-specific attribute had been overlooked, that some major scandal during the experiment might create a strong association of corruption or terrorism with one of these countries, or that some other country-specific stochastic event might bias results. Later statistical analysis confirmed the intuition that any country-specific effects did not alter the overall treatment effects. Using multiple countries also provided some insurance against the possibility that the same corporate service provider might receive two identical emails in the same round of approaches (perhaps because the same company maintained two separate websites) and become suspicious.

To further guard against the possibility that providers might detect the experiment, we drafted and randomly assigned 33 different base emails that varied the style, diction, and syntax of the approach. For the aliases hailing from non-English-speaking countries, we introduced two minor spelling and grammar errors to enhance authenticity. Individual names were selected in line with the most common male names from each origin country, making sure that they did not correspond with high-profile individuals like prime ministers, athletes, or other media celebrities. As with the basket of countries, later statistical analysis confirmed that the distinct letters did not alter the overall treatment effects.

Detailed discussion of the treatments is held over until Chapters 4–6, with only a summary listing here. The first treatment variation was simply to state that the international rules set by the Financial Action Task Force require that identity documents be collected for those forming shell companies. The second kept this same information, but added that there were penalties for non-compliance. A third replaced the mention of penalties with a normative appeal that all concerned want to "do the right thing" as reputable businessmen. In contrast to the public standards of the FATF, one treatment tested the influence of private standards with mention of the Association of Certified Anti-Money Laundering Specialists (ACAMS). A related condition referenced the transparency standards but attributed them to both ACAMS and the FATF.

Another treatment offered providers extra payment, a "premium," if they ignored the requirement to collect identity documents. A treatment for corporate service providers based in the United States claimed that the identity requirement was enforced by the IRS. Three treatments dispensed with the Norstralian origins and aliases to signal different kinds of risk. The first simply kept the basic frame of the Placebo email, but had the customer come from the United States. The next signaled a corruption risk with consultants hailing from one of eight corruption-prone countries: Guinea, Equatorial Guinea, Guinea-Bissau, Papua New Guinea, Kyrgyzstan, Tajikistan, Turkmenistan, and Uzbekistan, abbreviated as the "Guineastan" countries. Additionally, the corruption risk was raised still further by having the consultants work in government procurement, an area notoriously prone to bribery, kickbacks, and embezzlement. The last departure from the Norstralian template signaled a terrorism financing risk. Here the customers came from one of four countries that are perceived to host terrorist groups: Lebanon, Pakistan, Palestine, and Yemen. Having these consultants work in Saudi Arabia for a Muslim aid organization heightened the terrorism financing risk, as both transnational action and charities are listed as "red flags" in the FATF's risk guidelines.

Having all the fictitious individuals working in the consultancy business provided a plausible but usefully vague backstory. Not only are there many bona fide international consultants plying their trade, but it is a common alibi for those engaged in more nefarious pursuits. For example, when Gaddafi and his sons demanded bribes from foreign oil firms, these were often excused as payment for consultancy (Lichtblau et al. 2011). When British arms firm BAE offered illicit payments through middlemen to Saudi Arabia and other clients, these payments were again disguised as consulting fees. A "how to" guide to offshore tax evasion recommended that funds flowing between the tax evader and the shell company be disguised as consultancy payments (US Senate Permanent Subcommittee on Investigations 2006: 33). As related in Chapter 4, a corporate service provider secretly filmed in the Seychelles in 2012 explained to what he thought was a corrupt Zimbabwean official how setting up a shell company ostensibly in the consultancy business was the best way to launder looted wealth (*Al Jazeera* 2012). A 2009 World Bank study found that fake consultancy payments were the most common cover story for those seeking to launder the proceeds of large-scale corruption (Gordon 2009). Consultancy services are, of course, intangible and thus it can be hard to prove whether such an arrangement is really in place or serves only as a cover to conceal illicit financial flows.

By introducing a desire for limited liability, tax savings, and confidentiality in the basic frame of the emails we touch on the three most common rationales for incorporating shell companies, according to extensive interviews with corporate service providers and observing at their professional conferences (see also Finkelstein 1998; Economist Intelligence Unit 2002; Nolan and Crouch 2009; StAR 2011). The internet email accounts used to send the emails were registered to mobile phone numbers in an African country, arranged when student researchers bought 50-cent SIM cards at a local market. Each account was set up within a coffee shop after having entered a proxy server to mask the actual location even further.

To preserve the fiction that the individual emails were being sent from all over the world (rather than just the United States, as was actually the case) and enhance the realism of the approaches, we again employed proxy servers that ensured that anyone seeking the source of the emails, or the IP address, would be directed to a variety of locations in Asia and Europe. A small minority of replies to these emails voiced suspicions about the exercise being part of an advanced fee fraud like the unsolicited emails suggesting the recipient is the beneficiary of a Nigerian prince's estate or some other scam (see the example below), and threatened to inform the local police to this effect, but none guessed the possibility of their being part of a field experiment.

Also specified in the protocol, we used standard responses to other common queries to ensure consistency in the experiment. The consultants did not require any other products, such as trusts or more complicated corporate structures within which to hold the shell company, for example. There was no need for a bank account. Tax advice was also not necessary, because this had been provided for the consultant already. There was a need to deflect requests from corporate service providers for a phone or Skype conversation to finalize arrangements. Aside from it being practically difficult to maintain the fiction of a multinational cast of consultants in direct conversation, the advantage of having all communication carried out via email was having the record of every word exchanged. The conspicuous exception to this comprehensive record was the name of any individual or corporate service provider firm, which were deliberately deleted in line with the ethics requirements of the experiment. In this way, the experiment would not cause any individual to come to harm or impose financial or reputational loss upon any firm.

Coding responses

The email responses from corporate service providers to our Placebo and various treatment messages comprise the raw data on which this book is built, and thus it is crucial to explain how these thousands of emails were sorted, sifted, and organized according to procedures laid down in the protocol. In each case, the key point of information in the replies was whether or not identity documentation was required by the provider in order to form the shell company. When the initial response did not address this part of the approach email, firms received a standardized specific prompt asking once more what documents were required. Once this information was obtained, a final email thanked firms for their time and informed them that the consultant's business needs had been met.

Each approach could result in one of five outcomes: no response, refusal, compliance, partial compliance, and non-compliance. No response, where providers made no reply after being prompted twice, may seem like the most self-evident and uninteresting possibility, yet in fact how to interpret this outcome poses one of the main challenges of the experiments. This question is especially important given that some portions of the subject pool, especially US law firms, left roughly three-quarters of our emails unanswered. The average response rate was 51 percent across all conditions in the international sample.

Of particular importance is whether no response reflects a form of "soft compliance," that is, where firms judged that the profile of the client they were ostensibly dealing with was too risky, and they acted to uphold international standards prohibiting the supply of untraceable shell companies by the simplest expedient of not engaging at all. If this is one interpretation, however, there are certainly others. As noted above, some firms replied with suspicions that the approach email was some kind of scam or spam (one example reads: "Your original communication sounded like many of the phony Nigerian/Chinese 'debt collection' schemes which I receive every day"). It is very likely that others simply deleted the approach without replying on these same grounds.

On a couple of occasions providers accidentally included internal email threads in their reply to a second approach discussing their response to the first, wondering whether they should bother to reply or just pretend that the first message had gone through to their junk file. Other providers may well have decided that the approach was genuine, but calculated that it represented too small a business return to pursue. Others again may have failed to reply through simple oversight. The chapters discussing the results of the various treatments return to this issue of whether or not non-responses reflect a form of soft compliance.

When providers replied with refusal of our solicitation, some simply declined without further elaboration, while others offered reasons that shed light on the discussion above. One provider suggested that the offer was too "cloak and dagger" for them to accept, another noted, "It is a fact of life that many e-mail solicitations are actually money laundering schemes," and a third replied that they had reported our fictitious consultant to the local police. While some refusals were business-like, others were arch or even indignant. Thus the response below from one Incorporation Agent in Australia to the Danish consultant, Mikkel Pedersen (all typos being in the original):

Dear Mikkel
I am assuming that your email was completely fraudulent.

If I am incorrect and this is not the case, please contact me on the number below and I will endeavour to assist.

However, if you indeed your intention behind contacting me is to make a lazy, fraudelent buck at the expense of others, then please spare a thought for the prospect you will remain a complete, impoverished idiot for the res eof your life and die poor and sad.

I will be leaving you nothing in my will.

Regards,

In other cases that were coded as refusals, providers evinced some ambiguity as to whether a higher price might induce them to change their initial "no" into a "yes." One particularly striking case concerned one of the treatment emails, no longer to the relatively innocuous "Norstralian" but instead to an obvious terrorism financing risk (discussed at length in Chapter 4). As is the case with non-responses, the extent to which refusals represent a form of soft compliance is discussed in tandem with the substantive results in the chapters to follow. Curiously, very few corporate service providers responded with refusals, let alone with elaborate rationales justifying the withholding of service. Many more simply asked for the requester's credit card number but no accompanying certified identity documents.

At the heart of the book is an interest in when and why actors comply with international rules. In the context of the emails received in response to solicitations for shell companies, what counts as being compliant? As discussed earlier, the key to preventing the kind of criminality otherwise facilitated by shell companies is the ability to link the legal person with the real person in control, and in practice this means the corporate service provider requiring and retaining certified identity documents proving the identity of the customer. Providers are the public face of the company as recorded in the corporate registry, receiving official correspondence and paying the annual government fee. In many cases law enforcement authorities or other parties have been able to retrieve these identity documents from the provider to pierce the corporate veil (US Senate Permanent Subcommittee on Investigations 2006).[8] These documents must include a copy of government-issued official photo identity documents (typically the picture page of a passport, but perhaps also a national identity card), which has been notarized or otherwise certified as a true copy of the original. A secondary requirement might be the provision of utility bills to prove address and residency, and perhaps also bank or other professional references.

[8] Author interviews: Washington, DC, United States, April 24–25, 2012.

Of course there are such things as fake passports (and fake or stolen notarial stamps), but while no human system is perfect, imperfect safeguards are much better than none at all. With all this in mind, the basic coding rule was that any response that specified the need for notarized or certified government photo identity documents before the shell company could be formed was coded as (fully) compliant. A reply from St. Kitts and Nevis provides an example of a compliant response (again with typos preserved):

Herewith, the requisite forms for your to complete. The identifying documents you must send are as follows: 1. Certified copies of the information pages of your passport or of your driver's licence. 2. Certified copies of two utility bills or other, showing your usual place or residence. 3. Two reference letters, one from a bank and the other form a business or other associate. Have these sent directly to us from the persons giving the same. Please remit half of the fee at this time (see wire instructions below).

What if the provider had failed to specify that the passport copies or other official government photo ID must be notarized? Responses that asked for some proof of identity but did not meet the conventional international standard of certified copies of official photo identity documents were coded as partially compliant. While tracing the company back to the service provider would yield some information as to the real owner, the documents on file would convey less information and would be easier to falsify.

The last category, non-compliant, is in many ways the most important. Here the provider was willing to supply a shell company without any photo identification at all, meaning that in effect the resulting company was exactly the sort of untraceable entity so useful for the range of crimes discussed earlier. Those investigating the company would have few if any options in trying to connect the company with the real individual in control. This beneficial ownership information is not listed in the corporate registries. No amount of pressure on the provider after the fact would summon up information that had never been collected when the shell company was formed.

While tracing the flow of funds used to pay for the company may yield some information, various dodges like anonymous pre-paid credit cards, credit cards issued to another anonymous corporation, routing the payment through several intermediaries, or banks that routinely fail to include full details of the payer on wire transfers may well frustrate any attempt to follow the money trail. When asked by one of the authors whether it was possible to "beat" banks' customer due diligence requirements, one provider laughed so hard at the naïveté of the question that he had to take time to compose himself before confirming that this was indeed the case.

The non-compliant responses received were often very brief, and in many cases showed in breath-taking fashion how quick, easy, and cheap it is to form anonymous shell companies in direct defiance of international rules mandating corporate transparency. Three such responses provide a flavor of the non-compliant replies.

(1) It sounds like you want to form your company anonymously with the State, is that correct? We can do that for an extra $25. If we are just setting up a Corporation for you and that's it we don't require any documents from you at all.

(2) Thanks for your email of 17 May. We do not require any documents/information for our cooperation. Your above email is quite sufficient to learn of your activities.

(3) All that you need to do is to provide the name you want for you [*sic*] new company, that's it.

These kinds of responses raise very serious questions about the extent to which global rules on corporate transparency are dead-letter, pious hopes that mean little or nothing in the actual practice of transnational commerce.

A final point relates to a possible objection about taking the email responses received at face value. As noted above, the email correspondence ended when the provider specified what identity documentation, if any, was necessary for the shell company to be formed. We did not actually buy any shell companies, in part because of the expense, but even more so because signing legal documents like incorporation forms in a false name is a criminal offense.

What if corporate service providers were engaging in some "bait and switch" ploy, whereby they initially intimated that no supporting documents were required, but later made the transaction conditional on just the sort of identity material that international standards specify? Here the findings of an earlier audit study completed by one of this book's authors are important (Sharman 2011). This study again was based on solicitations for shell companies, but in 42 instances the author went through to the very final stage of forming a company through providers, bar actually paying the money. In no instance did providers change the requirement for identity documentation once correspondence had begun, including in the 17 cases where providers did not ask for any supporting documentation at all. Furthermore, in three other cases Sharman actually did pay the providers and form the companies under his own name as beneficial owner (André Pascal Enterprises in England, Gruppo20 in the Seychelles, and BCP Enterprises in Nevada). Once again, there was no change in the documentation required by the provider, which was none at all in the case of the English and Nevada companies. Inspired by the author's prior work (Sharman 2011), several media organizations replicated this process and found a similar consistency among providers (for example National Public Radio formed the memorably named shell companies UnBelizable and Delawho?). The audit study thus strongly suggests that the measure we have used here to judge compliance – the demand for notarized identification – is a meaningful measure of the outcome of interest: the ease of forming anonymous shell corporations.

Conclusion

Whether or not shell companies can be traced back to their real owners is vital for efforts to combat a range of related financial crimes, from the money laundering essential to all large-scale profit-driven crime, to major corruption offenses, to tax evasion, to sanctions-busting, and to the financing of terrorism. In practice, those firms whose business it is to form and administer shell companies are the essential locus of compliance if the global standards on corporate transparency are to be effective. The key questions following from this are whether, when, and why these standards actually work in practice.

Despite the significance of these questions, the answers so far from international organizations, governments, and other evaluations are largely guesses (Levi and Reuter 2006; Andreas and Greenhill 2010; Reuter 2012). Building on the experiment outlined above, the chapters to follow aim to answer these questions with much better evidence. While Chapters 4–6 deal with the effect of the various treatments, Chapter 3 looks at one of the most puzzling general results relating to patterns of compliance and non-compliance between rich and poor countries, as well as between tax havens and the rest of the world.

3 | *Overall compliance, tax havens, OECD and developing countries*

As discussed in Chapter 1, to the extent that untraceable shell companies are easily available, law enforcement authorities will find it very difficult to make progress apprehending money launderers, tax evaders, corrupt officials, and a wide range of other criminals. At the most general level, what do the overall descriptive findings from the field study tell us about how well or how badly global rules actually work in practice when they mandate that shell companies be traceable back to the real people in control? This chapter presents the broad-brush results from the 7,456 solicitations made to the corporate service providers, compares them to what might have been expected, and seeks to explain the patterns that emerged. The broad finding that almost half (48.2 percent) of the replies received did not require certified identity documents, and more than a fifth (22.1 percent) did not require any photo identity documents at all, provides evidence for a significant compliance problem. But is this result a surprise? Though based mainly on reading laws rather than assessing actual practice, FATF reports have long indicated that both member and non-member countries have had trouble meeting the standard whereby authorities must be able to identify companies' real owners. On this basis, perhaps non-compliance rates might have been expected to be even worse.

The next step is to break the results down to allow comparisons of compliance rates between rich developed countries, poor developing nations, and offshore tax havens. Unlike the overall level of compliance, this move reveals some definite surprises. Perhaps the greatest is that tax havens, long reviled as scofflaws of the global financial regulatory regimes, have an outstanding level of compliance far ahead of the average, and far above major OECD countries in particular. Also intriguing and running directly counter to expectations is the fact that poorer developing countries sometimes prove more compliant than developed nations (though not as compliant as tax havens). Given how wide of the mark it has proved to be, why has the conventional wisdom been that developed countries should have had much higher compliance rates than poor countries and tax havens? After describing the logic of these expectations, we explain the counter-intuitive results in terms of a campaign of international pressure against tax havens since the late 1990s.

Overall results

Of all the replies received from our 7,456 solicitations in the international and US subject pools, 22.1 percent were willing to provide a shell company without requiring any photo identification at all. International CSPs were significantly less likely to offer anonymous shells at 16.4 percent of replies compared to an astounding 41.5 percent non-compliance rate in the United States among the CSPs that responded to our inquiries. Given the minimal investment needed to find and approach providers of shell companies, the barriers to obtaining a prohibited untraceable shell company are thus very low, even though such companies are formally prohibited by international rules. Even without any expertise on the subject, a person searching for a provider willing to violate international standards in this regard could start searching at the beginning of the day and probably be finished by lunch. From this result, it is apparent that the standards on corporate transparency are relatively ineffective. A further 26.1 percent of the replies asked for some identity documentation (31.5 percent internationally, 7.9 percent in the United States), but did not specify that this had to be certified or notarized. Of the remaining replies, 24.9 percent were compliant (31.7 percent internationally, 1.5 percent in the United States), while 26.9 percent refused service (20.4 percent internationally, 49.1 percent for the United States).

One complication in interpreting our results is the large number of non-responses received: almost half (49.0 percent) in the international sample, and 77.3 percent from providers in the United States. If many or most of these non-responses are actually a form of "soft compliance," in that providers uphold the rules prohibiting the provision of anonymous shell companies by simply ignoring emails from insalubrious customers, then the pessimistic conclusion above concerning regime effectiveness might be misleading. As a proportion of all approaches made, not just the replies received, 8.7 percent of providers were willing to supply a shell company without any photo documentation (9.1 percent in the United States and 8.4 percent in the rest of the world). A generous view might be that all eventualities except non-compliance (i.e. no response, refusal, part compliance, and compliance) are consistent with the goal of preventing access to anonymous shell companies, and thus that the global rules are in fact more than 90 percent effective. Given that no human system can be expected to be perfect, this level of compliance might in fact represent a strong endorsement of the existing rules.

This generous view that takes all behavior save non-compliance to be rule-consistent is in fact the basis for our "Dodgy Shopping Count" measure of compliance. The Dodgy Shopping Count is a simplified measure of non-compliance gauging the average number of providers a particular type of customer would have to approach to receive a non-compliant response, i.e. be offered a shell company with no need to supply any photo identity documents whatsoever. A 5 percent non-compliance rate would thus equal a Dodgy Shopping Count of 20. Broadly speaking, the lower the Dodgy Shopping Count, the easier it is to get an anonymous shell corporation, though there are some definite limits to this simple yardstick noted later in the chapter and discussed in the Chapter 2 Appendix at the end of the book.

There are two caveats to this more optimistic, generous perspective, however. First, even an effectiveness rate in excess of 90 percent may not be good enough to have real policy impact. For example, take the treatment with the lowest rate of non-compliance, terrorism financing, where approximately one in twenty solicitations elicited a response from a provider willing to provide a shell company with no questions asked. Remember also that this is a blatantly obvious risk, where we did everything possible to indicate the danger of a terrorist connection barring only an outright statement of terrorist links. Even if this result is interpreted as the system being 95 percent effective, the search costs for an untraceable shell company are still relatively low in absolute terms, possibly a couple of days' work instead of half a day. Thus it may be that the system has to be 99 percent effective, or even more, to create a real barrier to criminals looking to obscure their illicit finances via shell companies. This rendering of the problem also ignores the possibility that risky customers might learn or compare notes, or that certain jurisdictions or certain providers might have a reputation for lax practices, and thus be disproportionately targeted by shady customers in searches. In this way criminals might reduce their search time and increase their success rate in obtaining anonymous shell companies far beyond what our Dodgy Shopping Count measure would indicate.

The second caveat more specifically regards counting non-responses as "soft compliance," a de facto form of deliberate risk-screening. We discuss a specific test of this possibility below, but it is worth noting that, to the extent many of the US law firms in particular are simply not in the business of forming companies for foreign clients, then their non-responses and refusals cannot be interpreted as evidence for compliance with the international Know Your Customer regime. If we had approached 1,000 US pizza delivery firms and asked for shell companies, presumably the result would have been nearly 100 percent non-response and refusal, but this would of course tell us nothing about the effectiveness of global rules governing shell companies.

The non-response puzzle presented a major obstacle to interpreting the results of our initial rounds of testing, and thus we designed a further approach to try to tease out the motivation beyond these silences. This approach was sent out only to those providers who had failed to respond after our initial email contact and second follow-up. It avoided all mention of tax, limited liability, confidentiality, or any other of the more specific risk factors in simply asking whether the firm was still in business and able to help clients interested in forming a company. Below is an example of one such email:

Good afternoon,
I am an international consultant living in [Norstralia]. After looking at the specific needs of our growing company, we were feeling that it would make sense for us to expand and to set up an international company. We were wondering if you will be able to help us with the incorporation.

I travel a lot for my work, so I communicate best via email. I hope to hear from you soon.

Yours,
[Alias]

The logic here was to strip away all possible risk factors that may have deterred providers from answering the first time around, and thus separate out the proportion of non-responses that were a form of soft compliance from those that had nothing to do with customer risk screening. The expectation was that those firms practicing soft compliance would reply to our innocuous approach, whereas those failing to

reply were simply not in the market, and thus their failure to respond
could not be taken as evidence of de facto compliance with international standards. In fact a large majority of those from the US and
the international subject pools again failed to respond (88 percent),
indicating that non-response is rather weak evidence of soft compliance. As such, the contention that our results are consistent with a
90 percent plus rate of compliance seems very unlikely.

Comparing aggregate results with expectations

Bearing in mind the differing pessimistic and optimistic interpretations
of the results explained above, to what extent do our findings fit with
other evaluations of the effectiveness of global rules governing beneficial ownership standards? The Financial Action Task Force is the most
important actor, given its responsibility for monitoring and enforcing
the effective application of anti-money laundering rules. As noted, the
FATF does not adopt anything like the method for testing effectiveness
employed in this book, instead preferring to read the laws on the books
and count convictions rather than assessing actual behavior. However,
even on this basis there have been long-standing reasons for disquiet.

The FATF Recommendation specifying that authorities must have
"adequate, accurate and timely" access to the identity of shell companies' real owners has long had one of the lowest overall levels of
assessed compliance. A compilation of evaluation reports of 159 countries indicated that only 7 percent were graded as Compliant with the
Recommendation of beneficial ownership, while another 15 percent
received the Largely Compliant rating (StAR 2011: 114) (interestingly
in light of our findings below, FATF members had slightly lower levels
of Compliant and Largely Compliant ratings than non-members). Only
one FATF member state, Italy, was rated as Compliant with this measure, while Australia and Norway were rated as Largely Compliant.

Recommendation 24 (denoted Recommendation 33 before the 2012
revision to the Recommendations) on the beneficial ownership of companies has been one of the most vexed for the FATF. A dedicated Expert
Group, formed to address disagreements over this Recommendation,
first reiterated its importance: "The FATF has for many years noted
the importance of corporate vehicles as one of the key mechanisms
used in money laundering schemes ... [and this] is also fundamental to
other important areas such as anti-corruption, corporate governance
and work to combat tax evasion, to name a few" (FATF Expert Group

2009: 2). The Group went on to note that this Recommendation was one of the last to be agreed to when the standards were first composed, and that this standard was rarely met in national evaluations.

As noted in Chapter 2, three FATF Recommendations relate directly to the identification of customers in corporate formation: Recommendation 10 (formerly Recommendation 5) on general customer due diligence, Recommendation 20 (formerly Recommendation 12) on customer due diligence for designated non-financial businesses and professions, and, especially as highlighted above, Recommendation 24 (formerly 33) on the identification of beneficial owners. Along with our collaborator Shima Baradaran, we culled statutory compliance levels from the FATF's Mutual Evaluation Reports on 47 countries and analyzed the statistical association with the compliance rates we found in our field study (Baradaran et al. 2013). Curiously, we learned that statutory compliance – as reported by FATF mutual evaluations – with Recommendations 10 and 20 was not significantly related statistically to the actual compliance rates we found in our experiments. Statutory compliance with Recommendation 24 was significantly related to actual compliance, but only at the most modest 0.1 threshold ($p = 0.08$), and the correlation was rather weak ($r = 0.26$). Regression analysis suggests that 93 percent of the variance in actual compliance rates remains unexplained by statutory compliance levels as reported by the FATF. These findings especially raise questions about standard measures of compliance relying on statutory faithfulness to international law.

The 2010–2011 debate within the FATF over what is now Recommendation 24 turned on whether to apply more pressure to countries to meet this standard or to water down the standard to match the actual laws obtaining in member states. Had this latter proposal succeeded, we note that it would have been a conspicuous example of the endogeneity problem on tracing the effectiveness of international standards discussed in Chapter 1, as the standards would have been changed to fit the practice rather than vice versa. The compromise decision in 2012 was to leave the content of Recommendation 24 unaltered, which was seen as a defensive victory by those most concerned with untraceable shell companies such as the World Bank/UN Stolen Asset Recovery Initiative and NGOs like Global Witness.[1]

---

[1] Author interviews: Washington, DC, United States, April 24–25, 2012; London, UK, May 17–18, 2012.

In part reflecting dissatisfaction with the FATF record of success on this question, the European Union Third AML Directive introduced in 2007 specifies that those forming companies must establish the true identity of the owners, but due to the delay in transposing this into national legislation the FATF evaluations do not yet capture the effect of this change, if any. Sharman formed a shell company with a British provider in September 2012 (Owens Saint Amans) and received the following reply, which may reflect this regulation:

Due to the implementation of 2007 Money Laundering Regulations we are required to ask for copies of the identification of company directors and beneficial owners of all newly registered companies via e-mail first and by post within 14 working days. We require: Valid proof of ID (valid passport, driving license, National ID card, firearms certificate or shotgun licence) for a company's beneficiary owner (who can be a company director and a shareholder); Proof of address (instrument of a court appointment, current council tax demand letter or statement, current bank or credit/debit card statements (but not ones printed off the internet), utility bills (but not ones printed off the internet) for a company's beneficiary owner.

The message ended with a further prompt: "You have a time frame of 14 days to comply with this procedure – failure to do so will result in receiving one more reminder from our side, and then – a notice of resignation and a further notification to the SOCA" (Serious and Organised Crime Agency). However, given that Sharman applied in his own name, and had earlier criticized this same firm in the media for their lack of diligence, it is impossible to tell what response another less visible customer might have received.

Given both this lack of confidence and the unflattering FATF evaluations of members and non-members alike, the overall results of the field experiment – showing more compliance than not – may actually prove surprising in that compliance rates are so high. If so few countries have imposed a legal duty on the firms that form shell companies to positively identify their customers, why might so many still require some form of ID? Here it is important to point out that, just as taking it for granted that the presence of corresponding domestic legislation will produce perfect compliance with international standards is a mistake, so too may be the assumption that the absence of such national law will produce complete non-compliance.

Some providers may feel a moral duty to take precautions in dealing with potentially shady customers. Thus one provider named in a 2006 US Senate report made no secret of his willingness to help customers illegally evade US taxes, but he refused to deal with foreigners from countries he perceived to be associated with terrorism, even though he had no legal duty to do so (US Senate Permanent Subcommittee on Investigations 2006). Others might fear reputational damage if a company they had set up was involved in spectacular malfeasance and the buck then stopped with the provider. Even in the absence of criminal law or regulatory penalties there may be civil law liabilities for reckless providers. Banks and trust providers that can be shown to be reckless or negligent in having dealt with criminal money may be sued by private parties who were injured by the crime. Depending on the laws of the specific jurisdiction, if the shell company provider has acted as a nominee director, as is often the case, this legal risk becomes more prominent, and the provider may have an incentive to show that at least some due diligence was performed.

Compliance by country type: the rich, the poor, and the havens

In contrast to overall global rates of compliance, this section discusses the expectations and descriptive results of our tests for compliance among three types of countries: rich, developed countries; poorer, developing countries; and tax havens. These results are not experimental, as we clearly could not randomly assign country type. We did, however, block randomize by five types of countries: OECD; tax havens; and three groups of developing countries categorized as hard, medium, and easy according to the World Bank's *Ease of Doing Business* index. So we are confident that the descriptive findings presented here are not biased by imbalances in assignment to conditions and any subsequent treatment effects.

The descriptive results are stark. The major contrast with the global findings covered above is that there were strong expectations as to which types of countries would exhibit better and worse levels of compliance. Specifically, the conventional wisdom on the subject suggests that, in general, poor countries are unable to comply with global financial standards (due to a lack of capacity), tax havens are unwilling to comply (as they attract business through lax regulation), and rich countries are both able and willing to comply (having both the means and the motive). Our results prove this conventional wisdom wrong on each count. Specifically, the tax havens demonstrated by far the highest levels of compliance. And, although rich and poorer countries showed similar levels of compliance, to the extent that there were differences, these tended to favor the developing rather than the developed world. Below we explain this three-part division in our results and the expectations for each group. Having done so, we then describe these findings. We devote a disproportionate share of the attention to the tax haven results, given that these constitute the biggest surprise and are thus most in need of explanation.

With the economic and political rise of countries such as China, India, and Brazil, the notion of a strict separation between rich, developed countries and developing poorer nations may be on its way to obsolescence, yet at present it still captures important differences, especially in finance. Our definition of developing country is taken from the World Bank's categorization of middle- and low-income countries. While China and India may have attained the first rank in manufacturing and some services, their financial sectors are much less sophisticated than those of even relatively small OECD countries (Mistry 2009; Sharman 2012), and they remain in the World Bank's middle-income category. The relatively under-developed state of the financial sector is often even more apparent in smaller developing countries (with the important exception of tax havens, many of which are high income according to the World Bank and all of which are categorized separately for the purposes of this study).

Poorer countries are commonly assumed to have particular difficulty meeting international financial standards. The lack of money and skilled professionals provides the first and perhaps most obvious reason for the shortfall. There may be very few of the lawyers, accountants, and banking experts necessary to effectively regulate a financial sector in a given country, especially as those few local financial professionals emigrate or are tempted into the private sector by higher pay. Regulators in developing countries commonly have to do without electricity and water in their offices, and even when there is power, internet connections, phone lines, and other office basics may be down more often than not.

Perhaps a little less obviously, developing countries may have much less incentive to regulate their financial sector. This sector may be fairly peripheral to the functioning of the real economy, especially the informal economy. Only 41 percent of adults in developing countries have a bank account (compared to 89 percent in developed countries), a figure that slips to 33 percent in South Asia, 24 percent in sub-Saharan Africa, 18 percent in the Middle East, and fewer than 5 percent in countries such as the Congo, Guinea, or Yemen (World Bank 2012: 11).

In contrast, as the crises from 2007 made abundantly clear, the economies of rich countries intimately depend on their financial sectors. Because financial crashes generate severe recessions and even depressions, developed countries have a strong incentive to regulate their financial sectors, and more generally to secure contracts, preserve ownership, and protect against fraud and other criminal activities. Furthermore, although private sector poaching may commonly be a problem, regulatory agencies in rich countries have a vastly greater pool of financial professionals to recruit from, and of course much greater government revenue to draw upon. Thus it has been reasonably assumed that rich countries would do a good job of corporate governance, especially relative to poorer countries.

While the basis for distinguishing between rich and poor states is reasonably clear-cut, that which separates tax havens (also referred to as offshore financial centers) from other countries is much less so. At first this difficulty might seem puzzling: stereotypical tax havens such as the Cayman Islands, the Bahamas, and Vanuatu have no personal or corporate income tax, whereas "normal" countries do. But most tax havens do in fact charge both kinds of income tax. However, crucially, most of these haven jurisdictions (many are not formally sovereign states) exempt non-resident investors from paying most or all of this tax. Hence they have a "ring-fenced" tax regime, meaning that local residents and companies are taxed, but only very low or zero taxes are levied on foreigners. If "pure" tax havens with no income taxes at all capture too few countries conventionally placed in this category, including all those with ring-fenced regimes captures far too many, given that almost every country in the world gives some kind of special tax concession to some kinds of foreign investment. The classic statement of this problem, and its resolution, is given in a 1981 US government report:

The term "tax haven" has been loosely defined to include any country having a low or zero rate of tax on all or certain categories of income, and offering a certain level of banking or commercial secrecy. Applied literally, however, this definition would sweep in many industrialized countries not generally considered tax havens, including the United States (the U.S. does not tax interest on bank deposits of foreigners). The term "tax haven" may also be defined by a "smell" or reputation test: a country is a tax haven if it looks like one and if it is considered to be one by those who care. (Internal Revenue Service 1981)

Though there is a large literature written by those seeking something better than the "smell test" (e.g. Orlov 2004; Zoromé 2007; Palan et al. 2010; Shaxson 2011), we pragmatically adopt the OECD's classification (OECD 2000), itself based in no small measure on the smell test (Sharman 2006).

Judging by the consensus among international financial policy circles, tax havens are the root of the problem when it comes to financial under-regulation and secrecy in general – and untraceable shell companies in particular. A variety of international reports at the turn of the century identified tax havens as incarnating "the dark side of globalization" in the way they allegedly aided and abetted money launderers, tax evaders, and their ilk (United Nations Office for Drug Control and Crime Prevention 1998; OECD 1998, 2000; Financial Stability Forum 2000; FATF 2000a). Tax havens were said to depend on foreign capital lured in by strict secrecy and lax regulation, commonly provided by anonymous shell companies.

The advent of the financial crisis from 2007–2008 forcefully revived this characterization. In their statement on financial transparency at the London G20 summit in April 2009, the heads of state noted: "We agree to take action against non-cooperative jurisdictions, including tax havens. We stand ready to deploy sanctions to protect our public finances and financial systems." Later that same year the same gathering again stated: "We are committed to maintain the momentum in dealing with tax havens ... We stand ready to use countermeasures against tax havens from March 2010." As well as co-sponsoring the Stop Tax Haven Abuse bill during his time as Senator, Barack Obama made his feelings about offshore shell companies clear during his first presidential election campaign: "There is a building in the Cayman Islands that supposedly houses 12,000 US-based corporations. That's either the biggest building in the world, or the biggest tax scam in the world – and we know which one it is."

Tax havens are routinely excoriated by various NGOs like the Tax Justice Network and Global Financial Integrity. For example, in 2008

Christian Aid claimed that the lost revenue due to tax haven-assisted corporate tax evasion and avoidance was responsible for the deaths of 350,000 children in developing countries each year and was the moral equivalent of "a new slavery" (Christian Aid 2008; see also Oxfam 2000; Association for Accountancy and Business Affairs 2002; Tax Justice Network 2011; Global Financial Integrity 2012; Henry 2012). Examples could be multiplied many times over, but technocratic institutions of global governance, rich country governments, and NGOs have largely spoken with one voice in condemning tax havens for being the main culprits in the provision of financial and corporate secrecy. Anonymous offshore shell companies have been portrayed as the primary locus of the problem.

Although the strong expectations of low compliance among tax havens have been built on a good measure of stereotype and prejudice, there is also a political economy logic to this view. Tax havens are almost always very small states or semi-sovereign territories with correspondingly small markets, largely unskilled labor, and poor natural resource endowments – and many are also very isolated (Palan et al. 2010). As such, the reason many and perhaps most tax havens legislate to adopt this offshore strategy is that they have little else to offer international investors except secrecy, low or zero taxes, and minimal regulation. Each of these factors presents a strong incentive to flout or evade international Know Your Customer standards. For individuals and many corporations, the tax advantages of an offshore shell company only accrue if their home country tax authorities are unaware that they really control the shell company in question. To put the same point differently, they are practicing secrecy-enabled illegal tax evasion by hiding income and assets, rather than legal tax avoidance. Absent the secrecy, the tax advantages disappear. As explained earlier, the surest way to guarantee secrecy is to make sure those forming the company have no information on the real owner.

Take the regulatory aspect alone. Individuals and firms seeking offshore incorporation face the inconvenience and delay of having to hunt down and notarize the relevant documents. Merely the postage on having the documents couriered to far-flung locales may raise the total cost of the transaction appreciably. After all, the shell company business is a high-volume, low-margin industry where the product may only cost a few hundred dollars or less. Tax havens face a cut-throat market of extremely mobile potential clients, especially compared to developed or developing states, both of which have something of a captive home market. Thus, economic logic would seem to dictate that tax havens have a stronger motivation to defy global corporate transparency regulations.

The results: confounding the conventional wisdom

Yet, as foreshadowed, the findings of this study on the relative compliance of rich nations, poor countries, and tax havens directly contradicts the prevailing expectations. Tax havens evince superior compliance rates, and developing countries are at least as compliant as developed ones – and in multiple analyses poorer countries demonstrate significantly greater compliance than rich nations. Table 3.1 and Figure 3.1 contain the basic results comparing the five outcome categories explained in the previous chapter (no response, refusal, compliant, part-compliant, non-compliant).

First, relating to the likelihood of getting any kind of reply, the response rate from tax havens is much higher (64.9 percent) than from either rich (49.4 percent) or poorer countries (44.6 percent). Unlike their "onshore" peers, providers based in havens are almost always in the business of forming companies for foreign clients. Thus it seems probable that their higher response may be because they are more used to and comfortable with replying to international inquiries like those from our fictitious consultants. For providers in non-haven developed and developing countries, their relative unfamiliarity in dealing with foreign clients and foreign laws may have made answering our responses more trouble than it was worth. The policy significance of tax havens' high response rate and high compliance rate is that it is possible to be both strictly regulated and internationally competitive, as opposed to the common complaint that to achieve one means to sacrifice the other.

On nearly every count, tax havens outperform the OECD countries: lower non-compliance, higher part-compliance, and higher full compliance – all at statistically and substantively significant levels. Refusal rates in tax havens are lower, but this could be a function of more providers offering strongly compliant responses rather than refusals, which can occur for various reasons. Be it in basic difference of proportions tests or more sophisticated statistical examinations (see Appendix Table A3.1), the differences between tax havens and OECD members are significant statistically and substantively and robust to alternative methods of analysis.

Table 3.1 *Contingency table of results by providers in OECD, tax haven, or developing country categories*

Country group	N	No response	Non-compliant	Part-compliant	Compliant	Refusal
OECD members	1086	549	140	141	129	127
Proportion		50.6%	12.9%	13.0%	11.9%	11.7%
Tax havens	1124	395***	45***	209***	387***	88***
Proportion		35.1%	4.0%	18.6%	34.4%	7.8%
Developing nations	2224	1232***	186***	361**	200***	245
Proportion		55.4%	8.4%	16.2%	9.0%	11.0%

Significant in difference tests compared to OECD countries: *0.1 level, **0.05 level, ***0.01 level.

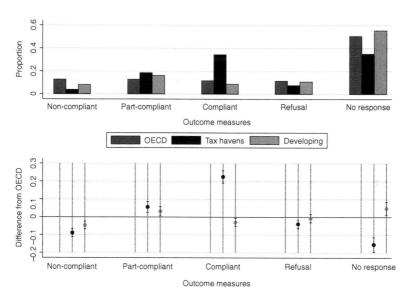

Figure 3.1 Comparison of results between OECD, tax haven, and developing countries as a proportion and difference from OECD countries.

By the broadest measure, the Dodgy Shopping Count, tax havens achieved a score of 25, developing countries 11.9, and rich countries 7.8 (remembering that the higher the score the harder it is to obtain an untraceable shell company and the more effectively the international

standards are apparently being enforced, see Figure 3.2). This suggests
that – in order to obtain an anonymous shell – a customer would
on average need to contact fewer than 8 providers in OECD countries, 12 in poorer nations, but 25 in tax havens. The implication: it
is more than three times more difficult to obtain an anonymous shell
in tax havens than in OECD member countries. This is exactly the
opposite of what the conventional wisdom would expect. Some of the
very best performers were the stereotypical tax havens of crime novels
and thriller movies such as the Cayman Islands, the Bahamas, and the
Seychelles, from which not a single non-compliant reply was received.
Other tax haven jurisdictions such as the Isle of Man, St. Kitts and
Nevis, Liechtenstein, the British Virgin Islands, Dominica, Belize, and
Mauritius outranked a large majority of OECD countries.

Perhaps just as surprising was the performance of poorer countries,
again with unlikely cases such as Vietnam and Uzbekistan surpassing
almost all OECD countries. Although not as strong as the tax havens,
the performance of providers in developing countries was generally
superior to that of their counterparts in rich countries, once again
confounding what policy-makers in general think they know about
this matter. Indeed, both the difference results (Table 3.1) and the
multinomial regression analyses (Appendix Table A3.1) confirm that
developing countries are non-compliant less frequently than OECD
countries. But the news is not all bad for the OECD – developing
countries, like OECD members, also appear to be somewhat less compliant than tax havens. Unfortunately, some of the OECD countries
we would most expect to maintain high regulatory standards do not
fare so well.

In contrast to developing countries, OECD countries were well represented at the tail-end of our league figure of compliance rates (see
Figure 3.3). Here, we take a more encompassing view of compliance,
so the compliance rate captures the proportion of responding firms
that demand notarized identity documents or refuse service. Of the
102 jurisdictions to which we made at least 15 approaches (including
three separate entries for US law firms, US business providers, and
the US overall), US law firms ranked 38th, Britain was 52nd, Canada
69th, Belgium 73rd, Australia 74th, the United States overall 86th, the
Czech Republic 91st, and US incorporation firms were dead last at
103rd. Figure 3.4 shows the distribution of compliance by US states
with the usual suspects – Delaware, Wyoming, and Nevada – showing
up at the bottom along with Alabama and Montana. The flavor of the

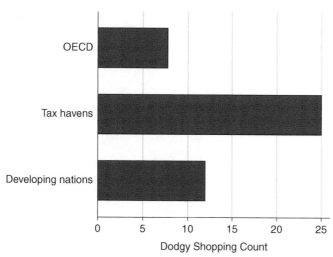

Figure 3.2 Dodgy Shopping Count: OECD, tax haven, and developing nation.

non-compliant results from the United States can be gauged by the following responses from three providers:

(1) We don't need a whole lot of info from you. You can place the order on our website under starting your company. It should only take 10 minutes and that is all the information we need from you.
(2) All that you need to do is to provide the name you want for you [*sic*] new company, that's it.
(3) We have many international clients with the same confidentiality concerns so I am happy to tell you that you have found the right service provider for your needs!

Although the Compliance Rates for different jurisdictions charted in Figures 3.3 and 3.4 below are helpful in providing a simple, concise picture of the big trends in the results, they also obscure some important differences. Take the example of three jurisdictions, the Cayman Islands, Utah, and Libya. These had very high rankings on the charts, but nevertheless exhibited a very different pattern of responses. Cayman providers almost always insisted on the suite of notarized copies of identity documents from the customer before they would form a shell company. Libyan CSPs, when they answered, nearly always refused service. Utah providers mostly did not reply at all. None of the three groups would provide an untraceable shell company, but very different processes seem to be at work.

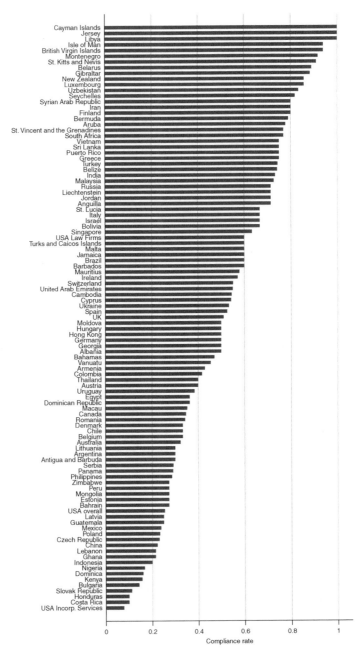

Figure 3.3 Compliance rate for countries with more than 15 email exchanges.

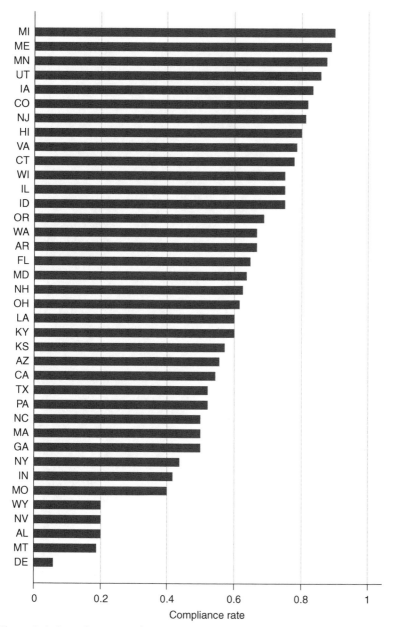

Figure 3.4 Compliance rate for US states with more than five email exchanges.

Explaining the results

How can we explain the surprising results on the relative performance of tax havens, developed and developing countries in applying
international rules on corporate transparency, especially given they
run directly counter to what most would have expected? The most
likely explanation hinges on a key trend: firms in tax havens comply at such high rates because the jurisdictions have been subject to
intense scrutiny and international pressure to improve their corporate transparency practices since the late 1990s. Clubs of rich states,
most notably the FATF, have applied this pressure. And the clubs have
tended to give their own members a much easier time than non-member tax havens. This unbalanced international pressure likely explains
the superior performance of tax havens relative to developed states.

A second explanation is also worth considering. Many developed
states, especially the English-speaking countries, have attempted to
remove barriers to business activity by deregulating, and one aspect of
this, it might be argued, has been to make the process of incorporation
as quick and easy as possible. Developing countries, in contrast, have
been much less likely to deregulate, either as a product of disinclin-
ation or inability, and forming a company is a much more bureaucratic
process. Below we produce evidence that reflects on this claim, and we
generally find it wanting. The difficulty of obtaining anonymous shells
does not appear to be related to the general ease of doing business nor
to the barriers in starting up a company.

Through the 1990s a variety of governments in Europe and the
United States began to worry about a purported "dark side of globalization," especially as related to financial liberalization. Though
these governments and the international clubs they dominated generally endorsed the free flow of capital across borders, they also worried about the malign consequences of this transformation, especially
in terms of their ability to tax their citizens and corporations and
their ability to counter increasingly internationalized criminal groups
(Gilmore 1995; Kerry 1997; Wechsler 2001; Naim 2006). Tax havens
were seen as greatly exacerbating both problems through their provision of financial secrecy, especially through their enabling anonymous
shell companies (United Nations Office for Drug Control and Crime
Prevention 1998). Indeed, there was a good deal of evidence that the
sharply increased number of offshore centers established since the late

1980s had led to something of a race to the bottom. Even those off-shore who now protest tax havens' virtues admit that in previous decades there was a "Wild West" ethos among financial centers.[2]

Customers could indeed fly in to deposit suitcases of cash with off-shore banks, no questions asked, and buy not only shell companies anonymously, but indeed shell banks as well. The advertisements of the period live down to every negative offshore stereotype. One that screams "FIND YOUR OWN OFFSHORE WEALTH HAVEN" promises "Live simply and easily making a tax-free fortune, using the world's most exotic islands ... Do all this legally with complete privacy using the world's best tax and offshore money havens" (www.quatloos.com/wealth-haven.pdf). The $100 set of audiotape seminars starred Jerome Schneider. Schneider was later convicted of assisting tax evasion, and despite offering clients "bullet-proof privacy," he struck a plea bargain that involved turning all his client records over to the IRS (further proof of the key distinction between providers who have client information but promise never to reveal it versus those who never collect it in the first place). Also featured in the ad were Kenneth Royce, billed as "the James Bond of privacy protection," and Howard Fischer, apparently also known as "Mr. Loophole." The advertisement further promises to show clients how to set up their own banks, "legally" eliminate all taxes, and change their identity.

In their defense, those offshore might point out that Schneider was an American operating from Vancouver, selling to US clients, and that it took the IRS 14 years after being alerted to Schneider's tax evasion schemes to prosecute him, even though he advertised them openly in the American Airlines in-flight magazine and the *Wall Street Journal*.[3] Yet Schneider and his ilk were often feted, or at least tolerated, by many offshore governments and financial institutions.

In response to such offshore schemes and more generalized fears about globalization, William Wechsler wrote a remarkably frank *Foreign Affairs* article. Wechsler was a former special assistant to the US Treasury Secretary with responsibility for combating international financial crime. In the article, he explained that the United

[2] Author interviews: Port Vila, Vanuatu, March 5, 2004; Vaduz, Liechtenstein, January 29, 2004; Douglas, Isle of Man, February 1, 2005; Panama City, Panama, April 2, 2008; Hong Kong, November 9, 2010; Miami, United States, May 1, 2012.

[3] Author interview: Miami, United States, April 30–May 1, 2012.

States could not defeat tax havens unilaterally, but also could not rely on universal membership bodies like the United Nations, because the United States would be outvoted by the tax havens and other countries.

The solution was coordinated action by clubs of like-minded developed states. Thus while the OECD targeted tax havens through its Harmful Tax Competition initiative from 1998, the FATF began work on a similar blacklist of jurisdictions alleged not to have "the right stuff" when it came to fighting money laundering. Though these OECD and FATF processes were formally and to some extent substantively independent of each other, they tended to converge on the conclusion that, whether it was tax evasion or money laundering, tax havens were the main problem. The solution was for such jurisdictions to commit to increased financial transparency. Because of the rise of borderless commerce, ratcheting up financial standards onshore was believed an expensive and counter-productive failure because of the escape valve provided by under-regulated offshore centers. Critics of tax havens asserted that mobile capital simply outflanked higher regulations by relocating offshore. Thus the FATF report on the issue began:

In today's open and global financial world, characterised by a high mobility of funds and the rapid development of new payment technologies, the tools for laundering the proceeds of serious crimes as well as the means for anonymous protection of illegal assets in certain countries or territories make them even more attractive for money laundering. Existing anti-money laundering laws are undermined by the lack of regulation and essentially by the numerous obstacles on customer identification, in certain countries and territories, notably offshore financial centres. (FATF 2000a: 1)

The solution: the OECD and FATF would publicly blacklist recalcitrant jurisdictions (FATF 2000b). These blacklists proved effective, but also partial, in that those targeted were held to higher standards than were members of the rich states' clubs. This explains at least part of the regulatory divergence between havens and OECD states. The blacklists were powerful in the way they damaged the reputation of those jurisdictions on the list and in the chilling effect they on had third parties who were potential investors in the jurisdictions that had been singled out. The listings tended to reverberate and be incorporated within private risk ratings, raising the cost of transacting with listed countries.

Although the impact on existing business was often marginal, interviews conducted in jurisdictions including the British Virgin Islands, the Cayman Islands, St. Kitts and Nevis, the Cook Islands, Liechtenstein, the Isle of Man, Panama, Vanuatu, Nauru, Samoa, and the Seychelles clearly revealed that both the government and the private sector regarded the danger or actuality of appearing on one or both of these blacklists as a serious obstacle in attracting new growth.[4] Of the two, the FATF list was regarded as more threatening than the OECD's. Even those tax havens that were not on one or both of the lists tended to pre-emptively tighten up standards, as the OECD and FATF deliberately encouraged the belief that other jurisdictions were at risk of facing the same fate. Coming off the list was conditional upon collecting more information on financial clients, including those forming shell companies, and sharing this information with OECD states.

What evidence is there to support the assertion that these initiatives were premised on double standards when it came to beneficial ownership? At the time the blacklists were launched and until 2003, the standard governing FATF members stated only that: "Countries should take notice of the potential for abuse of shell corporations by money launderers and should consider whether additional measures are required to prevent unlawful use of such entities" (FATF 1996: 5). As noted above, even when this requirement was strengthened for FATF members in 2003, only one member country actually met it.

In contrast, in setting out the criteria for being blacklisted the FATF specified much more demanding conditions: "Shell corporations and nominees are widely used mechanisms to launder the proceeds from crime ... The ability for competent authorities to obtain and share information regarding the identification of companies and their beneficial owner(s) is therefore essential for all the relevant authorities responsible for preventing and punishing money laundering" (FATF 2000a: 4). Why was the ability to look through to find companies' real

---

[4] Author interviews: George Town, Cayman Islands, January 19–20, 2004; Basseterre, St. Kitts, January 22, 2004; Vaduz, Liechtenstein, January 29, 2004; Port Vila, Vanuatu, March 4, 2004; Avarua, Cook Islands, June 14–15, 2004; Road Town, British Virgin Islands, January 20–21, 2005 and May 21–22, 2007; Douglas, Isle of Man, 31 January 31–February 2 2005; Victoria, Seychelles, May 30, 2005; Panama City, Panama, April 2–4, 2008; Apia, Samoa, July 31–August 1, 2008; Nauru, August 18–19, 2008.

owners "essential" for non-members, but only something that FATF members should vaguely "consider"? Some offshore governments directly posed this question to the FATF during negotiations, but were brushed aside.[5]

The FATF made abundantly clear that if jurisdictions wanted to be de-listed, they would have to meet the conditions. This required not simply legislating, but also setting up the relevant implementing institutions and providing concrete evidence of their effectiveness. A gap thus opened up between the high standards forced upon targeted offshore jurisdictions and the lax standards those countries within the club applied to themselves.

If outside pressure explains the superior performance of tax havens relative to rich states, what explains the discrepancy between developing and developed countries? Some poorer developing countries were targeted by the FATF's blacklisting process as it expanded beyond its initial offshore focus to include such states as Nigeria, Indonesia, Egypt, and Burma, as well as Russia and Ukraine. As noted above, even those developing countries not so listed may well have tightened up beneficial ownership standards pre-emptively.

An alternative explanation involves the trend towards deregulation in OECD countries. In contrast, incorporating a company in most developing countries remains both legally and practically an involved and often bureaucratic process. Thus, in an unanticipated way, the greater red tape in developing countries may make anonymous incorporation difficult.

Very laudably, some OECD countries have sought to reduce the burden of red tape and expense for small businesses and sole traders looking to incorporate. This has extended to moving the incorporation process online, and minimizing or eliminating the need for supporting documentation so as to provide a convenient, expeditious, and affordable service. There are sound economic reasons for these reforms, which enable small family and individual businesses to obtain the advantages of limited liability and possible tax concessions that have long been available to their larger competitors. In the United States in particular, where incorporation procedures are a state rather than federal responsibility, competition between states to encourage incorporation within their jurisdiction has further sharpened this

---

[5] Author interview: Road Town, British Virgin Islands, May 21, 2007.

trend toward making forming a company as quick and cheap as possible. The fee revenue that results may be substantial, with Delaware gaining more than $720 million a year just from its company registry alone.[6]

This raises the question of whether an unintended by-product of this deregulatory impulse has been to make it easier for criminals to form companies anonymously. A key measure of the business regulations is the World Bank's annual *Doing Business* report, which places a premium on facilitating business activity. In 2012 the survey included 10 measures, the first of which was starting a business, which is measured in terms of the number of procedures, time in days to accomplish business startup, and business startup costs as a percentage of per capita income (World Bank 2012).

Many countries put considerable stock in how they are ranked in this index. For example, on his first day after being reappointed Russia's President in May 2012, Vladimir Putin committed to improving his country's ranking from 120th place to 20th on this index by 2018 (Adelaja 2012). More specifically related to shell companies, even after the problem came to light of untraceable New Zealand shell companies used to smuggle North Korean arms to Iran and to launder the drug profits of the Mexican Sinaloa drug cartel, the relevant government officials were reluctant to reform the country's corporate laws. They explicitly feared jeopardizing New Zealand's *Doing Business* ranking.[7]

In contrast, forming a company in most developing countries remains a bureaucratic ordeal. Perhaps the starkest evidence of this kind of problem is that collated by teams led by Peruvian economist Hernando de Soto. De Soto and his colleagues started with the seemingly obvious but often overlooked premise that "Reading the laws as they are written gives no clue to how they will work in practice" (de Soto 1989/2002: xxii), a premise very much at the heart of this book also. Their work began in 1983 with the simple expedient of sending out researchers to impersonate those seeking a sole trader's license, a process that is very similar to forming a company. The researchers found the paperwork and administrative procedures for this supposedly simple task took 289 work days and cost 32 times

---

[6] Author interview: Washington, DC, United States, March 21, 2011.
[7] Author interview: Washington, DC, United States, April 28, 2012.

the minimum monthly wage in lost profits, fees, bribes and transport costs. Parallel exercises were later carried out in Egypt, Haiti, and the Philippines, with similar results (de Soto 2000).

Even in economically successful countries like China today the picture is similar. Rather than a day or two, the process of forming a company in China takes more than a month, and it requires surmounting many bureaucratic hurdles and often paying many bribes[8] (World Bank 2013). Developing countries suffer considerable economic costs due to these sclerotic procedures and through the corruption that results from attempts to fast-track applications for business licenses. Unlike in OECD members or tax havens, it may well be impossible to form a company without many in-person visits to the relevant offices, meaning that the beneficial owner usually has to be a resident. The silver lining of this otherwise unhappy situation is that companies from many developing states are less attractive to criminals, especially foreign criminals, and the Know Your Customer requirements are quite strict, even if they were not formulated to counter financial crime.

Thus, there is a compelling logic behind the argument that business deregulation may facilitate anonymous incorporation. However, in our study we find very little evidence that this is the case. We used the World Bank's 2013 *Ease of Doing Business* rankings (collated in 2012, when much of our study took place) and analyzed any statistical correlations with the compliance rates we found in our field study. Among OECD countries, we found no significant association between compliance rates and any of the relevant *Ease of Doing Business* ranks, including the overall ranking, the starting a business component score, the number of startup procedures, time of startup, or cost of startup as a proportion of GDP.

When analyzing all of the countries in our study that overlapped with the World Bank report (145 in all), again there was no significant association between actual compliance rates and overall ease of doing business, the category ranking for starting a business, the number of startup procedures, or the time to startup. The cost of startup, however, was significantly and negatively related to the compliance rate ($p = 0.006$, $r = -0.226$). This means that the more expensive it is to start a business, the higher on average the country's compliance rate. This result, however, may be an artifact of country wealth, as

---

[8] Author interview: Hong Kong, November 9, 2010.

poorer countries have lower GDPs per capita and thus higher proportional costs. In the final analysis, then, there is little evidence that the general ease of doing business or the difficulty of starting up a business affects the compliance rate with global corporate transparency standards.

Conclusion

This chapter has presented and discussed the broad patterns that emerge from the thousands of solicitations for untraceable shell companies. In the main, the formal standards mandating that authorities must be able to look through the corporate veil are ineffective. Although there is some uncertainty about how to interpret the large proportion of providers who did not reply, their failure to respond to even the most innocuous approach strongly suggests their unresponsiveness was generally not evidence of soft compliance. The low compliance rates of FATF mutual evaluations foreshadows our result, but these direct approaches provide a far more detailed and robust picture than has previously been available.

The strong performance of corporate service providers in tax havens relative to those in developing countries, and the fact that havens and, in some measures, developing countries perform better than developed countries, runs directly against dominant expectations. This means that most of the presumptions and pronouncements of the G20, OECD, FATF, and their major member governments on the subject of beneficial ownership over the last two decades are badly wrong. The rigorous Know Your Customer standards applied offshore are argued to be a product of a multilateral crackdown from the end of the 1990s mainly aimed at tax havens.

Yet for all the important lessons of this chapter, it is crucial to point out that all the data presented so far are descriptive rather than experimental. Descriptive data can tell us the overall level of compliance, and which types of countries do good, bad, or indifferent jobs in regulating their corporate service sector, but not when or why providers decide to follow or flout the international rule mandating that they require identity documents from customers.

To answer the question of what causes providers to comply, or not, with global rules, the following chapters analyze and explain the results of randomly assigning different email treatments across the pool of providers. Thus the chapter immediately following looks at whether corruption and terrorism risks make providers more risk averse or rule-compliant, and whether offering to pay providers to ignore the rules induces them to do so. Chapter 5 compares the relative effects of providing varying information about public and private standards, the former set by the FATF internationally and the IRS within the United States, the latter set by the Association of Certified Anti-Money Laundering Specialists. Finally, Chapter 6 tests responsiveness to penalties, norms and US origin in causing changes to compliance rates.

4 | *Terrorism and corruption*

In 2004 a gruesome video from Iraq went viral on the internet. It showed a 26-year-old American telecommunications worker, Nicholas Berg, seated on the floor in front of a phalanx of masked terrorists. One terrorist, believed to be Abu Musab al-Zarqawi, produced a long knife and promptly beheaded Berg in what must be one of the most graphic episodes ever aired on YouTube. In the ranks of al-Qaeda terrorists, few men descended to the depths of al-Zarqawi, who was linked to the deaths of more than 700 people before the US military killed him in a 2006 airstrike (BBC News 2004; Miklaszewski 2004; Burns 2006).

Like many terrorists, al-Zarqawi depended on financing from abroad, and his key lieutenant, Shaqwi Omar, apparently produced some of the funds through a set of elaborate money laundering and fraud schemes perpetrated by his brothers, nephews, and other accomplices in the United States. According to a US federal indictment, in one of several such conspiracies Shaqwi Omar's brother, Bassam, formed a shell corporation in Utah called Wasatch Front Construction Services. He and his nephew, Alaa Ramadan, used the shell to perpetrate an intricate mortgage fraud involving sham improvements on two Utah houses and a "straw buyer" to swindle a title company out of more than $121,000 at the closings on the sales of the homes, both of which quickly went into foreclosure. Multiple indictments placed the sum of all the known Omar schemes at more than half a million dollars. The FBI has traced some of the money to wire transfers to Jordan where, again, the trail has gone cold due to the multilayered shrouds common in modern international finance. Despite an ongoing FBI investigation, a definitive link to al-Qaeda has not yet been made (MSNBC 2006; NBC News 2006; Dollar 2006).

In this chapter we address the question of whether the problem of anonymous shells in terrorist financing generalizes beyond such anecdotes. We also probe the effects on corporate service provider compliance with global transparency standards of potential terrorism, possible corruption, and the offer of a premium payment. The distinguishing feature of this volume is that it is based on the first-ever global field experiments. As important as the findings of the previous chapter are in terms of debunking myths about which countries comply and which do not when it comes to corporate transparency standards, they are descriptive findings. In contrast, in this and the next two chapters we draw on the advantages of experimental research designs, as summarized in Chapter 1, to shed light on the causes of compliance and non-compliance among corporate service providers.

Specifically, in this chapter we present the results of our first three experimental interventions: the Terrorism, Corruption, and Premium treatments. For each treatment we make crucial modifications to the basic email template that constitutes the Placebo so as to signal terrorist financing or corruption risks, or to offer providers a bonus payment if they defy beneficial ownership rules. We test for the impact of these risks and inducements by comparing the results of these email treatments to our Norstralia Placebo emails. Following from the logic of randomized assignment of providers to either the Placebo or a treatment, we can be much more confident that any observed differences in their response rate (or non-response rate) are caused by the treatments.

In the use of the experimental method and the focus on non-state actors, what we call Experimental TR, such work is a major step forward in the study of global governance and compliance with international rules. But the findings presented here are also very significant for policy-makers. Few issues over the last decade have had the prominence of the fight against terrorism, and finance has been described as the "life blood" of such groups. Yet policy-makers largely have no idea if the raft of measures passed in the wake of the September 11 attacks designed to cut off terrorist funding have been effective in convincing financial firms to avoid business with those who pose such a risk. At least when it comes to the provision of shell companies, the data presented here provide the best evidence yet: providers are indeed often cognizant of and sensitive to the dangers of terrorist financing.

Beyond the financing of terrorism, the NGO Global Witness summarizes why shell companies are an especially vital mechanism for large-scale corruption, noting that they are "key to the outflow of corrupt money that keeps poor countries poor. Those who loot state funds through corruption or deprive their state of revenues through tax evasion need more than a bank: they need to hide their identity behind a corporate front" (Global Witness 2012: 6). How willing are providers to provide such a corporate front to obvious corruption risks? Again, despite a flurry of international rule-making and concern, we know remarkably little about the answer. Disturbingly, the results presented here suggest that those selling shell companies are almost completely insensitive to the danger of corruption.

The final treatment, Premium, similarly aims to shed light on illicit gain. But rather than service providers enabling the misuse of entrusted power by others, here they themselves are the target. To what extent are they tempted to violate the rules mandating that they practice Know Your Customer procedures by the prospect of direct financial gain? Alternatively, might such a blatantly inappropriate offer actually make the recipients more suspicious, and thus less willing to supply an untraceable shell company? In keeping with the earlier comments about heterogeneous responses, we find evidence of both mechanisms in play.

In discussing each of these three treatments, we begin by explaining the significance of the issue at stake. Next, we explain the design of the treatment in terms of the significance of the crucial wording changes made to the basic backstory of a consultant looking to incorporate to obtain tax benefits, limited liability, and confidentiality. Finally we present the results, both in terms of statistics on compliance (with the more technical robustness checks contained in the Appendices) and some examples of the email replies we received.

Explaining the Terrorism treatment

In some ways ambitions to cut the flow of funding to terrorist organizations predate the rise of the rest of the anti-money laundering agenda. In the early 1980s Western European governments faced far-left groups like the Baader Meinhof Gang and the Red Brigades, which funded themselves in part through bank robberies and other financial crimes (Pieth 2002: 365). The British government struggled with the Irish Republican Army, funded by criminal activities within Northern Ireland but also by a network of supporters in the United States. Some aid to the militants was funded through what were at least ostensibly charities, in particular Noraid, an expedient that would later become the central target for those looking to interdict the flow of money to Islamic terrorist groups. At this time the United States was largely uninterested in the issue of terrorist financing (except where it intersected with the "the war on drugs"). In the latter half of the 1990s the UN worked towards a convention to prohibit the financing of terrorism, yet this attracted very little interest in terms of signatories (Pieth 2002; Rider 2004). What changed, of course, was September 11.

The first move in the American counter-offensive against al-Qaeda was financial (Heng and McDonagh 2008). A few days after the attacks President Bush declared that "Money is the lifeblood of terrorist operations. Today we are asking the world to stop payment." There are, however, significant differences between the financing of terrorism and the sort of profit-driven financial crime that gives rise to money laundering. In part as a result of these differences, the effectiveness of these measures is highly uncertain (Biersteker and Eckert 2007; Eckert and Biersteker 2010; Gordon 2011).

To an even greater extent than the other sorts of financial crime discussed in this book, our knowledge of the financing of terrorism is tentative and disputed. Because of the national security aspect, even the cases that are detected are often shrouded in secrecy, with fewer court documents or other independent sources to draw on. Critics assert that much of what passes for policy knowledge reflects political agendas focused on magnifying the threat so as to boost various agencies' budgets and powers, as for example when lurid initial accusations released by authorities to the press are later quietly dropped for want of any evidence (Naylor 2004: Ch. 7; more generally see Mueller and Stewart 2012).

Unlike other criminals, terrorists are more often motivated by ideology than the profit motive (though Shapiro and Siegel 2007 present examples of mid-level terrorists skimming off funds for their own personal enjoyment). While some terrorist operations have been cramped by financial constraints, like running out of money to buy the desired stock of explosives for the 1993 attack on the World Trade Center (Shapiro and Siegel 2007: 405), terrorism is essentially cheap. Individual terrorist attacks require only tiny sums of money, sometimes only a few thousand dollars, that are very unlikely be detected by the financial surveillance apparatus first developed to fight the illicit drug trade. Thus although the September 11 attacks may have cost up to $500,000, bombings like those that occurred in Madrid, London,

Bali, and on dozens of occasions in Iraq, cost at most in the low tens of thousands of dollars (Strasser 2004; Gordon 2008). The example that opened the chapter, focusing on al-Zarqawi and his alleged accomplices in the United States, also involved relatively minor amounts of money. These small sums may mean that even the comparatively modest fees required to set up a shell company may be uneconomic, and the possibility of using cash or alternative remittance systems might render the use of shell companies unnecessary.

Furthermore, unlike money laundering, which is a process of taking "dirty" money and seeking to remove the taint of its criminal origin, the financing of terrorism is just as likely to involve the use of "clean" money obtained legitimately that is later directed to fund a criminal enterprise. The most typical scenario is commonly said to involve the use of charities, particularly Islamic charities, as discussed further below (FATF 2002, 2008; Council on Foreign Relations 2002, 2004; Ehrenfeld 2003; Biersteker and Eckert 2007; Gordon 2008).

In October 2001 the FATF had added a Special Recommendation specifically requiring governments to regulate charities to ensure they were not used to finance terrorists. Such activity might involve the diversion of money raised for genuine charitable purposes without the knowledge of the original donors, or those giving the funds may deliberately use an intermediary as a front organization. (Critics have pointed out that, whatever the genuine risk, this directive gives authoritarian governments a perfect excuse to crack down on civil society groups like NGOs.)

If charities are reputedly the vehicle of choice for terrorist financiers, the role of shell companies seems to be much less prominent. Unlike with corruption and tax evasion, there are few hard and fast examples of shell companies being used by terrorists and their sympathizers. Although the Russian arms dealer Viktor Bout was convicted on terrorism charges and used a network of shell companies, his motives were far more pecuniary than political. Larger armed groups classified as terrorist organizations that have something approaching standing military forces and control defined territorial areas like Hezbollah, Hamas, FARC in Colombia, and earlier the Tamil Tigers have correspondingly greater financial needs and thus may need to engage in more complicated schemes to obscure their finances, potentially including shell companies.

For the purposes of our experiment, however, the actual importance of shell companies in financing terrorism and the extent to which
this issue is analogous to or different from money laundering are to
some extent irrelevant. Rightly or wrongly, the US government and
the FATF have decided both that attacking terrorist financing is a
crucial front of the war on terror and that charities are a primary
mechanism for funding Islamic terrorist groups. They have repeatedly conveyed this understanding through the 40 Recommendations,
the commentary and guidance that has arisen around the application
of the Recommendations, and in the policies of national Financial
Intelligence Units and related bodies charged with applying these
international standards on countering the financing of terrorism at the
domestic level. Countering the financing of terrorism has made financial transparency, especially where it is related to shell companies, a
political priority.

In response, the FATF mandates that private financial institutions
must gauge the terrorist financing risk of actual and prospective clients
by their country of origin. Thus a clear red flag is when customers are
from "Countries or geographic areas identified by credible sources as
providing funding or support for terrorist activities, or that have designated terrorist organizations operating within their country" (FATF
2012: 63). An earlier report again mentioned "locations of specific
concern" for terrorism as a major risk factor (FATF 2008: 32). Each of
the four nations we selected to signal this risk hosts significant terrorist groups responsible for attacks both within and beyond these countries. Pakistan and Yemen host noteworthy al-Qaeda groups, Palestine
is home to Hamas and smaller groups such as Islamic Jihad, while
Hezbollah is a major force in Lebanese national politics and maintains
its own military forces. Saudi Arabia was famously the home of 15
of the 19 September 11 hijackers, and it has provided the religious
inspiration and financial support for many radical Islamic groups,
some of whom have turned against the Saudi state. The combination
of a national from a high terrorism risk country working in another
country notorious for its support of terrorism in the past serves to
strengthen the terrorism risk.

Some other obvious candidate countries for signaling a terrorist
financing risk like Iran, Sudan, and Syria were excluded to avoid the
potential confound of sanctions. For example, if providers had been
much more likely to refuse business from fictitious Iranian consultants
relative to the Norstralian control email, it would have been impossible

to tell if this reluctance was a product of the terrorist financing risk or the sanctions risk. (In our pilot version of the study we had a fictitious US client asking an Iranian provider to set up a company in the Islamic Republic so as to improve the former's business; the provider was understandably very skeptical.)

The second terrorist financing risk was the Islamic charity. The initial FATF guidelines on countering the financing of terrorism note: "The misuse of non-profit organizations for the financing of terrorism is coming to be recognized as a crucial weak point in the global struggle to stop such funding at its source … Within the FATF, this has rightly become the priority focus of work to implement Special Recommendation VIII (Non-profit organizations)" (FATF 2002: 1). Richard Gordon, who helped to both design and evaluate UN and IMF standards to counter the financing of terrorism, has written: "Special Recommendation VIII suggests that some charities appeared to be involved in terrorism-financing transactions. This was emphasized repeatedly in material that could be referenced by financial institutions, their supervisors, and law enforcement, including FATF reports and guidance issues by national regulators" (Gordon 2011: 544). As a direct result, "hardly surprisingly, financial institutions tended to focus on charitable organizations and, in particular, nonprofits that involve Islamic organizations and wire activity to or from 'suspect' states. If you are a financial institution and you need to report on *someone*, you might as well report on an Islamic charity" (Gordon 2008: 700).

A third risk involved cross-border activities, signaled by the alias hailing from one country but working in another. The FATF enjoins companies to screen "[c]harities and other 'not for profit' organisations which are not subject to monitoring or supervision (*especially those operating on a 'cross-border' basis*)" (2006a: 22, emphasis ours). Given these three risk factors – coming from a terrorism-prone country, being associated with an Islamic charity, and working on a cross-border basis – we designed the following treatment email, with the key treatment language highlighted in bold:

Dear [Provider],
I am consultant with a business seeking to incorporate a new company internationally. **We consult for a number of Muslim aid organizations. Though we are from Pakistan, my co-worker and I live in Saudi Arabia, where our company is based, but our international clientele is growing, especially in your area.** We would like to form a new company in your area as private

individuals. Could you please inform us what your costs are like for this? Also, what are the identifying documents we would need to establish this corporation? By way of information, we are seeking to form this company confidentially.

We are hoping that by incorporating we can limit business liability and have a more favorable taxes outlook. I will be doing extensive business travel for the next few weeks so I would ask that you please contact me through email.

Sincerely,
Omar Rana

More than just the additive effects of different risk factors, it is the interaction of the country of origin, charity work, and cross-border activity together that constitutes the strong cue of terrorism financing risk. The combination of a would-be customer hailing from a country associated with terrorism, working on a cross-border basis, and consulting for the type of charitable institution conventionally assessed as providing the main conduit for terrorist funds, who is asking for a product that serves to screen his identity, constitutes a strong and unequivocal risk of terrorist financing. Any firm or individual with even a vague sensitivity to terrorism financing should have picked up on this and either responded by refusing business or by strictly applying Know Your Customer procedures.

Terrorism findings

The terrorism findings reflect the response and compliance levels to this obvious terrorism financing risk, as defined by international standards and guidelines. If such international standards are effective, we would thus expect that rates of non-response should increase, and for those that do respond, non-compliance should decrease. In contrast to many of the findings reported in this book, there are some encouraging signs in the data in that at least some of the results follow the expected direction for response and compliance. A significant proportion of providers do indeed seem to be sensitive to the risk of terrorist financing.

As shown in Table 4.1 and Figure 4.1, non-response rates increase in the international sample from 44.5 percent in the Placebo condition to 58.3 percent in the Terrorism treatment – a non-trivial increase of nearly 14 percentage points. In the US sample, shown in Table 4.2 and Figure 4.2, there is a similarly large increase in

Table 4.1 *Contingency table of results by Placebo, Premium, Corruption,
and Terrorism with difference tests for the international sample*

Condition	N	No response	Non-compliant	Part-compliant	Compliant	Refusal
Placebo	1112	495	97	184	210	126
Proportion		44.5%	8.7%	16.5%	18.9%	11.3%
Premium	385	191*	24	66	56*	48
Proportion		49.6%	6.2%	17.1%	14.5%	12.5%
Corruption	428	225***	38	61	64*	40
Proportion		52.6%	8.9%	14.3%	15.0%	9.3%
Terrorism	424	247***	24**	46***	64*	43
Proportion		58.3%	5.7%	10.8%	15.1%	10.1%

Significant in difference tests compared to the Placebo condition: *0.1 level, **0.05
level, ***0.01 level.

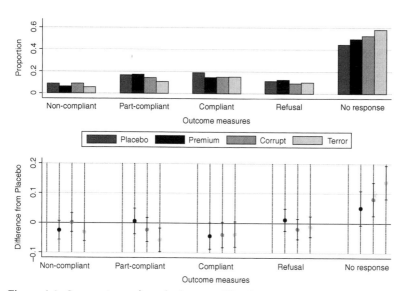

Figure 4.1 Comparison of results between Placebo, Premium, Corruption,
and Terrorism groups as a proportion and difference from Placebo group
(international sample).

non-response – 73.8 percent in the Placebo to 83.3 percent in the
Terrorism treatment – more than 9 percentage points higher. Recall
that because each of the treatments was randomly assigned, any difference between treatment and control should be due to the information

Table 4.2 *Contingency table of results by Placebo, Corruption, and Terrorism treatment groups with difference tests for the US sample*

Condition	N	No response	Non-compliant	Part-compliant	Compliant	Refusal
Placebo	816	602	92	13	3	106
Proportion		73.8%	11.3%	1.6%	0.4%	13.0%
Corruption	532	417*	54	8	1	52*
Proportion		78.4%	10.2%	1.5%	0.2%	9.8%
Terrorism	550	458***	32***	8	2	50**
Proportion		83.3%	5.8%	1.5%	0.4%	9.1%

Significant in difference tests compared to the Placebo condition: *0.1 level, **0.05 level, ***0.01 level.

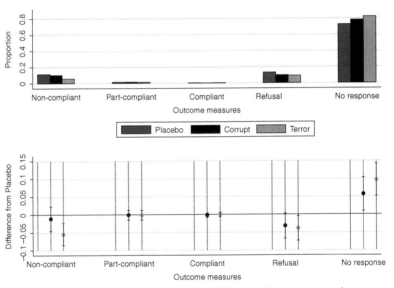

Figure 4.2 Comparison of results between Placebo, Corruption, and Terrorism groups as a proportion and difference from Placebo (US sample).

provided in the treatment. We thus interpret these statistically significant increases in non-response as a reaction to the increased risk posed by the customer that may have potential ties to terrorism. In this sense, the result may be a form of "soft compliance" in which the provider simply complies by not engaging the potential customer any further.

Despite the advantages of randomization, it bears repeating that the non-response category is complicated to interpret because we ultimately do not know why some providers respond whereas others do not. As discussed earlier, our non-response follow-ups suggest that the vast majority of the non-responses cannot be interpreted as a form of soft compliance, given that 88 percent of those firms who had failed to respond to our earlier approaches also failed to reply even to a completely innocent business inquiry. However, in relation to the *variation* in the non-response rate in the Terrorism treatment compared with the Placebo it seems very likely that the lower response rate is caused by the treatment email's appearing riskier.

For providers that did respond to the Terrorism prompt, the levels of compliance are mixed, but there is at least some evidence that when faced with higher risks providers do not ignore international standards so readily. Admittedly, some of the responses we received showed a breath-taking disregard for the obvious terrorism financing risk. Thus one reply to the Pakistani alias went as follows:

If you are looking for discretion, do not incorporate in Nevada. The preferred state is Delaware. The yearly fees are ($110 agent fee and $125 franchise tax fee = $235). And Delaware does not put all of your corporate information on their website for the world to see. We don't need any identifying documents. Just the name of the entity. Who you want me to send the documents to (name and address). And a credit card (MasterCard, Visa, American Express). We do not accept Bank transfers. Let me know if you have any other questions.

But relative to the Placebo condition, non-compliance levels in response to the Terrorism treatment were significantly lower, dropping from 8.7 to 5.7 percent, which is more than a one-third reduction from the baseline. The introduction of a terrorism risk is associated with a 3.0 percentage point decrease in non-compliance for the international sample, which is a statistically meaningful result based on standard significance thresholds. The decrease in non-compliance is even greater in the US sample, dropping from 11.3 percent in the Placebo to 5.8 percent in the Terrorism treatment for a difference of 5.5 percentage points, which represents a drop in the base non-compliance rate of nearly one half (see Tables 4.1 and 4.2).

While the decrease in non-compliance is encouraging and suggests some possible success in the fight against terrorism financing being

waged by countries and organizations such as the FATF, the other outcomes are not as clear-cut. In particular, rates of partial compliance
also decrease in the international sample (from 16.5 percent to 10.8
for a drop of 5.7 percentage points, which is one-third of the base rate),
meaning that providers were less likely to ask potential terrorists for
at least some form of identification. Even some of the partially compliant responses were not especially reassuring, as per this reply from
a Balkan country to the Pakistani alias, Omar Rana: "I need copy of a
passport of the owner of the company, power of attorney, and money.
My fees are 3058 euros, and 5000 euros deposit for the account of the
company. You are paying 50% in front and 50% after. If you want to
start this write an email in order to send you a fee invoice."

Furthermore, there is a marginal decrease in the compliance rate
from 18.9 per cent to 15.1 percent, meaning that providers did not
demand full, certified documentation as often as in the Placebo condition. However, this result is statistically significant only at the most
modest 0.1 threshold, so the treatment effect is less certain. While
one would hope that the compliance levels would increase, the results
instead show a decrease in compliance. In the US sample, so few
firms are compliant or partially compliant that there are no meaningful differences on these measures. Notably, refusal rates in the US
sample decreased significantly from 13.0 in the Placebo to 9.1 for the
Terrorism treatment, a drop of nearly one-third from the base rate
that is statistically significant at the 0.05 level. A few of the refusals
are almost as worrying as the non-compliant responses, however. The
reply below again to the Pakistani alias, Omar Rana, accurately dis-
cerns the nature of the risk, but then suggests his "no" might become a
"yes" if the price were right (a logic we test for more broadly with the
Premium treatment later in this chapter):

Your stated purpose could well be a front for funding terrorism, and who
the f*** would get involved in that? Seriously, if you wanted a functioning
and useful Florida corporation you'd need someone here to put their name
on it, set up bank accounts, etc. I wouldn't even consider doing that for less
that 5k a month, and I doubt you are going to find any suckers that will do
it for less, if at all. If you are working with less than serious money, don't
waste anybody's time here. Using a f***ing [internet email] account also
shows you are just a f***ing poser and loser. If you have a serious proposal,
write it up and we will consider it. Your previous message and this one are
meaningless crap. Get a clue. Just how stupid do you think we are?

Optimism in the non-compliance results is bolstered when recasting the results in terms of the Dodgy Shopping Count. An individual seeking an anonymous shell, as represented by the Placebo, would need to approach 11.5 providers on average in the international sample before successfully finding one that would not demand any photo identity documents whatsoever. By contrast, a potential terrorist as represented by the Terrorism treatment would have to approach 17.5 providers on average. The Dodgy Shopping Count for the Terrorism condition in the US sample is similar at 17.2. However, the Dodgy Shopping Count for the Placebo in the US subject pool is 8.9, which means that the terrorism risk had stronger treatment effects in the United States compared to the baseline. See Figures 4.3 and 4.4 for the Dodgy Shopping Counts.

This is good news. It is also bad news. The good news in these results is that potential terrorists should indeed find it more difficult to obtain a shell company without producing any photo identity documents. The bad news is that, as noted earlier, it does not take long to approach 11 or even 18 companies. The fact that it is relatively more difficult for people posing terrorism financing risks to obtain untraceable shell companies than our strait-laced Norstralians does not mean it is very difficult in absolute terms.[1] What is more, while the Terrorism condition increases non-response rates and decreases non-compliance rates (and thus boosts the Dodgy Shopping Count), it also decreases rates of part-compliance and compliance in the international subject pool and reduces refusal rates among US providers. While non-compliant firms appear to drop out when facing a potential terrorist threat compared to the Placebo, it seems that more law-abiding firms also dropped out in similar proportions. Curiously, the terrorism criminal risk induced very different actions from our subject CSPs than corruption and bribery, to which we now turn.

---

[1] We supplement the basic difference in proportions tests with multinomial probit models as well as selection models that directly analyze compliance as a function of those that respond. The results of these additional models are reported in Appendix Tables A4.1–A4.4 for the international and US samples. The multinomial models show that the results for the Terrorism treatment are fully robust. Moreover, the only statistically insignificant result from Table 4.1 (for refusals) becomes significant. The multinomial results for the US sample (Table A4.3) also bolster those reported here in Table 4.2. Finally, selection models also show that response rates are lower for the Terrorism treatment, and compliance is also less likely (see Tables A4.2 and A4.4).

Explaining the Corruption treatment

Along with wire transfers, shell companies are the most common laundering device in major corruption cases, whether it is giving or receiving bribes and kickbacks, or embezzling state funds. A 2009 report for the World Bank (Gordon 2009) confirmed that shell companies were the most important means by which the proceeds of large-scale corruption offenses were laundered (see also FATF 2011). The *Puppet Masters* report from the World Bank–UN Stolen Asset Recovery Initiative reaffirms the same conclusion (StAR 2011). It notes that of 150 cases of corruption involving more than a million dollars the "vast majority" involved the use of shell companies to disguise the transfer of dirty money. We describe two cases illustrating common examples of shell companies in corruption. The first is in transferring bribes from multinational firms to government officials in return for government business, while the second deals with misappropriation of public funds by state leaders.

The first example involves the Reserve Bank of Australia (the central bank, equivalent to the US Federal Reserve) and bribes paid for bank note printing technology. Two private companies, Note Printing Australia and Securency, marketed and sold the technology for printing Teflon bank notes to foreign clients. Note Printing Australia was wholly owned by the Reserve Bank, which also had a 50 percent stake in Securency, and the Reserve Bank audited the accounts of both companies. Foreign sales of the note printing technology were initially disappointing. Seeking to boost this lackluster performance the Australian government's export promotion agency, Austrade, introduced agents to assist in winning contracts in Bangladesh, India, Angola, Botswana, Dubai, Madagascar, Mauritius, Mozambique, Namibia, South Africa, Swaziland, Uganda, China, Argentina, Uruguay, Chile, and Nigeria. According to the Australian Federal Police every single case involved bribery ("Securency Bribe Allegations Widen." *Canberra Times* October 24, 2012). The "consultancy fees" or "commissions" to agents were often paid via shell companies in the Seychelles, the Isle of Man, and the Bahamas. After the scheme came to light thanks to whistle-blowers disgusted by the complicity of the Reserve Bank, the Australian police were able request and obtain information on the true owners of the company from the Seychelles provider that had formed the company via the Seychellois government.[2]

A second, more generic case explains how local senior officials can extract bribes from foreign oil companies. Previously this may have been done by direct payments, or monetary transfers via a shell company, but the energetic application of the US Foreign Corrupt Practices Act has made this riskier (though by no means unknown), even for non-US oil firms. Instead the local official, perhaps the oil minister, sets up a shell company controlled directly or via a family member or close associate. The official then writes a requirement into legislation, tender guidelines, or a particular contract that all foreign oil projects must have a local partner with a 10 percent share. Many kinds of foreign investment arrangements contain requirements for local participation, and thus prima facie this is unlikely to attract attention. The process of choosing the local partner is rigged in favor of the minister's company (if there is any process at all). The foreign oil company is then presented with the local partner company, which supposedly will provide ill-defined consultancy services or something similar, but in practice does nothing.

The minister's shell company then enjoys 10 percent of the revenues for the entire life of the project, which may amount to many millions or even hundreds of millions of dollars. The foreign oil firm may well have a shrewd idea what is going on, but has a strong incentive not to try to find out who is behind the shell company, as if they found out then they may be vulnerable to knowingly participating in a corrupt scheme. Of course the oil company could reject the whole deal, but local content requirements are common and non-negotiable, and there are other oil companies that will then step in to exploit profitable opportunities.[3]

With disarming candor, Obiang (the kleptocratic Michael Jackson fan) explained how the system worked in testimony before a South African court:

Cabinet ministers and public servants in Equatorial Guinea are by law allowed to own companies that, in consortium with a foreign company, can bid for government contracts. And should the company be successful,

---

[2] Author interview: Brisbane, Australia, October 2, 2012.
[3] Author interview: Bergen, Norway, November 21, 2012.

then what percentage of the total cost of the contract the company gets, will depend on the terms negotiated between the parties. But in any event, it means that a cabinet minister ends up with a sizeable part of the contract price in his bank account. (US Senate Permanent Subcommittee on Investigations 2010: 24)

Finally, secret film footage of two service providers in the Seychelles again underscores the relationship between large-scale corruption, shell companies, and sham consultancy arrangements. Two journalists impersonate a corrupt senior official from Zimbabwe ("George") looking to launder funds embezzled from that country's diamond mines, and the official's lawyer and front man ("Prince"). They explicitly based their strategy on the authors' approach used in this volume and in prior research (Sharman 2011), first asking the providers if they were required to supply identity documents. The providers said yes, in accord with Seychellois law and international standards. Then Prince suggested that he provide the relevant documentation, even though George would be in control.

The first provider from Zen Offshore Services (whose website offers shell companies for $637) replies to George, "You will be the beneficial owner and we don't even ask about your name or address or anything." In a separate meeting with the same provider, Prince explains, "My client is from Zimbabwe and then he's the liaison officer between the Zimbabwean government and the rich diamond mines." The provider replies, "Yep, we don't want to know that. That's the sort of thing we can't have knowledge of. If we had knowledge of that we'd have to put it forward, so I haven't heard a word you've said in the last couple of minutes" (both sides laugh at this point). The provider then sells them a shell company, Kind International Consulting, to own a series of other shell companies and receive the money (George pays in cash, and hence the transaction is untraceable).

The second provider is even more explicit. After suggesting the formation of one shell company with an associated bank account he goes on:

Assume you have one million dollars you want to deal with. It's there with you in cash, OK? We may have to create another company, and that company will be a consultant company. It charges you monthly or weekly "X" amount on all sorts of transactions, and you organize for payments to be deposited into that company's account, OK? For payment of your fees and charges. And, as such, you finally get your money, quietly. (*Al Jazeera* 2012)

Both providers had their licenses suspended shortly after the documentary aired (an option not available in the United States, where there is no license required to sell shell companies). Ten other providers in the Seychelles contacted by the two journalists had earlier refused to do business ("Govt Decries Unfair Al-Jazeera Report on Money Laundering." *Nation* November 10, 2012). Other shell company journalistic stings carried out by National Public Radio and BBC Panorama involving onshore providers are similarly damning.

The Corruption treatment email closely parallels the examples above in signaling corruption risk via two modifications to the basic template. The first relates to the nationality of the prospective customer, the second to the particular industry. As noted, the Placebo emails were ostensibly from eight relatively interchangeable, minor OECD countries with low levels of perceived corruption. In place of these low-risk "Norstralians," however, the Corruption treatment substitutes one of eight personas, each from a different high-corruption-risk country, as adjudged by Transparency International's Corruption Perceptions Index. These countries are Guinea, Guinea-Bissau, Equatorial Guinea, Papua New Guinea, Kyrgyzstan, Tajikistan, Turkmenistan, and Uzbekistan, abbreviated as the "Guineastan" countries. For most people outside the regions concerned (West Africa, the South Pacific, and Central Asia), these countries are relatively obscure. Each country ranks in the bottom one-fifth of the Corruption Perceptions Index as among the most corrupt countries in the world.

For the same reason that the incidence of non-compliance with Know Your Customer rules is essentially unknown absent field experiments, we do not know the actual incidence of corruption offenses in any of these eight countries, or the accuracy of Transparency International's measure. Yet this uncertainty is largely irrelevant to our aim of signaling corruption risk to providers. FATF guidelines state that financial institutions should judge the corruption risk of prospective customers by the degree to which their home countries suffer high levels of corruption ("Countries identified by credible sources as having significant levels of corruption or other criminal activity," FATF 2012: 63). Transparency International's ranking is by far the most commonly used measure of corruption, despite provoking a lively academic debate over its accuracy as a measure (e.g. Larmour 2006; Andersson and Heywood 2009; Atkinson 2011).

We designed the second change to the email to signal the danger of corruption by claiming that the client is a consultant involved in government procurement, which according to the OECD is one of the most corruption-prone industries (OECD 2007: 1). It is important to note that due to an administrative error, the mention of government procurement was inadvertently omitted from our experiment in the United States, so the results there hinge on country origin alone. In the larger international subject pool, subjects received both elements of the treatment. Our logic for including reference to government procurement stemmed from the fact that the senior officials who have discretion over allocating millions of dollars of public procurement funds may be sorely tempted to seek bribes from the private firms competing for their favor, or these firms may offer inducements unsolicited. The costs of the public money wasted on overpriced or substandard goods and services (if they are delivered at all) are borne by society at large, while the officials in question take all the benefits for themselves. And so our Corruption treatment takes the following shape in the international experiment, exemplified by an approach from the Equatorial Guinea alias, Bartho Rodrigues, again with the relevant text in bold:

Dear [Provider]:

I have a consultancy firm which I operate in **Equatorial Guinea** with some colleagues where we reside. We have multiple clients in different countries. **We focus specifically on public-sector consulting for government procurement.** Since some of our outside business is in your area, we were hoping to see some saving on our tax by setting up an international corporation. Also, our business has been growing of late and we would like to reduce unforeseen liabilities. We would like to form a new company in your area as private individuals. We were wondering if you could provide us with some more information. Specifically, we are very interested in keeping the process of setting up this company as confidential as possible. That said, what are the kinds of identifying documentation would you require of us as we set this up? Also, how much do you usually charge for these services? I will be travelling extensively over the next period and will prefer to communicate via email.

Warm regards,
Bartho Rodrigues

As with the Terrorism treatment, even more than the presence of these two separate elements signaling corruption risk is the combination of these elements with the rest of the email approach. For any provider with any sensitivity to corruption risks at all, the prospect of a customer from a notoriously corruption-prone country, in a line of work characterized by endemic bribes, kickbacks, and associated malfeasance, asking for a shell company so as to screen his finances should set alarm bells ringing as a blatantly obvious invitation to aid and abet criminal behavior (unknown non-resident customers from distant regions are further risk factors, according to the FATF).

Whether providers do in practice have any such sensitivities, however, has previously been unknown. If they do, relative to the Placebo email this should be reflected in some combination of fewer responses, more refusals, higher rates of compliance, and lower incidence of non-compliance, jointly acting to raise the Dodgy Shopping Count. On the other hand, a failure to observe marked differences in these outcomes compared with the Placebo email would provide powerful testimony that providers are either incredibly uninformed about corruption risks, or, much more likely, see the prospect of incorporation fees as sufficient to quiet any moral qualms or fears of penalties attached to their facilitating serious corruption offences. Below we present and explain the results.

Corruption findings

Despite having done all we could to produce a strong treatment effect while maintaining the essential realism and believability of the approach email, the treatment effects we actually see for the Corruption condition are small and largely insignificant statistically (See Table 4.1 and Figure 4.1). For the international providers the non-response rate does increase significantly, from 44.5 percent to 52.6 percent – an increase of 8 percentage points that boosts the proportion of non-respondents by almost one-fifth. Likewise, among US providers the Corruption condition causes a significant increase in the non-response rate, raising the proportion of subjects who ignored the emails from 73.8 percent in the Placebo condition to 78.4 percent for the Corruption treatment (statistically significant at the 0.1 level) (See Table 4.2 and Figure 4.2). Apparently, a meaningful group of corporate service providers preferred not to respond to customers from corruption-prone countries who are involved in a questionable enterprise.

As with other treatments, this variation in the non-response rate suggests some "soft compliance," where subjects may seek to prevent shady dealings by ignoring the inquiries altogether. We reiterate here that our follow-up checks suggest that the vast majority of non-responses likely were not complying in a soft way by ignoring the emails, but there are still significant increases in the non-response rate of 8 to 15 percentage points for some key treatments, including Corruption and Terrorism, compared to the Placebo. This indicates that some meaningful set of subjects do appear sensitive to customer profiles.[4]

Beyond response rates, in a pattern that repeats for some other treatment conditions and that again demonstrates the importance of heterogeneous effects, apparent corruption causes *both* a decrease in response rates *and* a decrease in compliance rates. Among the international providers, the Corruption treatment caused a drop in compliance from 18.9 percent to 15.0 percent, which equates to a decrease

---

[4] This may be a corruption effect, or it may be simply a product of poverty: CSPs may simply disregard inquiries where the benefits from the new business may prove less lucrative. Since poverty and corruption are highly correlated, this potential confound is hard to disentangle. If providers are chiefly concerned about profit, however, then they may also be aware of the extreme levels of economic inequality in the Guineastan countries. Inequality implies that, while many citizens of the Guineastan countries are very poor, some significant proportion are likely quite wealthy – and consultants in government procurement probably belong to the latter category. Nevertheless, the poverty hypothesis can be tested more systematically since there is variation in the GDP per capita levels among the Guineastan countries. According to the International Monetary Fund's statistics, Guinea, Guinea-Bissau, and Tajikistan are among the 30 poorest countries in the world with GDPs per capita of $488, $576, and $836, respectively. On the other hand, Equatorial Guinea, with its significant oil revenues, ranks among the 50 richest countries at $14,500 (though in practice the majority of this wealth is held by the ruling family and its cronies). Turkmenistan, with a GDP per capita of $5,078, is decidedly middle income, and Kyrgyzstan (GDP per capita of $1,070), Uzbekistan ($1,559), and Papua New Guinea ($1,900), while not as poor as Guinea, Guinea-Bissau, and Tajikistan, also reside on the lower end of the global income distribution. When we test for the effects of alias-country income, however, we find no systematic differences in treatment effects among the Guineastan countries. This also holds for the income differences among the nations in the Terrorist condition: Lebanon, Pakistan, Palestine, and Yemen, where Lebanon is relatively wealthy and the other three nations are in the bottom 50 for GDP per capita. We found no significant differences in treatment effects among the nations by income. We thus feel more confident about attributing differences to corruption or terrorism rather than wealth or poverty.

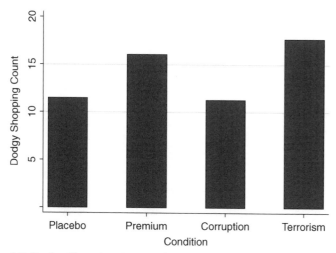

Figure 4.3 Dodgy Shopping Count: Placebo, Premium, Corruption, and Terrorism (international sample).

of nearly one-fifth from the baseline compliance rate – a result that is significant in a statistical sense at the 0.1 level. We interpret this to mean that, among the providers who failed to reply, a significant share would have demanded certified identification like their counterparts did in the Placebo condition. The corrupt customer profile apparently deterred compliant providers from responding at a higher rate than non-compliant firms. After all, the non-compliance rate showed essentially no change between the Corruption treatment and the Placebo (the slight increase from 8.7 to 8.9 percent is not statistically significant). Indeed, the Dodgy Shopping Count actually decreases slightly, from 11.5 to 11.3, but again this change is not statistically significant. (See Figure 4.3.)

Part-compliance and refusal rates also dropped in the Corruption condition, though likewise not to statistically significant degrees. As we discussed above for terrorism, we interpret this as a collusion effect. The fictitious consultant appears to be asking for something inappropriate, and some providers appear willing to accommodate the request despite possible criminal intent. The examples of such providers in this chapter demonstrate that this sort of collusion is hardly unknown.

We see a similar effect in the US pool of providers. Where the Corruption condition causes a significant (at the 0.1 level) upsurge in non-response from 73.8 to 78.4 percent, it simultaneously causes a significant drop in

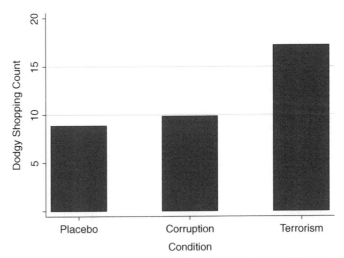

Figure 4.4 Dodgy Shopping Count: Placebo, Corruption, and Terrorism (US sample).

the refusal rate from 13.0 to 9.8 percent – a reduction from the refusal baseline of nearly one-fourth (statistically significant at the 0.1 level). This grows in importance because refusal was virtually the only way that US providers complied with international standards. The total number of compliant responses that demanded certified ID in the United States was only 10 of 2,996 requests, or about one-third of one percent. And the part-compliance rate was not much better: 52 requests for some form of ID out of 2,996 inquiries, or less than 2 percent.

The significant drop in the refusal rate thus looms ominously for a US system that appears indifferent to enforcing global standards. On the whole, providers appear willing to enable corruption. Indeed, the Dodgy Shopping Count in the United States scarcely budges from 8.9 in the Placebo condition to 9.8 for the Corruption treatment, a statistically trivial difference that does not reach any significance threshold. (See Figure 4.4.) Customers posing obvious corruption risks can obtain anonymous shell companies from US providers at roughly the same rate as the innocuous customers from the Norstralia countries.[5] Another way to probe the willingness of CSPs to aid and abet criminal

---

[5] We also estimated multinomial models to consider the robustness of the results reported in this chapter. Again, the results (Appendix Tables A4.1 and A4.3) corroborate those reported here. Levels of non-response increase in both the

activity is to simply offer them what essentially amounts to a bribe for providing an anonymous shell. This was our intent behind the next treatment.

Explaining the Premium treatment

The Premium treatment notes the international Know Your Customer requirement, but offers providers an unspecified extra payment if they waive this rule.[6] At one level the Premium treatment appeals to the simple cost–benefit logic. By increasing the rewards for non-compliance, it should increase the proportion of providers who are willing to defy international rules by supplying a shell company without requiring any photo identity documents. According to this view, every provider has its price. The non-compliance rate should thus be increased, as the increased monetary pay-off stifles any moral qualms providers might have, and outweighs their fears concerning the costs of being discovered and sanctioned for non-compliance. This draws upon the notion of the logic of consequences (discussed in Chapter 6), according to which the main driver of human behavior is allegedly a rational process of cost–benefit calculations to determine the option with the highest net benefit. On this reading, the treatment might be thought of as a crude measure of the elasticity of supply of untraceable shell companies, though only a very rough approximation because we do not specify how large the premium payment might be.

An example of the treatment language, employing the Danish alias Mikkel Pedersen, is reproduced here with the key treatment language in bold:

Dear [Provider]:
I am contacting you as I would like to form an international corporation for my consulting firm. I am a resident of Denmark and have been doing some international consulting for variuos companies. We are now growing to a

---

international and US samples. Levels of compliance (or compliance/refusal for the US sample) are lower. The selection models provide still further evidence supporting the findings reported in this chapter (see Appendix Tables A4.2 and A4.4). The multinomial model brings out one effect not evident in the difference of proportion tests: partial compliance is more likely to be lower in response to the Corruption treatment relative to the Placebo. This only deepens worries about the potential for corruption to weaken international standards.

[6] We thank Robert Keohane for suggesting this treatment.

size that makes incorporation seem like a wise option. A lot of our newer business is in your region.

My two associates and I are accustomed to paying Denmark income tax, but the rising tax rates make incorporation in another country a more economic alternative. Also, our contracts grow larger and more complicated, so reducing personal liability through incorporation seems more attractive. We would like to form a new company in your area as private individuals. As I am sure you understand, business confidentiality is very important to me and my associates.

We desire to incorporate as confidentially as we can. **I am willing to pay a premium to maintain confidentiality.** Please inform us what documentation and paperwork is required and how much these services will cost? I would like to start the process of incorporation as soon as possible. Also, how much can we expect your fees to be? Due to numerous professional commitments, I would prefer to communicate through email. I hope to hear from you soon.

Thank you very much,
Mikkel Pedersen

Something of the effects behind the instrumental logic of this treatment can be seen in the ambiguous but profane refusal from the Florida provider to the Pakistani alias reproduced earlier in this chapter. Here the provider correctly identifies the serious terrorism risk signaled in this treatment through the nationality, residence, and occupation of the fictitious customer. However, rather than refusing the business or not replying, the provider seems to respond to the higher risk by asking for a higher price: $5,000 a month. A higher chance of being caught and/or more severe penalties requires a greater pay-off to compensate.

Certainly there are many examples of lawyers and other financial intermediaries being paid either to turn a blind eye to the misdeeds of their clients or to go further and actively assist in the laundering and concealment of illicit funds. For instance, Riggs Bank in the United States established shell companies to hide true ownership of accounts controlled by Augusto Pinochet after he was indicted by a Spanish judge on charges of crimes against humanity (US Senate 2004, 2005).

An even more blatant case concerns Bhadresh Gohil, a lawyer for the London firm Arlington Sharmas. Gohil had responsibility for exercising the firm's anti-money laundering precautions, but instead earned generous fees as he sold his services as a money launderer to (among others) corrupt Nigerian governor James Ibori. Ibori was convicted in 2012 in London of corruption-related laundering offenses, with £50 million frozen, the police currently in pursuit of another £200 million, and estimates of Ibori's total take running as high as $3 billion. Ibori's official salary as governor of Delta state was £12,000.

In November 2010, Gohil himself had earlier been convicted of being paid to help launder Ibori's money after external hard drives found by the police in a hidden compartment behind the fireplace in his office revealed crucial evidence. Shell companies set up by Gohil were key to both misappropriating the money and spending it. Gohil set up a shell company (Africa Development Finance, Nigeria) in 2005 for Ibori and another corrupt Nigerian state governor in relation to a publicly owned telecommunications company, V Mobile. Africa Development Finance received $37 million from V Mobile, ostensibly for consultancy and due diligence work, plus a success fee. This money was then passed through shell companies and trusts set up by Gohil in Nigeria, Guernsey, Jersey, and the Seychelles, disguised as loans between ostensibly independent parties, and deposited in accounts held with Citibank in New York and HSBC and Barclays in London. Gohil set up another shell company, Haleway Properties Limited (Gibraltar), to own one of Ibori's London properties. A further chain of companies was set up by Gohil to purchase a private jet for Ibori. Gohil was paid handsomely for his services, as indicated by the assets later confiscated from him by the police (Sowore 2007; Sahara Reporters 2008, 2011, 2012).

The premium to the provider does not necessarily have to be monetary, however. Obiang's lawyer Michael Berger, who set up a variety of California shell companies to hold bank accounts, a private jet, and a $33 million Malibu mansion, seemed to be at least as impressed by the fringe benefits of participating in his client's lavish lifestyle as by his $5,000 a month retainer and other lump sum payments. Thus in 2007 Berger writes to Obiang:

Thank you very much for inviting me to your party and for being so nice to me at the party. I appreciate the super VIP treatment that you gave me. I appreciate you telling your friends that I am your attorney. I am proud to work for you ... The food was great, the drinks were better than great, the house, the view, the DJ, the white tiger were all SO COOL! Best of all were the people that I met there because of you.

And on another occasion:

Dear Mr. Nguema:
Thank you very much for inviting me to the Kandy Halloween party @ The Playboy Mansion and getting me the VIP treatment. I had an awesome time. I met many beautiful women, and I have the photos, e-mail addresses and phone numbers to prove it. If the word gets out that you are looking for a bride, women all over the world will go even more crazy for you …
Your loyal friend and attorney,
Michael Berger. (US Senate Permanent Subcommittee on Investigations 2010: 47–48)

If corporate service providers are willing to be actively complicit in laundering money by setting up chains of shell companies, there are presumably many other providers who would at the very least be willing to turn a blind eye to funds they may suspect are the proceeds of corruption. On the other hand, offering to pay a premium may actually make providers more wary and therefore raise the Dodgy Shopping Count. On common sense grounds, someone who explicitly offers payment to break rules should raise suspicions. Providers may be normatively troubled by the inappropriateness of buying their complicity in violating rules. Or they may fear that such a suspicious approach may leave them vulnerable to a higher chance of more severe penalties imposed by regulators or law enforcement. Although national laws vary, money laundering offenses usually include provisions that those who assist in concealing what they reasonably ought to have suspected to be criminal funds are themselves guilty of money laundering and thus vulnerable to criminal prosecution. Arguably, this provision might catch providers doing business with the Premium clients. More particularly, the FATF specifically identifies customers offering to pay extra as a red flag that should raise suspicions among financial institutions. The FATF instructs CSPs to screen customers who offer "to pay extraordinary fees for services which would not ordinarily warrant such a premium" (FATF 2006a: 22). Thus, for both principled and pragmatic reasons the offer of a premium payment may raise compliance rates and lower the Dodgy Shopping Count.

Of course, remembering heterogeneous effects, none of these responses is mutually exclusive. While some providers may be tempted by the premium to violate rules they otherwise would have followed, others may calculate that the increased risk is not worth it, while others again may be morally offended by such a shady approach. In this manner the net effect of the treatment depends on the proportion of providers falling into each category.

Findings for the Premium condition

If international standards are being observed, we would expect the Premium treatment to produce an increase in non-response and refusal and be associated with a decrease in non-compliance. Consistent with the expectations, we do indeed observe higher levels of non-response in the Premium condition relative to the Placebo. The results are significant in the statistical sense. Non-response increased from 44.5 percent to 49.6 percent (a 5 percentage point change that is significant statistically at the 0.1 level). This change is where any sliver of good news ends.

Disturbingly, the results reveal that offering to pay an extra fee reduces compliance. Whereas compliance in the Placebo condition is 18.9 percent, when providers received the Premium condition they were only compliant 1 percent of the time – a 4.5 percentage point decrease in compliance, which is statistically significant at the 0.1 level. Indeed, this result means that we can with some certainty reject the notion that this finding is just a fluke (though as we discuss below the result may not be robust to more sophisticated regression analysis).

In response to one of our Premium inquiries from Daan Visser, the Netherlands alias, a US law firm simply responded: "You don't need 'identity' documents." If ever there were a blatantly non-compliant response to a blatantly non-compliant solicitation, then this is it. As the results show, the essence of the response is not atypical – indeed, we received 24 non-compliant responses after the Premium approach.

As with other treatments some of the other results are less clear. In particular, part-compliance and refusal rates both increase relative to the Placebo when providers receive the Premium treatment, but the differences are not large and are insignificant statistically. And the non-compliance rates actually decrease relative to the Placebo, but again the difference is trivial. Indeed, other than non-response and compliance, all other results are not statistically strong. Because the Dodgy Shopping Count is derived from the non-compliance rate, it appears to be more difficult to obtain a shell when a Premium is offered (16.1 approaches needed rather than 11.5 for the Placebo), although to reiterate these results are not statistically meaningful (see Figure 4.3).[7]

The clearest result that emerges from the Premium condition is that offering to pay a premium leads to a pronounced decrease in the rate at which providers demand full, certified identify documentation. At first blush, the result is not that surprising. People respond to financial incentives, acting in their own self-interest for financial gain. But the results also suggest that people are cognizant of the risks they face in facilitating the establishment of anonymous shells. And they are more likely to undertake those risks only when appropriately compensated.

Conclusion

Having presented and discussed the results of the Terrorism, Corruption and Premium treatments, what general patterns emerge? All three treatments prompted mixed responses, with evidence that different types of providers responded to the same treatment in different ways. While some shied away from suspicious approaches relative to the Placebo, others seemed attracted by the prospect of collusion.

To the extent that there are clear-cut results, the Terrorism treatment did cause an increase in the Dodgy Shopping Count in both the international and US samples relative to the Placebo benchmark, indicating that there is significant sensitivity among providers concerning the risk of terrorist financing. However, the system is far from watertight, and in absolute terms it does not seem that it would be especially difficult for even an obvious candidate for the financing of terrorism to come by an untraceable shell company. The statistically significant results for this treatment demonstrate that providers do indeed pay attention

---

[7] Multinomial models are less consistent about the robustness of the Premium results. They actually suggest that non-compliance could be lower in response to the Premium treatment and compliance levels may not actually be lower. The selection model is similarly inconsistent with the difference in proportions tests reported here. Compliance does not appear to be statistically different in response to the Premium treatment. (Again, see Appendix Tables A4.1 and A4.2.)

to the text of our email approaches. Corresponding decreases for the Terrorism treatment in compliance and part-compliance among international CSPs, and a reduction in the refusal rate in the United States, however, temper the encouraging treatment effects for non-compliance and the Dodgy Shopping Count.

The mildly optimistic findings for the Terrorist treatment do not extend to our Guineastan approach, however. Given the fact that the pool of providers pay attention to the text, their general indifference to very unsubtle hints about the fictitious consultant's aim of laundering the proceeds of corruption is striking. As discussed, shell companies are the most common and important enablers of large-scale corruption. But either providers are not aware of this problem, and the international policy measures designed to respond to it, or they simply do not care. Indeed, taking into account the paucity of examples where the financing of terrorism has been facilitated by the use of shell companies compared with the dozens of examples of their use in embezzlement and bribe-giving and taking, it is possible to argue that those selling shell companies are alert to the less important risk of terrorist financing but not the much more important one of corruption, which generates vast illicit flows and equally massive damage to many countries' development prospects (United Nations Office on Drugs and Crime/World Bank 2007).

Finally, we tested whether non-compliance can be bought with an offer of extra money through the Premium treatment. Certainly, there are lurid examples of lawyers and other financial intermediaries being induced either to turn a blind eye to their clients' illegal dealings, or to actively further them. But are these cases of the proverbial few bad apples or do they reflect a more general phenomenon? The results suggest that some providers were obligingly willing to drop the requirement for notarized identity documents, indicating that the prospect of enrichment quieted any doubts they may have had about the risks such an offer posed to society at large and themselves in particular. More broadly, the extent to which behavior can be explained as a product of rational cost–benefit calculations relates to fundamental issues in political science that are taken up in detail in Chapter 6.

5 | *Laws and standards*

In June 2011 we sent a Placebo email from our Denmark alias, Mikkel Pedersen, to a service provider in Indiana. Shortly thereafter we received a response indicating that the information needed for incorporation was the name of the company, the "assumed" name of the company, the company address, the dissolution date (the provider recommended "perpetual"), whether the company would be managed by its members, and the name and address of the registered Indiana agent. The provider offered to serve as the agent for no additional charge. Finally, the provider complimented us on our English, praising it as "better than some Americans!" Nothing else was required save the payment by check or credit card. As per our protocol, we coded this response as non-compliant: the provider required no proof of identification for the beneficial owner. This type of non-compliant response was quite common for our US subjects. Indeed, as noted earlier, more than 40 percent of providers replying to our inquiries in the United States required no photo identification documents whatsoever.

But a curious thing happened with the same firm in May 2012, when we sent a second inquiry. The email came from the Norwegian alias, Lukas Hansen, and it was equivalent to the first email save for one additional sentence, which read, "My internet searches show that United States law, enforced by the Internal Revenue Service, requires disclosure of identifying information when forming a company." How did our genial service provider so complimentary of our English skills react? We received no response, even after we pestered with two follow-up emails.

Similarly, in May 2012 we received a response from a service provider in California to our Netherlands alias, Daan Visser, which had sent a Placebo email. The provider asked us to complete "the secure online form" at an indicated link. Trying to be helpful, the provider added, "Links contain a form to fill out for incorporation, but make no reference to required documents." Interestingly, we had sent a substantively similar inquiry from the Australia alias, Thomas Smith, to the same provider in June 2011 – but that email also contained the key sentence about the IRS. The California firm had ignored the IRS treatment email but was only too happy to help in the Placebo condition. This pattern repeated many times throughout our US experiment: a non-compliant response in the Placebo condition but no response at all to the IRS treatment.

As we describe below, this result generalizes beyond these individual cases: the IRS condition caused a significant increase in the non-response rate and a corresponding decrease in the non-compliance rate. Curiously, it also caused a decrease in the rate of refusals, though this decrease is smaller and less significant statistically. The IRS treatment thus probed the treatment effects of information about domestic law enforcement, and it allows a comparison of the effects of domestic law with international rules and private standards.

Whether and when actors in the international system follow laws and regulations is a fundamental concern to a field defined and divided by the concept of international anarchy. The state-centric nature of the field of international relations has been discussed extensively already, and thus it will come as little surprise that the traditional focus on international law and international standards more broadly has been on states as both the authors and objects of these laws and standards (Vogel 2008; Schafferhof et al. 2009; Avant et al. 2010; Simmons 2010). For scholars of international law and international politics alike, the focus has been almost exclusively on treaty and international customary law. Since the end of the Cold War, however, many scholars have reacted to this state-centrism by stressing the importance of private authority in international affairs (Cutler et al. 1999; Haufler 2001; Biersteker and Hall 2002; Cutler 2003; Avant et al. 2010).

Our idea of Experimental TR aims to bolster and refine this trend. The very idea of global governance refers not just to practices where the object of governance is something other than national units, but also to where the agent of governance is something other than the state or clubs of states. We thus encourage research on governance without government (Rosenau and Czempiel 1992).

This chapter briefly summarizes the relevant literature on public authority and private rules in global governance. The main aim, however, is empirical: to present and explain the results of three treatments designed to compare the relative effects of prompting providers about each type of standard. All three treatments are similar insofar as they inform providers of the international rule they should be following in responding to the solicitation, i.e. requiring identification documents from the customer. The three treatments thus test whether telling providers what they should be doing makes any difference to their propensity to do it.

The theoretical rationale for these treatments is that two key strands of literature on international law suggest that often rule-breaking is a result of ignorance about the proper rule-compliant course of action, either because the rules are vague and under-specified or, by extension, because actors are simply unaware of the rule they should be following. These legalization (Abbott et al. 2000) and managerial perspectives (Chayes and Chayes 1995) are summarized below. If ignorance is a significant cause of non-compliance when it comes to Know Your Customer procedures for those forming shell companies, a little knowledge in the form of a prompt from the customer should go a long way in reducing non-compliance, raising compliance, and reducing the provision of untraceable shell companies.

If the three treatments share the same focus on providing information on the rules that apply, however, the key difference among them is the source of the standards. The first FATF treatment references the rule as that of the public, inter-governmental Financial Action Task Force. The second, the ACAMS treatment, relates that the same standard is that of the private for-profit Association of Certified Anti-Money Laundering Specialists. The third treatment, which we assigned randomly only to the providers in the US subject pool, attributes the standards to the Internal Revenue Service. This enables us to discern differences in treatment effects between an international enforcer, the FATF, and a domestic agency well known for its enforcement rigor. This book departs from the state-centric canon in seeing private actors, rather than states, as the locus of compliance, but the ACAMS treatment goes one step further in also testing the notion of private agents as global rule-makers, not just rule-takers.

Before detailing the three treatments we briefly put them in the context of the relevant scholarly thinking about why private authority might be important in translational relations. The next section explains related work from international relations and international law, arguing that the more knowledge relevant actors have about international rules the more they will comply. This is the key contention to be tested in this chapter.

In testing whether private rules are any more effective than inter-governmental FATF or domestic standards in limiting the supply of untraceable shell companies, we present the specific logic behind the design of each treatment. Following this the results indicate that the FATF treatment, where the inquiry explicitly references international identification standards promulgated by the FATF, does not significantly affect responses for any outcome. The ACAMS treatment, where the standards are attributed not to the FATF but instead to the private association, ACAMS, causes an increase in the rate of compliance compared to other conditions, although the result is not strong statistically. Finally, the IRS treatment, where the standards are attributed to the US Internal Revenue Service, exerts a significant effect in reducing both response rates and non-compliance rates, suggesting that at least one domestic agency has much more influence over corporate service providers than the international body governing the domain.

Private authority, non-state actors, and transnational relations

While states may ultimately rely on coercion to enforce compliance domestically, to the extent private actors affect compliance beyond the level of the state, the concept of authority is central. Absent the ability to force parties to follow rules, some measure of inducement, persuasion, or other consensual mechanism is required. For Biersteker and Hall (2002), the varieties of authority are market, moral, and illicit. Avant et al. refer to five types of authority through which "global governors" (including both public and private actors) may make rules count: institutional, delegated, expert, principled, and capacity-based (2010: 11). Of these, the most relevant for private actors are delegated authority—when states or inter-governmental organizations employ private agents, expert, when private actors have superior knowledge to public ones, principled, a form of moral authority, and capacity—when the actor can get the job done and solve a given problem. It is important to note here that for these authors the private actors in question are at least as often NGOs as for-profit corporations.

Those studying global environmental governance and the governance of multinational corporations in particular have emphasized private actors as the targets of international regulatory regimes, whether it is logging firms (Bartley 2007) or those in the diamond trading business (Kantz 2007; Haufler 2010). As such, there is a useful parallel with the corporate service providers at the heart of our study. But those writing on environmental and corporate governance have also increasingly looked at private agents as standard-setters and -enforcers, as holding authority in their own right.

Such "private-to-private" global regulation, where non-state actors are both regulators and regulated, can rely on mechanisms like codes of conduct, market-based strategies, private monitors, and specialized expertise that may not be available in the public sector (Büthe 2010; Haufler 2010). A prominent and powerful example of a private standard-setter might be the big credit-rating agencies, Standard & Poors, Moody's, and Fitch (Sinclair 2005). Through their rating of private and sovereign debt offerings these agencies have significant influence over the economic behavior of firms and states. The Internet Corporation for Assigned Names and Numbers and the International Accounting Standards Board provide other examples of influential private global regulators (Büthe and Mattli 2011). Büthe (2010) explains the presence of private authority with reference to a supply and demand model. The demand may come from governments keen to delegate highly specialized tasks, private firms looking to reduce transaction costs, or NGOs seeking to address transnational ills. The supply of such regulation may be motivated by firms clubbing together to self-regulate so as to pre-empt government regulations, or establish barriers to entry, or create a valuable specialized expertise in the resulting standards, as well as NGOs motivated by more altruistic ends.

Yet even those writing about the power of private global governors often stress the limitations of private authority (e.g. Lipschutz and Rowe 2005). The same uncertainties about selection effects and endogeneity that bedevil the study of public international law often frustrate attempts to determine whether private rules make any real difference to actors' behavior, either in absolute terms, or relative to the rules set by states and inter-governmental organizations. The same factors that make field experiments both desirable and possible in addressing these uncertainties would seem to apply even more strongly in private-to-private regulation than in public international law, given that private actors are in principle more easily assigned to control and treatment groups than states or inter-governmental organizations.

Knowledge, rules, and compliance

One of the most important schools of thought in international law, called the managerial approach, holds that significant non-compliance with international law is unusual, but when such breaches do occur they stem from ambiguity, incapacity, or built-in expectations that actors will comply incrementally over time (Chayes and Chayes 1993; see also Henkin 1979). If the rules are clear to the actors and they possess sufficient capacity, the argument goes, they will conform.

Chayes and Chayes argue that much non-compliance with international law arises from the lack of clarity in the rules themselves. If significant room exists for competing interpretations of the law, parties can hardly be faulted for acting in conformity with the interpretation that best suits their interests – even if a competing party might allege non-compliance. It is only after the actors have taken the necessary measures to reduce ambiguity in the rules that actions clearly outside the law's boundaries can be identified as non-compliant (Chayes and Chayes 1993).

Closely related to the managerial school's argument about ambiguity is the discussion of *precision* advanced by proponents of the "legalization" approach. As Abbott et al. explain, "A precise rule specifies clearly and unambiguously what is expected of a state or other actor (in terms of both the intended objective and the means of achieving it) in a particular set of circumstances" (2000: 412). Greater precision entails greater legalization, which implies a stronger injunction for actors to follow the law. Legalization increases when the law is precisely stipulated, and compliance should naturally follow.

While neither foundational work in the managerial or legalization schools made the point explicitly, a logical extension of both arguments suggests that the most extreme form of ambiguity or imprecision is ignorance. That is, if parties fundamentally lack knowledge of the rules that apply in a given context, actions that fall outside the bounds of the rules certainly cannot be labeled deliberately non-compliant. By extension, informing ignorant parties about the rules dramatically reduces the extreme ambiguity and imprecision resulting from unawareness.

Perhaps a key reason that neither Chayes and Chayes (1993) nor Abbott et al. (2000) discussed ignorance explicitly is that the key units of analysis for managerial and legalization schools are nation states. Since states negotiate international law, thus by design they are knowledgeable about its boundaries. But the managerial and legalization logics should encompass individuals and organizations that do not know the law on the grounds that this is equivalent to having very imprecise or ambiguous laws. Removing ignorance disambiguates in the extreme. And this suggests observable implications that can be tested experimentally. Indeed, an important part of the managerial school was built upon psychological and sociological foundations (see Chayes and Chayes 1993, fn. 30), and these have rich implications for individuals and suggest that this extension is defensible.

We emphasize here that our experiments should not be read as a definitive test of the managerial or legalization arguments or any other theoretical tradition. Rather, the experiments test observable implications derived from the theories, leaving many other observable implications of the same theories unexamined. Nevertheless, we maintain that we are testing important observable implications of these leading theories in the domain of financial transparency, so any anomalies that accumulate should compel reexamination of the theories, however minor or domain-specific. As we argued in Chapter 1, this is the best way to accumulate knowledge within international relations.

The text below first gives some background on the FATF to reinforce the material in Chapter 2 and describes the related treatment, then explains the ACAMS treatment in relation to the discussion of private standards above, and finally presents the IRS treatment and results.

Explaining the FATF treatment

At the height of his power and wealth in the late 1980s and early 1990s, Medellin drug lord Pablo Escobar controlled as much as 80 percent of the global cocaine trade and was named one of the ten richest people on earth by both *Fortune* and *Forbes*. Besides ordering the deaths of Colombian presidential candidates, supreme court justices, hundreds of judges, and thousands of policemen, Escobar also invented many international money laundering practices. Drug kingpins like Escobar faced a significant problem: how to get billions of dollars in cash from drug sales in the United States converted to pesos and back into Colombia. As convicted cocaine trafficker George Jung revealed, "It became more of a problem to count the money and stack it ... Money became an obstacle. You know, it started to take the fun out of the whole thing, believe it or not" (Zill and Bergman 2000).

At first Escobar merely had his agents deposit cash from US drug sales into American banks, and then he wire-transferred the money to Colombia. As he famously noted, the drug trade was "simple – you bribe someone here, you bribe someone there, and you pay a friendly banker to help you bring the money back" (Cockburn 1993). But in the 1980s, the United States began to crack down on money laundering. This is when Escobar got creative. He flew planeloads of cash to Caribbean tax havens and made use of more relaxed banking laws there to deposit the money into accounts of bankers and businessmen willing to trade with him. He later co-opted the black market currency exchanges in both the United States and Colombia. Through creative and evolving tactics he brazenly thwarted official efforts to stop the flow of laundered money (Zill and Bergman 2000).

To counter the threat posed by Escobar and his ilk, the wealthy countries of the world established the Financial Action Task Force in 1989. US officials clearly saw money laundering as a global problem, and addressing it would require the cooperation of other countries. In particular, the tax havens such as the Cayman Islands and the Bahamas would need to be brought to heel. So the United States and its key allies attacked the problem in the conventional way – through the use of international agreements focused on compelling member countries to reform domestic laws and align them with a global standard.

Few international institutions have done more with less than the Financial Action Task Force. In its early years, the FATF worked with a staff of three and a budget of a few hundred thousand dollars, and in 2012 the permanent staff was only twenty and its budget $4 million. Yet from the beginning the FATF's mandate was sweeping: it was charged with halting cross-border money laundering, particularly the financial flows associated with the global narcotics trade. The FATF's response was ingenious in many ways.

One of its first actions was to issue its mission-defining 40 Recommendations for the detection and prevention of money laundering. The Recommendations were sweeping in scope, first detailing the approach for scrutinizing financial transactions, but also defining money laundering, outlining customer due diligence practices, dictating appropriate record keeping, recommending the organization of domestic financial and law-enforcement agencies, and sketching the parameters for international cooperation on the issue. In particular, as reviewed in Chapter 3, what is now Recommendation 24 mandates that "Countries should ensure that there is adequate, accurate and timely information on the beneficial ownership and control of legal persons [i.e. companies] that can be obtained or accessed in a timely fashion by competent authorities" (FATF 2012). To repeat, the "beneficial owner" is the person who actually controls the company and profits from its activities, so it cannot be merely a nominee director as in the example of Lu Zhang that opened this book. Recommendation 24 requires the penetration of the corporate veil and the revelation of the actual person or people in charge of the company.

But with its very minimal staff and operating budget, how was the FATF to enforce such a sweeping set of standards? The answer: by leveraging its focal position and marshaling the resources of its member states through "mutual evaluations" or peer review. Every few years all states that have signed onto FATF standards – and 180 countries have agreed to date – undergo a thorough appraisal of the degree to which they are in compliance with the FATF recommendations. Member governments second personnel to perform the reviews, which vastly amplifies the reach of the FATF's staff, which are also supported in these evaluations by the World Bank and International Monetary Fund.

The mutual evaluations in essence provide report cards on the level of country compliance with financial transparency standards. When countries are found out of compliance, the FATF indicates the deficiencies in the report, and even leading countries – such as the United States – can receive strong admonitions from the FATF. For countries that were especially non-compliant, in 2000 the FATF created a blacklist of "Non-Cooperative Countries and Territories" (NCCT), as discussed in Chapter 2. Early blacklisted jurisdictions included tax havens such as Panama, the Cayman Islands, and the Bahamas. Later, the FATF added more powerful and populous countries to the list, including Russia, the Philippines, Israel, Hungary, Nigeria, and Ukraine. The blacklist appeared to get government leaders' attention: all of the countries moved quickly to reform domestic laws and policies in order to be removed from the NCCT, and by 2007 all had succeeded (Drezner 2007; Sharman 2011). But in 2011 the FATF's International Co-operation Review Group created a new blacklist and targeted a set of "pariah" countries including Iran, Pakistan, and

North Korea, so the institution's "naming and shaming" strategy is ongoing. The response to the blacklist indicates that the FATF is very effective in promulgating its standards, and the evidence we presented in Chapter 3 suggests that the global rules on financial transparency have significantly improved compliance levels in tax havens.

But the key focus in this project centers not on the degree of national statutory compliance with international law but with adherence to global standards at the level of individual firms. Indeed, as discussed in Chapter 3, levels of statutory compliance reported in the FATF's Mutual Evaluation Reports correlate only weakly with the levels of actual compliance we find in our field study. Thus, we want to learn if knowledge of international laws and standards causes corporate service providers to follow the rules. The FATF treatment originates from the Norstralia aliases and also randomly assigns the 33 base email texts. But it adds two sentences that we believe capture the key observable implication from managerialism while maintaining the essential believability of an approach from a prospective client. To the base email we added the passage in bold below. The approach reveals information about global standards but also asserts continued interest in confidentiality. We copy a typical example of the treatment language here.

Dear [name/company]: I am contacting you regarding a business I am trying to set up. I am a consultant and my colleagues and I are seeking to establish an international corporation. I am a [Norstralia] resident, but I do business both locally and with some international client, including some in your region. Our business has been growing substantially, and our goal is to limit tax obligations and business liability. We would like as much business confidentiality as possible in these early stages of formation. **My internet searches show that the international Financial Action Task Force requires disclosure of identifying information. But I would rather not provide any detailed personal information if possible.**

So, we would like to know what identifying documents will be required to establish this company. We would also like to know what start-up costs will be. Due to my travel schedule, email will be the best way to reach me. I look forward to hearing from you soon. Regards, [Alias]

A skeptic might worry that our subjects already possess knowledge of the FATF and its rules, so we are not testing what we claim. This seems a reasonable objection, and we acknowledge that in such cases our experiment does not provide a direct test of the managerial or legalization logics. Rather, in the cases where subjects already possess knowledge of the FATF standards, the treatment functions as what psychologists call a "priming" manipulation: key information is called to mind for subjects, and that process of recall – however subtle – induces behavioral change (see Decoster and Claypool 2004).[1] Any priming effect of international law, however, is consistent with a managerial logic: knowledge of the rules, even if that knowledge is called to mind from memory, should still affect behavior. And given that much more subtle priming treatments than this one produce robust results in social psychology subjects (Decoster and Claypool 2004), any effects from a priming treatment should remain interesting and relevant.

However, our conventional survey that followed the experiment suggests that a sizable proportion of subjects did not possess prior knowledge of FATF rules. Indeed, of the 301 CSP representatives that answered the question on our survey, 193, or 64.1 percent, answered that they had never been briefed on FATF recommendations or policy. For subjects like these, to the extent they are representative, we would argue that the intervention is a direct treatment that serves to inform subjects about rules of which they are unaware.

We caution against extrapolating too far from these survey results, however. We sent the survey to the same 3,771 firms in the experimental subject pool. But only 342 subjects, or 9.1 percent, actually completed the survey. Given the answers we received to many of the survey questions, including the embedded survey and list experiments, we strongly suspect that the subjects responding to the survey were a biased sample of the subjects that answered the experimental emails. So the proportion of experimental subjects with knowledge of the FATF rules may have been significantly lower than the 36 percent the survey indicates.

FATF findings

If we take the survey at face value, it suggests that for roughly two-thirds of the subjects the FATF treatment served to inform them of the

---

[1] We note here that the priming experiments performed in psychology often involve much more subtle treatments. Our prime is significantly less subtle and therefore may not induce the same unconscious reactions.

global standards. For the remaining third the treatment should be seen as a priming intervention that calls to mind key information. It turns out that the point about direct versus priming effects ends up being rather moot. We saw no significant treatment effects.

In the global experiment, the outcomes across the board were statistically equivalent for the FATF and Placebo conditions (see Table 5.1 and Figure 5.1). The proportion of firms requiring no documentation whatsoever – and thus offering anonymous shells – was 8.7 percent in the Placebo condition and 9.0 in the FATF condition. This slight increase in non-compliance from Placebo to the FATF treatment was not statistically meaningful, however. Similarly, the part-compliant outcome, where firms required some form of ID, was 16.5 in the Placebo condition and a statistically similar 15.9 for the FATF treatment. The percentage change in compliance by demanding certified ID and the proportion refusing service altogether decreased by larger amounts from Placebo to treatment (from 18.9 to 16.9 percent for compliance and from 11.3 to 9.5 percent for refusal), but neither drop was statistically significant. The proportion of firms not replying increased from 44.5 percent for the Placebo to 48.7 percent for the FATF treatment, but again the difference is statistically trivial. In essence all of these results suggest that directly informing (or priming) CSPs in the global subject pool about international law did not cause any meaningful differences in their behavior.

We saw the same pattern for the US corporate service providers (see Table 5.2 and Figure 5.2). Once again, invoking the FATF and its identification standard increased the non-response rate from 73.8 percent in the Placebo condition to 76.4 percent for the FATF treatment, but once more the bump is not statistically consequential. The same was true across the other outcomes. Non-compliance decreased from 11.3 to 9.9 percent, part-compliance ticked upward from 1.6 to 2.0 percent, compliance remained constant at 0.4 percent, and refusal fell from 13.0 to 11.4 percent. Yet again, the pattern holds: all differences are statistically trivial.[2]

---

[2] Nearly all of these results are qualitatively the same when estimating multinomial probit or selection models as reported in Appendix Tables A5.1–A5.4. One possible exception in the United States, is that the FATF treatment is associated with lower levels of refusal.

Table 5.1 *Contingency table of results by Placebo, FATF, ACAMS, and ACAMS + FATF treatment groups with difference tests for international providers*

Condition	N	No response	Non-compliant	Part-compliant	Compliant	Refusal
Placebo	1112	495	97	184	210	126
Proportion		44.5%	8.7%	16.5%	18.9%	11.3%
FATF	390	190	35	62	66	37
Proportion		48.7%	9.0%	15.9%	16.9%	9.5%
ACAMS	109	50	9	19	27	4**
Proportion		45.9%	8.3%	17.4%	24.8%	3.7%
ACAMS + FATF	114	59	13	16	18	8
Proportion		51.8%	11.4%	14.0%	15.8%	7.0%

Significant in difference tests compared to the Placebo condition: *0.1 level, **0.05 level, ***0.01 level.

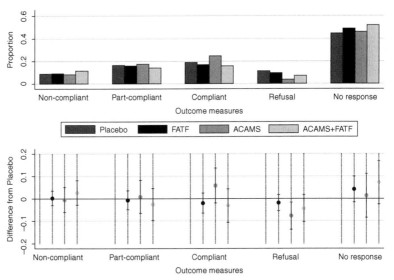

Figure 5.1 Comparison of results among Placebo, FATF, ACAMS, and ACAMS + FATF treatment groups for international providers.

The Dodgy Shopping Counts for the international and US samples are displayed in Figures 5.3 and 5.4. While they provide an intuitive sense of number of firms one would need to approach before finding a non-compliant firm, they are of course derivative of the

Table 5.2 *Contingency table of results by Placebo, FATF, and IRS treatment groups for US providers*

Condition	N	No response	Non-compliant	Part-compliant	Compliant	Refusal
Placebo	816	602	92	13	3	106
Proportion		73.8%	11.3%	1.6%	0.4%	13.0%
FATF	546	417	54	11	2	62
Proportion		76.4%	9.9%	2.0%	0.4%	11.4%
IRS	552	442***	42**	12	2	54*
Proportion		80.0%	7.6%	2.2%	0.4%	9.8%

Significant in difference tests compared to the Placebo condition: *0.1 level, **0.05 level, ***0.01 level.

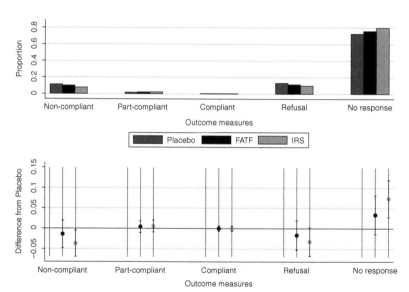

Figure 5.2 Comparison of results among Placebo, FATF, and IRS treatment groups as a proportion and the difference from the Placebo group for US providers.

non-compliance rate. As such, the Dodgy Shopping Count is effectively identical between the Placebo and the FATF treatment.

These results surprised and puzzled us. The logic of ambiguity and precision advanced by the managerial and legalization schools seems unassailable. Obedience to the law should improve when the precise boundaries of the law are known, and compliance should especially

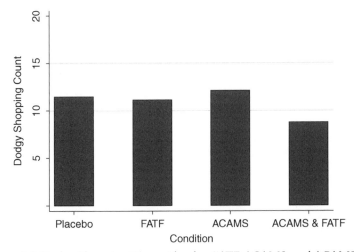

Figure 5.3 Dodgy Shopping Count: Placebo, FATF, ACAMS, and ACAMS + FATF, international sample.

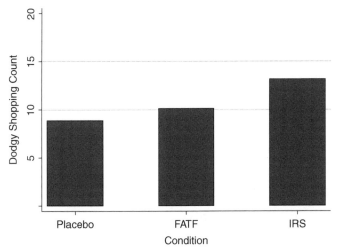

Figure 5.4 Dodgy Shopping Count: Placebo, FATF, and IRS, US sample.

improve if a law is revealed that was previously unknown completely. But this is not what we found in the domain of financial transparency. Making clear that global standards require customer identification did not meaningfully alter subjects' compliance with those standards. Even more interestingly, this null result did not hold when we attributed the standards to other bodies, one private in the form of the Association of Certified Anti-Money Laundering Specialists (ACAMS) and one domestic when we invoked the Internal Revenue Service.

ACAMS treatment

Sounding like a professional educational association akin to the American Political Science Association, the Association of Certified Anti-Money Laundering Specialists is a for-profit entity that confers a certification and organizes conferences and a range of other bespoke training courses. It is fundamentally the product of one person: Charles A. Intriago. The Association grew out of Intriago's newsletter, *Money Laundering Alert*, which was launched in October 1989, just before the FATF was created, and at a time when the United States was almost the only country that had criminalized money laundering. The newsletter grew into a subscription website (www.moneylaundering.com), and series of conferences. The discussion to found the Association began in the late 1990s and came to fruition in 2001, just before the terrorist attacks of that year. An important model was provided by the Association of Certified Fraud Examiners, founded in 1988, which similarly is a for-profit concern selling a qualification and running conferences (Association of Certified Fraud Examiners 2012).

By capitalizing on its first-mover advantage in the field of anti-money laundering, ACAMS has pulled itself up by its bootstraps. Despite the "Certified" moniker, the certification is self-referential, given that ACAMS itself has no delegated authority from either the FATF or any national government, though increasingly it does garner endorsements from both. Intriago himself sold out of the organization for $12 million, leaving in 2008 to found the Association of Certified E-Discovery Specialists and the Association of Certified Financial Crime Specialists, whose mission seems to overlap that of ACAMS. In 2011 ACAMS was acquired by Reuters Thomson, a Canadian-owned firm operating in more than 100 countries (which also provides the Institute of Scientific Information's citation database and ranking of academic journals).

The founding of ACAMS came at a time when the coverage of the anti-money laundering (AML) regime had grown exponentially. Successive deepening of international AML standards and national laws meant that banks had to do more and more to stay compliant with regulations, for example in terms of screening for a wider range of crimes. Thus according to a KPMG survey of 1,000 international banks, the cost of complying with these regulations increased an average of 61 percent for 2001–2003, 58 percent for 2004–2006, and a further 45 per cent for 2007–2010 (KPMG 2004, 2007, 2011). Beyond banks, hundreds of thousands of other financial and non-financial firms came to be included within the regulatory framework, necessitating the retraining of staff or the hiring of new staff with AML expertise. Finally, more countries adopted AML laws, thus creating an international market for specialists in this area. Having a certification became a relatively reliable way of communicating one's credentials in this new and highly lucrative labor market, with the cost of certification currently running at $1,670 plus an ongoing annual membership fee of $265. In this sense unlike many of the private standard-setters discussed in the more general literature on private standards (Büthe 2010), ACAMS is providing an excludable private good, even if it is one that may well have positive externalities for society at large. The certification confers expert authority on the recipient in other contexts beyond the labor market, as for example, "Jane Smith, FBI agent and Certified Anti-Money Laundering Specialist" is apparently more highly regarded by juries than "Jane Smith, an FBI agent with 20 years' experience in investigating money laundering cases."[3]

ACAMS is headquartered in Miami, and it now has more than 12,000 members worldwide. Although the majority of members are from the United States, there are significant ACAMS nodes in Latin America, the Caribbean, Europe, Asia, and Africa. In Britain, however, a rival organization, the International Compliance Association, offers a similar anti-money laundering qualification held by 10,000 individuals and has a presence in 30 other countries, so ACAMS does not enjoy the same dominance everywhere. The centerpiece of ACAMS is the certification process, aimed at individuals in banks and other private firms as well as government agencies. Indeed, increasingly it is public bodies that comprise much of the business growth for ACAMS.[4]

Through its training, the Association serves to diffuse and entrench FATF standards among the target private financial firms that are the

---

[3] Author interview: by phone, March 29, 2012.
[4] Author interviews: by phone, March 29, 2012, and in Washington, DC, April 25, 2012.

crucial "last mile" in terms of compliance, exactly those that the
FATF finds it most difficult to reach. There is no formal relationship
between ACAMS and the FATF. Indeed, despite the AML regime relying on private actors for most of the implementation, the FATF had
no formal outreach to any part of the private sector before 2007, and
it is still very much focused on inter-governmental processes. States
have created the demand for credentials in this area by mandating
that Money Laundering Reporting Officers receive AML training,
but they do not specify who should provide it, or even the particular
contents. Although it is international public standards that define
that there should be private sector representatives in the front-line
of the fight against money laundering, it is private associations like
ACAMS that help to determine what these representatives are actually doing.

Yet although distant, there is a relationship between ACAMS and
the FATF. Many members of the ACAMS board are former US government employees who had roles within the FATF and maintain
close contacts with the organization.[5] Some FATF Mutual Evaluation
Reports explicitly praise ACAMS training. Nevertheless, if ACAMS
has wide latitude in determining its certification requirement, and thus
how the broad principles of international AML standards are set in
practice, what difference does this make to compliance?

Below we reproduce the ACAMS treatment with the key sentence
in bold.

Dear [name/company]:
I am an international consultant living in [Norstralia]. My associates and
I have been based in [Norstralia] for some time and we have done extensive international work, especially in your area. After looking at the specific
needs of our growing company, we were feeling that it would make sense for
us to expand and to set up an international company.

We especially hope to limit taxes and reduce liability. We were wondering
what you require us to give in order to do this.

**My internet searches show that the Association of Certified Anti-Money
Laundering Specialists requires disclosure of identifying information when
forming a company.** But I would like to avoid providing any detailed personal information if possible.

[5] Author interview: by phone, March 29, 2012.

We would like to form this corporation as privately as possible. What identifying documents will you need from us? We would also like to know what your usual prices are. We appreciate the help.

I travel a lot for my work, so I communicate best via email.

I hope to hear from you soon.

Yours,

[Alias]

As is apparent, aside from the usual minor stylistic differences, the basic structure of the email has all the common elements. Half of the key modification is to prompt corporate service providers about their Know Your Customer duty, just as that in the FATF treatment. The key difference with the latter, of course, is the mention of the Association of Certified Anti-Money Laundering Specialists. Why might presenting exactly the same information from different parties evoke different responses? As discussed above, key to the idea of private rule-enforcement, and probably any kind of rule-enforcement at all, is the notion of authority. Even when saying the same thing, some speakers will carry more weight than others because of who they are and the way they are perceived. Condemnation of a particular human rights abuse is likely to have more effect in coming from a Nobel Peace Prize laureate than an average journalist or academic. So too it might be that, as the club of the world's strongest states, the FATF might have a prestige and authority that no firm could match, in which case the FATF treatment would have a significantly greater impact in raising compliance than the ACAMS treatment. Or if ACAMS graduates and trainees are strongly represented among those who receive our emails, they may put far more stock in this body's standards than in what they may perceive as some remote, unengaged talk-shop in Paris like the FATF. In this case, we should see a positive difference in compliance rate produced by the ACAMS treatment relative to the FATF email, perhaps more in countries where the Association is strong (especially in Latin America and the Caribbean), relative to those where its presence is tenuous (Britain, Africa, or Asia).

ACAMS findings

The results for the ACAMS treatment are not strong and generally mixed. Certainly despite the prompt on what they should be doing there were still providers happy to supply untraceable shell companies in defiance of international rules. Thus in replying to our fictitious Danish consultant Mikkel Pedersen, one exuberant if constitutionally ill-informed American provider responded: "Regarding what information is required. None! Hard for Europeans to understand we have a word in our constitution which is privacy! You simply need to fill in our form ****, regarding bank account an appearance is now required." Despite requiring a copy of Pedersen's passport (though not that it be notarized), another partially compliant response indicated that at least some Europeans do understand the concept of privacy:

First allow us to introduce ourselves. We are a Swiss based Fiduciary company located in the heart of Geneva ... List of our clients includes some of the world's renowned personas as well as prosperous, dynamic businesses. Our location is not accidental. In today's turbulent world, Switzerland is for many the haven for both business and personal financial affairs. Its unique location at the heart of Europe combined with its reputation of financial freedom, privacy and stability is an excellent harbor for investors and depositors from all over the world ... Combined with Switzerland's low taxes (Switzerland is by many considered to be the world's Tax haven) and the highly sophisticated bank service, including the famous 'banking-secrecy', **** offer an unique business opportunity.

The message went on to offer ready-made Swiss shelf companies and Liechtenstein foundations. But to ascertain the more general patterns, and consistent with the results presented in other parts of this book, we compare the ACAMS treatment against the Placebo to learn what differences there are. Additionally, we also consider the ACAMS treatment in comparison to the FATF and a treatment where we combined reference to both the FATF standards and ACAMS in the same email to learn if there are any additive treatment effects from combining mentions of the two institutions and their standards. Generally the ACAMS treatment does not produce big differences relative to the Placebo, but there are some differences when compared with other treatments.

First consider the results in Figure 5.1 and Table 5.1. In contrast to the previous chapter and many of the results in this book, but in line with the FATF results just presented, the ACAMS treatment does not alter response rates in meaningful ways. Thus, the mention of international standards – public or private – does not decrease the rates at which firms respond.

For those services that do respond, across all of the outcomes, the ACAMS treatment is not statistically different from the Placebo at conventional levels except in one case: refusal rates are lower for ACAMS than for the Placebo. Mention of ACAMS does produce greater levels of compliance (5.9 percentage points higher), but the result does not reach standard levels of statistical significance ($p = 0.14$). However, if we use the looser one-tailed significance test, compliance for ACAMS is significantly higher at the 0.1 level compared to the Placebo. And if we consider ACAMS compliance against other treatment conditions, ACAMS produced significantly higher compliance at the 0.1 level in two-tailed tests compared to the FATF condition and also compared to a treatment where we attributed the standards to both ACAMS and the FATF together. The ACAMS condition also caused significantly higher compliance rates in two-tailed tests at the 0.05 level compared to both the Penalties and Norms conditions (see Findley et al. 2012b).

Thus, there is some evidence that invoking private certification standards produces greater levels of compliance. However, because the Dodgy Shopping Count is based on the non-compliance level alone, which is similar for these conditions compared to the Placebo, there are only slight differences in the estimated number of firms one would need to approach with FATF, ACAMS, or the Placebo (see Figure 5.3).[6] Thus, reference to the international standards body does not significantly affect rates of response or compliance; reference to a private certifier may produce an improvement in compliance, but it is likely small. Domestic laws and enforcement, tested through the IRS treatment, however, produced much stronger effects.

IRS treatment

As noted, this chapter is devoted to two main aims. The first is discovering whether telling actors about rules they should be following makes them any more likely to do so. The second is to determine whether varying the attribution of the source of the rules has any impact on compliance. Might the same information produce different effects when attributed to different institutions? This section explains the rationale for the IRS treatment. Unlike the FATF and ACAMS, the Internal Revenue Service

---

[6] The multinomial and selection models are no more encouraging than these results. The ACAMS condition is associated with statistically lower levels of refusals, but that is the extent of the differences. See Appendix Tables A5.1 and A5.2.

has an obvious public profile in the United States and also possesses strong enforcement powers, which are likewise widely known.

Both common sense and the IR realist school of thought might argue that the ultimate mechanisms of enforcement against individuals (e.g. police and prisons) and companies (e.g. fines) are wielded by the state. In contrast, and to paraphrase Stalin's famous quip about the Pope, those of this view might ask how many army divisions the FATF commands. As discussed elsewhere in the book, the FATF sets standards for states and can blacklist those countries that are adjudged to be in violation of these standards. But the FATF certainly does not have the power to wield military force, to imprison people, or to levy fines. In a strictly legal sense, the FATF does not exist since, unlike shell companies, it not have legal personality. As a private company ACAMS does have legal personality but of course has no coercive powers.

Historically, much of the realist skepticism about international law and international organizations has been based on the point that such arrangements are not backed by hard enforcement mechanisms (Mearsheimer 1994/95). Following from this, realists focus on states precisely because they do have such tools at their disposal. So to test whether and to what extent the prospect of penalties might motivate corporative service providers to require proof of identity from prospective customers where they otherwise would not apply this standard, it may be necessary to bring the state back in. Even if one does not accept the view that state dominance of the means of legitimate violence is the essential and defining feature of political life, it is important to see what difference, if any, the prospect of national enforcement makes in this domain – both relative to the prospect of FATF enforcement and of course in comparison with the Placebo.

In order to test this idea, we developed a treatment based on the US tax authority, the Internal Revenue Service (or IRS). In the IRS treatment, as well as the usual template of why the customer wants a shell company, we again noted the international Know Your Customer requirement, but this time identified the IRS as the enforcer (the relevant text in bold).

Dear [Corporate Service Provider],
I am writing on behalf of myself and the other two associates of our small consulting business, currently based in [Norstralia]. We do work in your area, so my purpose in writing is to request assistance and direction on incorporation internationally – although we live and operate in [Norstralia],

international incorporation is the best thing for our business right now since we are taking on more clients, and for tax purposes, as well as to limit liability. We would like to form a new company in your area as private individuals. Additionally, we'd like to make this process as private and confidential as possible. My internet searches show that United States law, enforced by the Internal Revenue Service, requires disclosure of identifying information when forming a company. But I would like to avoid providing any detailed personal information if possible.

Can you please inform me which identification documents will be required by you and how much your services will cost? It will be much easier for you to reach me via email than on the phone. Thanks in advance.

[Alias]

Importantly, this treatment was only directed at the US section of our pool of providers. Although, as some of the examples considered below demonstrate, the IRS does engage in enforcement actions against foreign companies and individuals, the overwhelming majority of its attention is devoted to US individuals and companies, and US nationals are most vulnerable to the coercive measures the IRS has at its disposal. There are certainly many other parts of the US government with an interest in the misuse of shell companies. But all US nationals will have had at least some experience with the IRS and know what it is, unlike, say, some of the more esoteric parts of the US government that also have a role in this area (e.g. the Office of Foreign Asset Control). In the recent past the IRS has enthusiastically used its coercive powers to apply very strict penalties to those found in violation of the rules.

Chapter 6 to follow discusses and tests the role of penalties and sanctions in promoting compliance, but given that coercive powers are perhaps the key distinguishing feature of the IRS relative to the other treatments in the chapter, some discussion of this aspect is called for.

The basic logic of this treatment closely parallels that described in the Penalties treatment in Chapter 6. Once again, the aim is to see whether the increased salience of punishment is enough to counter the temptation of increased profit through rule violation. A further similarity is that it draws on the idea that human behavior should be explained in rational choice terms, i.e. that actors decide on a course of action by calculating and comparing the costs and benefits of the various options open to them. According to this view, rules are upheld through the prospect of sanctions for violation rather than, for example, by any principled belief in the rightness of the rules in question or habitual compliance produced by socialization (March and Olsen 1998; Simmons 1998, 2010).

An example of why the IRS might well scare US providers concerns the Offshore Compliance Initiative. The most public face of this program was the $780 million penalty levied against the Swiss bank UBS for assisting thousands of American clients to evade taxes. As part of this settlement UBS also had to hand over the names of more than 4,000 of these clients (something the bank had solemnly promised these individuals it would never, ever do) (Sheppard 2009). The clients in turn had the choice of voluntarily divulging the true state of their financial affairs to the IRS in return for a lesser punishment or facing criminal prosecution. Crucially, a condition of the voluntary disclosure program was that those confessing to past misdeeds have had to provide full details of all the professional intermediaries who assisted them in concealing their assets, including corporate service providers. The IRS has now developed something of a model of indicting a foreign bank, settling with the bank in return for client names, extracting the details of other financial institutions, and then indicting these other financial institutions so as to get access to further lists of those evading US taxes. As a result, more than 18,000 individuals have come forward to strike a deal with the IRS, in each case providing full details on all parties involved.

The targets of this kind of enforcement action are by no means limited to large banks, however, but extend to the kinds of service providers that fall within our subject pool. A recent example of the IRS employing its enforcement powers shows the relevance to shell companies and those who sell them. For example, in June 2012 three tax preparers were charged with conspiring to defraud the IRS after the firm they managed, United Revenue Services, was alleged to have helped clients evade US taxes due on foreign accounts (Department of Justice 2012). According to the indictment, this was done through the simple expedient of forming shell companies in Belize to hold their American and Israeli clients' funds lodged in the Luxembourg branches of two Israeli banks. These funds are alleged to have been transferred to the companies disguised as investment losses and business expenses. Such a scheme relies on the now-familiar ruse of dissociating the ostensibly independent shell companies from their actual beneficial owners. The penalties for such a fraud range up to five years in prison. The *Wall Street Journal* noted that the timing of the IRS indictment in mid-June might well have been a not-so-subtle reminder to taxpayers that the annual deadline for declaring foreign bank accounts is the end of that month (Saunders 2012).

A second example of why the IRS treatment might be expected to catch providers' attention relates to the intermediaries (both American and those from third countries) currently trying to strike a plea bargain concerning charges that they provided "abusive tax shelters" to US citizens, schemes that are often premised on the use of shell companies. This can involve some very unpleasant tradeoffs, the general contours of which are illuminated by confidential interviews and suggest that those convicted of the large-scale provision of such abusive tax schemes can face 20 to 30 years in prison as well as loss of all their assets, not just the profits from the schemes. In discussing plea bargains, the IRS Criminal Investigation division is apparently reluctant to even concede in advance to "only" 20 years of prison time. Because those above a certain age or with any sort of serious health condition realize that such a sentence means they will never be released, they go on the run and seek to disappear. Apparently, however, in such cases justice always catches up with the fugitive.[7] While the details of these particular examples will probably not be known to any given US provider, all will know that getting on the wrong side of the IRS can easily result in fines or jail time. We would expect this association to obtain even in the relatively neutral phrasing of the treatment that does not explicitly mention penalties and sanctions.

Before going on to the results of our IRS treatment, there are two important aspects of this approach to be explained. The first is that, despite our prompt in the email, in fact the IRS does not require providers to collect official identity documents to establish the true identity of a company owner. The IRS may require a foreign owner of a US company to apply for an Employer Identification Number, and this application calls for details like the individual's name and address, but there are no supporting documents of any kind that are required. In general, US federal law does not require identification and verification of beneficial ownership, and the same is true of almost all states' laws as well (GAO 2006; FATF 2006b; Verret 2010). In this sense again, the

---

[7] Author interviews: Washington, DC, United States, March 22, 2011 and April 25, 2012; Bridgetown, Barbados, May 25–26, 2010; Miami, United States, April 30–May 1, 2012.

fictitious claim of IRS enforcement of beneficial ownership standards directly parallels the fictitious claim about FATF enforcement in the Penalties treatment. In both we prime the providers by raising the salience of prospective punishment, rather than communicating accurate factual information about the true legal situation.

The second aspect relates to why the IRS would care about a foreigner looking to use a shell company purchased from a US provider to avoid foreign taxes. The IRS treatment deals with domestic enforcement to the extent that both the state agency and the provider are in the United States, but the prospective customer is not. The examples of IRS enforcement presented above are mainly to do with US citizens evading US taxes. The US government has a clear material interest in collecting all the revenue to which it is entitled, but has no such interest in helping other governments collect their revenue. Given these points, the rationale behind using a foreign customer rather than our fictitious American Mark Brown is two-fold.

First, and most importantly, to ensure comparability, all of the treatments involve a customer in one jurisdiction approaching a provider in a different jurisdiction. As outlined in Chapter 1, for reasons of both policy and theory, having this as a domestic interaction where both parties are in the same country is a very different kind of problem. The international nature of the interaction is key, getting at the central international relations contention that rule enforcement in an international context is fundamentally different from domestic rule enforcement. Domestic politics is seen as a rule-governed environment characterized by hierarchy and authority, while the absence of a world government means that the international system is anarchic. Comparing domestic and international inactions would thus be comparing apples and oranges.

The second point is that US authorities do in fact have an interest in preventing foreigners from using US shell companies purchased from American providers in perpetrating financial crime. The action taken against Russian arms trader Viktor Bout, former Ukrainian Prime Minister Pavlo Lazarenko, and Teodoro Obiang of Equatorial Guinea has been described already. More generally, the idea that governments have no obligation to help their foreign counterparts collect tax income (the fiscal interest criterion) is no longer current. When faced with requests for tax assistance from abroad, governments can no longer legitimately ask, 'What's it in for us?' (Eccleston 2013;

Sharman 2006). Relatedly, according to current international rules, US providers helping foreign nationals to evade foreign taxes are guilty of a money laundering offense under US law, given that the FATF has defined tax evasion as a predicate crime for money laundering and the rules on mutual legal and administrative assistance (FATF 2012).

IRS findings

The results so far in this chapter have suggested that presenting information about international laws and standards has no significant effects when associated with the FATF or ACAMS. What occurs when we associate the standards not with an international organization or private standards body but with a domestic agency well known for its enforcement rigor?[8] On its website the Internal Revenue Service identifies itself as the US domestic agency that liaises with the FATF and implements FATF standards in the country (see Internal Revenue Service 2012a, 2012b). In reality, as previously noted, the US federal government's ability to enforce global transparency standards is hamstrung by the US states' dominance of incorporation law. Still, it appears that mention of the IRS makes a significant difference for CSPs.

Critically, non-compliance rates dropped from 11.3 percent in the Placebo condition to 7.6 percent for the IRS treatment. This decrease is statistically significant at the 0.05 level. The non-compliance rate measures the ease of obtaining anonymous shell companies, so the drop from the baseline of one-third is substantively meaningful. Anonymous shells are significantly harder to get when the IRS is invoked. Indeed, the Dodgy Shopping Count increases from 8.9 for the Placebo to 13.2 for the IRS treatment. See Figure 5.4. As was the case for the other conditions in the US experiment, there were no differences across conditions for part-compliance or compliance, likely because such responses were so rare.

As with many of the treatments, the IRS condition caused a significant jump (at the 0.01 level) in the non-response rate, from 73.8 to 80.0 percent. But offsetting the hopeful IRS treatment effect on non-compliance, the IRS condition also caused a significant (at the 0.1 level) drop in the refusal rate, from 13.0 percent in the Placebo to 9.8 percent for the IRS condition. Of course, refusal is not as normatively positive

---

[8] We thank Jessica Preece for suggesting this treatment.

as compliance, where identifying information is collected on beneficial ownership in a way that can later be tracked by law enforcement, so the offsetting numbers here should perhaps cause less concern than if non-compliance and compliance rates were dropping equally.[9]

Conclusion

This chapter probed the treatment effects of informing corporate service providers about laws and standards. Specifically, the experimental design enabled a direct comparison of international rules with private standards and domestic enforcement. As such, it speaks directly to the ongoing debates about the comparative effectiveness of international law, private certification, and domestic prosecution. To our knowledge this is the first instance where the effects of information about these different sources of standards have been directly tested in a comparative way using a field experiment.

We find the results very interesting. It appears that informing (or priming) CSPs about international standards does not cause them to comply more readily. Rather, there is no evidence of treatment effects. Likewise, attributing the global standards to a private certification body, the Association of Certified Anti-Money Laundering Specialists, did not cause an appreciable difference from the Placebo condition where no mention of identification standards was made. In stark contrast, referencing the standards and ascribing them to the US Internal Revenue Service had significant treatment effects in decreasing both response rates and non-compliance rates (while also marginally decreasing refusal rates, which offsets the hopeful effect on non-compliance to some degree). Apparently, raising the specter of a powerful domestic enforcer like the IRS deters CSPs from offering anonymous shells.

In many respects these results may not surprise political scientists or policy wonks. Of course domestic laws, propagated under a hierarchical system with identifiable enforcement, should matter. But significant work in sociology and psychology suggests that people are generally law-abiding and quite sensitive to social norms, so informing them of standards – whether they be international or domestic, public or private – should induce compliance. We found the non-effects of the

---

[9] The multinomial and selection models are consistent with the results reported on the IRS here. See Appendix Tables A5.3 and A5.4.

FATF and the small effects of the ACAMS treatments surprising for just this reason. CSPs apparently do not conform to the expectation that non-compliance results from ignorance.

Of course, it may be the case that the incorporation industry is particularly venal and its denizens immune to legalistic appeals. While this may be so, we suspect rather that this is a case where domestic laws and practice have simply not yet caught up with international standards. Both the tax havens and the United States and other OECD countries appear to reflect this pattern, as discussed in Chapter 3. The tax havens likely evinced poor compliance with Know Your Customer standards until they were compelled by the United States and FATF to reform their domestic laws and enforce them rigorously. We fear that OECD countries will continue to act as the most attractive and welcoming sites for anonymous incorporation until meaningful reforms in policy and law enforcement occur at the domestic level. Yet the effects and non-effects of information about laws and standards on compliance rates beg the question of the causal mechanisms suggesting why subjects might comply with the rules. The next chapter – focused on penalties, norms, and power – attempts to probe the causal effects of those mechanisms.

6 | *Penalties, norms, and US origin*

In 1998 behavioral economists Uri Gneezy and Aldo Rustichini performed a now-famous experiment at ten daycare centers in Israel. Many parents at the daycares had been arriving late to pick up their children, so Gneezy and Rustichini, after a four-week observation period, imposed a fine of three dollars on late parents at six of the ten daycare centers – randomly assigned, of course. The result? The rate of late arrivals *increased* significantly, and the tardiness did not diminish even after the fines were removed (Gneezy and Rustichini 2000). The experiment illuminates one of the core debates in the social sciences: Do actors behave more appropriately when threatened with penalties for violating the rules or when they are normatively constrained?

Gneezy and Rustichini's findings suggest that, before and during the observation period, parents were inclined to feel socially obligated to show up on time so that the daycare workers would not have to stay after hours to wait for them. But once a fine was imposed, it implied that tardiness could be recompensed by paying a monetary price, and it induced the unintended consequence of increased late arrivals. The threat of penalties can therefore backfire. The experiment also presents an illustration of the possibility that the effects of social norms and penalties may be more complicated than commonly assumed in international relations, especially when considering sub-national actors (March and Olsen 1998; Checkel 2001). Furthermore, this study illustrates how experiments can surprise us and confound our preconceived notions of how the world works. The experimental results presented in this chapter are similarly surprising in disconfirming many of our expectations (some derived from IR theory, others just simple intuitions) about why actors comply with or defy international rules. In some instances treatments we thought would make a big difference to compliance rates made none, whereas in other instances the effect was exactly the opposite of what we had expected.

Two of the three interventions examined in this chapter, the Penalties and Norms treatments, are derived from theoretical debates in IR. During the 1990s and 2000s some scholars argued for the primacy of a rationalist "logic of consequences" in explaining behavior, whereas an opposing group maintained that a constructivist "logic of appropriateness" was more important (March and Olsen 1998; Checkel 2001; Barnett and Duvall 2005). Jon Elster captures the essence of these two contrasting logics when he suggests that the first kind of consequential behavior is motivated by the formula of "Do X to get Y," or in the case of sanctions, "To avoid penalty Y, don't do X." Action motivated by appropriateness, however, fits the form of "All good people do X" or "No good person does Y" (1989). According to this second logic, actors may and often do pass up opportunities for material gain in order to abide by norms, defined as commonly shared beliefs about appropriate behavior for an actor with a given identity.

We are less interested in the competing "isms" associated with these different logics, seeing the disputes as both overwrought and under-tested. What is more, our study of financial transparency certainly cannot hope to settle the big debate. But we are keenly interested in the observable implications of central arguments made by rationalists and constructivists, including the contentions that actors may respond to penalties on the one hand or might feel compelled by norms on the other.

After all, there is nothing inherent in arguments advocating penalties or norms that suggests that they are mutually exclusive. Actions may often be motivated by a combination of instrumental calculation and a normative sense of appropriateness. It strikes us, however, that statements holding that penalties and norms ought to induce behavioral change are precisely the types of hypotheses conducive to experimental testing.

In this chapter we therefore describe and present the results for three treatments – Penalties, Norms, and US Origin – that we designed to probe some of the core ideas of IR theory related to compliance with international law. On the one hand, the Penalties treatment draws on the idea that actors follow the rules when it pays to do so because non-compliance is sanctioned. Along these lines, to corporate service provider subjects in the global sample we randomly assigned a treatment that invoked the FATF's transparency standards requiring customer identification, as in the treatments discussed in the previous chapter, but also made a further crucial change in adding a line stating that violation of the standards might result in legal penalties, but that nonetheless requested confidentiality.

Alternatively, those arguing for the importance of norms suggest that actors comply with standards because they habitually and reflexively seek to follow social rules and conventions (see March and Olsen 1989, 1998; Wendt 1999; Kelley 2008). Thus, we randomly assigned another condition, the Norms treatment, where we raised the FATF identification standards, noted that the standards were widely accepted, and expressed a desire to do "the right thing" as "reputable businessmen." This rendering of our template attempts to test the observable implications that invoking standards of behavior and social roles can prime subjects to behave appropriately according to international rules.

We also designed a third treatment intended to probe an additional observable implication from international relations theory. For a set of subjects in the global sample, we sought to learn if origin in the United States would make an appreciable difference in compliance rates. Our intent was to test the effects of US power, especially given that the United States is widely perceived to exercise extra-territorial jurisdiction in prosecuting financial crime, as discussed in Chapters 2 and 5. But we acknowledge upfront that it is also a rather ambiguous test, since many factors accompany US origin besides projected US power, including relatively low corruption rates and high wealth, so there are many potential confounds embedded in the treatment. Following the same pattern as in the previous two chapters, we explain the rationale for each of these treatments in greater detail, present the results from our solicitations, and discuss implications for both IR theory and policy.

As foreshadowed, the results of the three tests provided plenty of surprises. The clear expectation was that bringing the notion of penalties for non-compliance to providers' attention would increase the rate of compliance and decrease the rate of non-compliance. In fact we found little evidence of this impact, and some worrying signs that the Penalties treatment might have actually *reduced* compliance. Something of the same dynamic seemed to be at work when we appealed to the providers' better natures through normative claims; again, there was little evidence of positive change, and some indications that this appeal actually made compliance rates worse. In both cases, the issue of heterogeneous effects may have again been at work. We explore the possibility that some providers who would have otherwise made a compliant response backed off altogether and refused to engage, whereas the more unscrupulous end of the market actually saw the approach as an invitation to collude in prohibited but profitable conduct.

Interviews with many providers prior to the conduct of the experiment indicated a wariness when it came to selling shell companies to US nationals for fear of being caught by the long arm of US extraterritorial law enforcement. Foreign financial institutions would seem to have good reason to be cautious in enabling US nationals to flout US law. In addition to the examples of the Swiss banks mentioned elsewhere, in 2012 alone the US government levied fines of $619 million against Dutch ING Bank, $667 million against Standard Chartered Bank, and a massive $1.92 billion against UK-based HSBC for different money laundering offenses. Yet directly contrary to what interviews had led us to expect, providers were at least as willing to supply anonymous shell companies to Americans as they were to our minorpower Norstralians, and it appears that they were also significantly less likely to demand identity documents from Americans than from Norstralians. All of these findings cause us to rethink expectations for the rational behavior of corporate service providers.

Penalties treatment

The rational choice approach has played a prominent, if not dominant, role in international relations for at least the past half century. At its most general level, rationalist theories explain behavior and outcomes as a result of goal-seeking behavior by individuals, often subject to some constraints. Rational choice is not a single, narrow theory, however; it refers rather to a general approach or large class of theories that make assumptions about individual instrumental calculations to achieve goals, often in their material self-interest (Green and Shapiro 1995; Snidal 2002).

Like the international relations literature more generally, much of the work on international compliance begins from a similar rationalist perspective (Fearon 1998; Simmons 2000, 2010). A wide variety of possible instrumental considerations are considered (Von Stein 2012), including inducements (Leebron 2002; Hafner-Burton 2009;

Lebovic and Voeten 2009), reciprocity (Axelrod 1984; Schachter 1991; Morrow 2007), reputation (Henkin 1979; Keohane 1997; Simmons 2000; Guzman 2008), credible commitments (Elkins et al. 2006; Long et al. 2007; Simmons and Danner 2010), and domestic politics (Putnam 1988; Slaughter 1995; Dai 2006, 2007; Simmons 2009).

In what follows, we do not take a rationalist perspective as given, but rather we test whether observable implications derived from a rationalist logic may be at work. We compare the effect of signaling the prospect of penalties to a variety of other possibilities, including the effect of norms. We thus explore some aspects of the mechanisms that might underlie rational or normative dimensions of compliance.

Often drawing on the work of economists, rationalist scholars in international relations posit that individuals act in accordance with their preferences as well as expectations of consequences (March and Olsen 1989). Individual choice is one of the most basic elements of this logic; individuals have the ability to choose, and they choose those options that they believe will lead to the most beneficial consequences. As such, we fashioned the Penalties intervention to capture the notion that providers of incorporation services would respond to avoid penalties as they engaged in rational, utility-maximizing behavior (Elster 1986). This approach falls more closely in line with the studies of compliance emphasizing possible costs and punishments, which means we capture to a much smaller extent other possible rationalist mechanisms, including reciprocity and reputation.

Of course, our approach differs from other accounts of compliance with international rules in the unit of observation. As discussed in Chapter 1, most IR scholarship sees states as the key actors and evaluates interstate behavior as if states were goal-seeking individual people. The compliance literature has largely followed this state-centric approach (Simmons 2010). Our experimental approach to the study of transnational relations, however, shifts the emphasis away from state to non-state actors, the primary locus of compliance in issues of financial transparency.

The Penalties treatment makes reference to possible legal consequences that service providers could suffer from failing to follow the FATF standards. By raising possible legal sanctions, we expected that service providers would consider possible government enforcement when responding to shady business inquiries. This treatment explicitly provides two pieces of information to service providers: (1) the email explicitly cites the Financial Action Task Force (FATF) and (2) it raises the legal penalties that are a possibility for those violating international law.

The prospect of legal penalties is not a far-fetched intervention to capture a rationalist logic of consequences. The FATF not only mandates particular standards, but also mandates that states introduce a range of administrative, civil, and criminal "effective, proportionate and dissuasive" penalties against private firms and individuals that do not follow these standards. The following example from the Austrian alias, Lukas Wagner, illustrates the introduction of legal penalties in the context that service providers would see (again with the relevant treatment language in bold):

Dear [name/company]
I am seeking information on how to incorporate an international company. I hope that you might be able to offer what I need.

I am a consultant, and my business associates and I live in Austria. Much of our business originates here, where we operate, but our company also grows quickly among international clients. Many of them are in your area. So, we feel that incorporation is a necessary option for us. We hope to limit taxes obligations and business liability.

We would like to know if you feel that you will be able to service us with a corporation. What identifying documents will you request for this transaction? We would prefer to limit disclosure as much as possible.

My internet searches show that the international Financial Action Task Force sets standards for disclosure of identifying information when forming a company. I also understand that legal penalties may follow violation of these standards. But I would like to avoid providing any detailed personal information if possible.

If you could answer these questions and also let us know about your prices, we very much appreciate it. Thank you for the time to address our query. Business obligations make communication difficult, so we would prefer to correspond with email.

Until we speak again,

Lukas Wagner

The prompt is both strong and subtle at the same time. Mentioning the Financial Action Task Force along with possible legal penalties signals that an authoritative body has set standards and mandated punishments for failing to abide by those standards. If providers searched on the FATF to learn more, they would easily find that the FATF has indeed set standards and that possible consequences would be in order for violating those standards.

The treatment is subtle in the sense that not all governments have indeed legislated all the standards set by the FATF, as discussed in Chapter 2. We thus need to rely on the prompt to evoke the strong possibility that legal penalties could follow, be it from a domestic source or even possibly from an international body or another country.

If providers behave according to rationalist expectations, then we would expect response rates and the incidence of non-compliance to decrease and compliance rates to increase. That is, service providers worried about legal penalties of failing to follow Know Your Customer guidelines may not even respond in the first place. Those that do respond should be more likely to require certified identity documents in order to avoid any legal sanctions.

Of course even if these expectations held true they may only do so for the median provider. But if, as seems likely, there is heterogeneity in the sample of service providers, CSPs could vary along a number of different dimensions, including their level of risk aversion/acceptance. It is possible that some providers have a greater risk tolerance and are willing to pursue or even seek out various business options even with possibly serious consequences as with individuals like Gohil and Berger described earlier in the book. Indeed, our results show some evidence of a subgroup of providers who are attracted to the prospect of bending or breaking the rules.

Penalties results

The likelihood that some providers will respond to the same prompt in very different ways is thus strong and should be kept in mind as we consider the results of the Penalties treatment. As seen in Figure 6.1 and Table 6.1, it appears that those selling shell companies are somewhat more inclined to refuse service or to drop out and fail to respond when receiving the Penalties treatment (the change in the response rate falls just outside conventional significance levels where $p = 0.11$). The refusal rate changed more markedly, dropping from 11.3 to 7.7 percent from the Placebo to the Penalties treatment, a decline of nearly one-third from the base rate that is statistically significant at the 0.05 level. None of the other outcomes saw statistically significant differences when compared to the Placebo condition.

Table 6.1 *Contingency table of results by Placebo, US Origin, Penalties, and Norms groups with difference tests for the international sample*

Condition	N	No response	Non-compliant	Part-compliant	Compliant	Refusal
Placebo	1112	495	97	184	210	126
Proportion		44.5%	8.7%	16.5%	18.9%	11.3%
US Origin	413	189	31	84*	58**	51
Proportion		45.8%	7.5%	20.3%	14.0%	12.3%
Penalties	379	187	28	75	60	29**
Proportion		49.3%	7.4%	19.8%	15.8%	7.7%
Norms	391	192	41	58	61	39
Proportion		49.1%	10.5%	14.8%	15.6%	10.0%

Significant in difference tests compared to the Placebo condition: *0.1 level, **0.05 level, ***0.01 level.

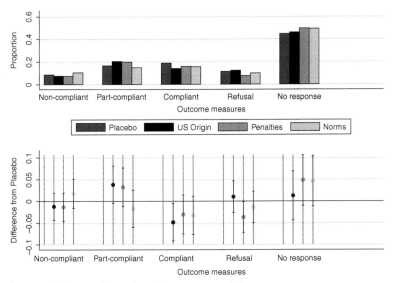

Figure 6.1 Comparison of results across conditions.

This suggests that there may be heterogeneity in the subject pool. One type of provider could be wary of suspicious customers and therefore predisposed to refuse service in the Placebo condition and ignore inquiries in the Penalties condition. But another type could be relatively untroubled by customers raising potential legal penalties, especially those providers inclined to offer untraceable shell companies. Thus one Kenyan respondent initially mentioned some identification require-ments, but then helpfully suggested a way around these (remembering from Chapter 3 that Kenyan providers keep company with the set of countries least likely to abide by international standards):

> Thank you for your inquiry. We confirm that amongst the particulars are required for incorporation would be the full names and addresses of the company's proposed shareholders and directors. The applicants would also require to furnish an Income Tax PIN registration number. It is possible to list a corporate entity as a director and as a shareholder and thus avoid hav-ing to declare individual names. It would cost US$ 2,500 to incorporate a local entity. This is an all inclusive fee that would cover all disbursements, taxes professional and official fees. We look forward to hearing from you.

The non-compliance rate for the Penalties treatment was largely unchanged from 8.7 percent in the Placebo to 7.4 percent in the treat-ment – a difference that is not significant statistically. Accordingly, the Dodgy Shopping Count (Figure 6.2) is not meaningfully different for Placebo versus Penalties. Likewise, the non-response rate increased from the Placebo base of 44.5 percent to 49.3 percent for the Penalties treatment, the part-compliance rate increased from 16.5 to 19.8 per-cent, and the compliance rate dropped from 18.9 to 15.8 percent. Again, however, none of these differences proved significant statistic-ally in two-tailed difference-in-means tests.

However, we performed a battery of statistical robustness checks to learn whether these results are sensitive to different specifications. The results reported above are mostly consistent in the robustness checks (see Appendix Tables A6.1 and A6.2). In the multinomial model the worrisome results for the Penalties treatment increase (though not without raising other questions). Here, we not only see a significant drop in the refusal rate, but we actually observe a statistically sig-nificant decrease in the compliance rate. This suggests that it is the compliant firms that drop out under the Penalties condition, but the non-compliant firms like the Kenyan one quoted earlier remain virtu-ally unchanged.

This is not exactly what we expected. We predicted that firms would be more inclined to ignore inquiries in the Penalties condition, yet while we saw an increase, it was not significant statistically except in the multinomial model. And critically, we also expected to see a

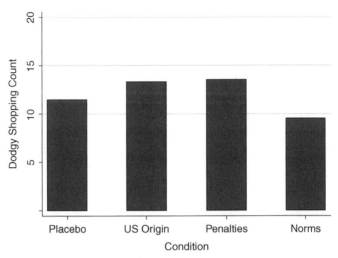

Figure 6.2 Dodgy Shopping Count by condition.

significant decrease in non-compliance and an increase in compliance and refusal. And yet some of our expectations are confirmed in the multinomial results. Indeed, the multinomial model predicts a lower response rate and a lower non-compliance rate, results that are significant in the multinomial model, thus offering some potential but qualified optimism for the prospect that legal penalties will alter behavior.

Unlike most of the other multinomial models in the book, the results here differ to a small extent from those in the basic difference tests. If we take the difference tests at face value, it is possible that those results reflect a collusion effect. More scrupulous firms ignore inquiries when penalties are invoked, but less honorable firms seem happy to provide anonymous shells even to customers that know they are breaking the rules and understand that penalties may ensue. Curiously, we saw some similar evidence of a collusion effect for the Norms treatment.

Norms treatment

Since the late 1980s, the study of international politics as the study of rational actors behaving instrumentally to maximize material goals has been challenged by an alternative account holding that the identity and behavior of states and other actors in the international system are crucially shaped by culture, ideas, and discourse. Those working in such a "constructivist" vein often emphasize the importance of non-instrumental action and non-material goals, as well as the way shared beliefs may come to constitute norms that are more than just the sum of the individuals' beliefs that created them. Though constructivists first made their mark in the realm of rather abstracted theory (Onuf 1989; Wendt 1992; Ruggie 1998), then the study of security questions (Katzenstein 1996; Price 1998; Tannenwald 1999), then human rights and international organizations (Keck and Sikkink 1998; Barnett and Finnemore 2004), more recently there has been a flowering of constructivist work on political economy (Blyth 2002; Best 2005; Seabrooke 2006; Weaver 2008; Abdelal et al. 2010; Chwieroth 2010).

Explaining economic phenomena and behavior in terms of rational utility-maximizing actors seeking material ends may seem so natural and obvious that it is difficult to conceive what an alternative perspective based on culture and shared beliefs could offer. Yet some of the most consequential changes in the international political economy have been driven by changes in norms, rather than changes in technology, relative factor scarcity, or price movements. A prominent example is the end of slavery. Slavery was a widespread and profitable economic institution that nevertheless came to an end largely because it became culturally unacceptable for one person to own another (Crawford 2002; Keene 2007; though not a constructivist, economist Douglass North makes the same argument in North 1990). According to constructivists, the value of goods and services – the utility derived from them, is not so much defined by scarcity as by cultural judgments that vary from time to time and place to place. Rationalist scholarship holds that the resources and information in states' and firms' possession determine their economic behavior. Alternatively, constructivists are more likely to argue that, even when actors have identical resources and information to interpret their circumstances, their different interpretations may lead to radically different outcomes (Abdelal et al. 2010).

The treatments based on inserting mention of material sanctions and inducements for breaking Know Your Customer rules fit neatly in the logic of consequences. As explained earlier, providers are hypothesized to be more likely to violate rules on collecting beneficial ownership information when there are increased profits associated with this option, but more likely to follow these rules with the mention of penalties for non-compliance. How does the Norms treatment map onto the logic of appropriateness and constructivism?

Constructivists suggest several mechanisms through which norms may affect behavior. The first is that widely shared, deeply internalized norms prescribing or proscribing certain actions are taken for granted by actors, and thus these actors unthinkingly act in accord with the norm in question. Taking an example from the security sphere, even when facing adversaries without nuclear weapons, currently nuclear-armed states do not include the use of such weapons in their military decision-making, because there is an international consensus that nuclear weapons are fundamentally distinct from other armaments (Tannenwald 1999).

Recently, however, some constructivists have criticized the idea of taken-for-granted norms as being excessively static and rendering actors as cultural automatons lacking any agency (Sikkink 2011). The alternative model contends that actors engage in moral reasoning to determine the appropriate course of action in the particular circumstance in line with extant norms (March and Olsen 1989: 160–161). A further supplementary notion is that norm compliance may be bolstered by individual feelings of shame and guilt for transgressing norms, or of enhanced self-worth and rectitude by upholding norms, even (or especially) when this involves some material cost.

Finally, another factor that may interact with those above in affecting behavior involves social sanctions or rewards (Schimmelfennig 2001). Those caught defying norms may be subject to disapproval or ostracism from their peers, whereas norm adherence promotes enhanced standing and status. Here, however, there is a danger of fundamentally different arguments bleeding into each other; if social standing or status are taken as commodities akin to money to be maximized via rational, instrumental action, then we are back to a logic of consequences, and there is no need for a logic of appropriateness (Tolbert and Zucker 1996).

Given the complexity and variation of constructivist theory there is no way a brief email approach can test such a body of work. Yet we do maintain that our treatment can prime respondents in such a way as to raise the salience of norms. Below we reproduce our Norms treatment with the most relevant text in bold, before relating it back to the discussion of the scholarship summarized above.

Dear [Corporate Service Provider],
I am an international consultant living in Norway. My associates and I have been based in Norway for some time and we have done extensive international work, especially in your area. After looking at the specific needs of

our growing company, we were feeling that it would make sense for us to expand and to set up an international company. We would like to form a new company in your area as private individuals. We especially hope to limit taxes and reduce liability.

We were wondering what you require us to give in order to do this. We would like to form this corporation as privately as possible. My internet searches show that the international Financial Action Task Force requires disclosure of identifying information when forming a company and most countries have signed on to these standards. As reputable businessmen, I am sure we both want to do the right thing by international rules. But I would like to avoid providing any detailed personal information if possible. What identifying documents will you need from us? We would also like to know what your usual prices are. We appreciate the help.

I travel a lot for my work, so I communicate best via email. I hope to hear from you soon.

Yours,
Lukas Hansen

The treatment first makes reference to commonly accepted standards of behavior, namely that most countries have committed to FATF regulations. A norm only functions as a norm if it is reasonably widely shared in a community. Second, the reference about "wanting to do the right thing" alludes to the process of moral reasoning and interpretation whereby actors seek out the appropriate course of action for particular circumstances. It not only suggests that the client has engaged in such a process, but it invites the respondent to do the same. In making mention of being "reputable businessmen," the email expresses an identity claim about the customer, suggests how the recipient may identify her- or himself, and raises the issue of standing or regard among one's peers, reputation being an irreducibly social concept of how some group of others regards the actor (Mercer 1996; Sharman 2007). Once again, this is not only a statement about the would-be customer; it also raises the same issues for the person reading the email, and deciding on the response.

Some might object that such a fleeting, impersonal exchange between strangers might not be strong enough to cue the mechanisms discussed above. Indeed, modesty is in order here, to repeat this is not styled as a test of constructivism per se. However, in everyday economic life norms do shape economic behavior even in fleeting, impersonal exchanges between strangers. People tend to tip according to cultural cues, even in restaurants they are unlikely to ever return to. In the laboratory, the "dictator game" consists of a two-player game where the first decides how to split a sum of money, and the second accepts the split proposed by player one, or rejects the whole deal, in which case neither player gets anything. Results consistently show that strangers reliably divide the stake on a more even, "fairer" basis than rational utility-maximizing would predict (Bohnet and Frey 1999).

Similar to the Penalties treatment, our initial expectation was that the Norms treatment would raise compliance with international rules. This expectation of more rule-abiding responses and fewer offers of untraceable shell companies could be a product of reflexive or unreflexive compliance with a generally accepted standard of behavior, some concern for self-esteem or the regard of others, or some combination of these.

Norms results

Having appealed to shared expectations about the right way of doing business, something that actors in the roles of reputable businessmen would want to do given international standards, the results are shown in Figure 6.1 and Table 6.1. Like many of the treatments we employed in the experiment, the Norms condition is associated with a higher non-response rate compared to the Placebo, though not statistically significant at conventional levels. We have suggested the extent of the variation in the non-response rate could be a "soft compliance" mechanism in which a subset of providers choose not to respond as a way of avoiding doing business with someone asking to incorporate anonymously. Here it is important to clarify that although the non-response checks described in Chapter 2 mean that the majority of this group cannot be assumed to be practicing a form a soft compliance, the change in the level of non-response from the Placebo to the treatments might indicate a minority group whose silence does indicate a form of risk management, though additional inquiry would be needed to establish this definitively.

The other four outcomes capturing levels of compliance are also not definitive. In particular, providers are less compliant when presented with the Norms treatment relative to the Placebo (15.6 percent for Norms vs. 18.9 percent for the Placebo), a result that is just outside the standard levels of significance.

Some of the compliant responses tried to square the circle of abiding by international Know Your Customer standards, while also providing the anonymity requested in the approach email through the use of a nominee director, as in the case of Lu Zhang and the GT Group that opened this book. The following compliant reply from a Belize service provider to our man in Oslo, Lukas Hansen, illustrates these conflicting priorities:

By law, we are required to keep in our confidential records, a copy of the passport page containing a picture and biographical information of each director and shareholder in the International Business Company as well as a recent utility bill showing a current address, and a bank or attorneys letter of referral. Please note that all these documents must be duly notarized. This information is kept in our records. We also offer the service of nominee directors and shareholders which allows for further anonymity. In the event you choose to go with nominee directors and shareholders, a power of attorney is then issued to you or nominee giving you control over the company.

Providers receiving the Norms treatment also respond with higher rates of non-compliance (10.5 percent for Norms vs. 8.7 percent for Placebo), though this result is not statistically significant. The Dodgy Shopping Count differs by 2, 11.5 for Placebo versus 9.5 for Norms, but is not statistically significant. Partial compliance and refusal rates are also lower than the Placebo, but again neither is statistically significant.

That the Norms treatment may be associated with marginally lower levels of compliance and higher levels of non-compliance is in some sense puzzling, and also potentially disturbing. The implication of IR theory on the subject indicates that invoking such a norm should motivate more legitimate behavior. It is possible the norm has not spread or been adopted well enough. It is also possible that the wording about appropriate behavior signaled the possibility of colluding on an inappropriate response. Once again, different providers may have responded to the same cues in different ways. Ultimately, the results are not clear-cut and leave open some questions about the precise mechanisms at work. What is clear is that once again compliant service providers are relatively difficult to find. The results of the Norms treatment add greater heft to the emerging claim that international standards are not effective overall and that attempts to foster greater compliance through appeals to shared norms may actually make the situation worse. Some of these disturbing findings persist when our approach originated in the United States.[1]

US Origin treatment

In the US Origin treatment the customer purports to be a US national rather than a citizen of one of the eight small OECD countries ("Norstralia") as in the Placebo. This treatment draws on the idea that since World War II and currently the United States represents the hegemonic international power (Gilpin 1981; Lake 1993; Mearsheimer 2001; Ikenberry 2011). Many international relations scholars argue that the hegemon in the international system provides a range of economic public goods. Hegemons are said to do so by setting basic rules and institutions that correct or prevent market failures and reduce transaction costs (Kindleberger 1973).

Providing such public goods is in the enlightened self-interest of the dominant power, either because it more than recoups its costs through its dominance of the larger, more stable markets that result from its interventions, or because it coercively extracts contributions from the other states in the system to cover its costs. In this rendering, the hegemonic United States might act to solve the collective action problems whereby every state suffers from money laundering, tax evasion, etc., but individual action is irrational for each state because of concerns over free-riding.

An associated realist view might suggest that even if the global corporate transparency regime as a whole may not be effective, it should most likely work when it comes to those parties of interest to the United States. Although some of these would clearly be foreigners involved in crimes that affect the United States (terrorist financiers, drug traffickers, etc.), US citizens would definitely be of interest because of their responsibility to pay tax on all worldwide income, and because interposing foreign shell companies is a common ruse by which to evade this requirement. According to this logic, the US government would

---

[1] In a multinomial probit regression model the results above are all consistent, meaning that the Norms treatment is not significantly related to any of the outcomes at standard levels. When collapsing the set of categories to estimate a selection model (compliance and refusal vs. non-compliance and part-compliance), Norms is associated with statistically significantly lower levels of compliance ($p = 0.09$). See Appendix Tables A6.1 and A6.2.

care little or nothing if assorted Norstralians were evading taxes properly owed to their governments, but would take a radically different and less favorable view of US citizens engaging in the same behavior. It would target providers helping individuals and firms to evade US taxes with strong punitive action. Anticipating this disposition, foreign providers would once more be disproportionately wary of solicitations from US customers.

A further connection with realist theory is the way it privileges power and anarchy (Gilpin 1981, 1987; Krasner 1991; Mastanduno 1998; Kirshner 2009). According to these and other realists, economic prowess provides the basis for buying the military means of survival in the anarchic international system, and international economic rules are said to reflect this imperative. A global regulatory regime that acts to redistribute wealth, and especially tax revenue, to the single most powerful state would closely fit realist expectations. Tax revenue might be considered particularly important to states, given that it can directly be translated into military spending, unlike private economic activity that first has to be captured by the state. Such a regime would act to punish those firms and countries that sapped US revenue by providing untraceable shell companies to US tax nationals, while the potential earnings of other governments would be allowed to drain away as their citizens hid behind the still-intact corporate veil.

As well as being the world's dominant power in setting global financial rules in general, the United States has been the driving force in setting and enforcing the particular FATF rules designed to counter international money laundering, including those relating to shell companies (Drezner 2007). The United States has robustly enforced these international standards outside its borders, especially through the extra-territorial application of domestic law when transactions involve Americans or the US financial system. As explained below, it has done so through such measures as the USA PATRIOT Act and the Foreign Account Tax Compliance Act, as well as more general foreign policy levers. US action against foreign financial institutions and their employees for breaches of financial transparency standards has resulted in a series of highly publicized massive fines and long jail terms for individual employees.

The coercive measures available to the US government that may deter firms from providing shell companies to US customers can roughly be divided into two categories: (1) actions to disrupt access to US dollar-denominated financial networks and (2) criminal prosecutions. One of the provisions of the USA PATRIOT Act passed in the immediate aftermath of the September 11 attacks allows the US Treasury to designate individuals, firms, or even whole countries as being of "primary money laundering concern." This may impose a duty of extra record keeping and due diligence for US institutions transacting with such an entity, which thus increases the cost of dealing with that entity. Or, the Treasury Department may rule that an entity is barred from transacting with any US institution and excluded from all US dollar-denominated financial networks. This last measure was invoked against individual banks associated with the governments of Syria, Iran, Burma, and North Korea, as well as against all private and government financial institutions in Nauru and Ukraine for these countries' anti-money laundering deficiencies.

More recently in 2010 the Foreign Account Tax Compliance Act (FATCA) requires that all foreign financial institutions determine whether any of their clients are US citizens, or whether any of their corporate clients have US beneficial owners, and report all these individuals' balances and transactions to the US IRS. Foreign institutions that fail to do so are subject to a special 30 percent withholding tax on all their transactions with any part of the US financial system. Both these foreign firms and their governments have been predictably unimpressed about being dragooned into an expensive compliance exercise in which they bear all of the costs, which are considerable, while all the benefits accrue to the US government. FATCA thus closely fits the realist view of international economic "cooperation."

Turning to the criminal law options, the case of the Swiss banks UBS and Wegelin assisting US clients to evade taxes was described in Chapter 2. These and other Swiss banks either directly set up shell companies for clients, or steered clients to closely associated corporate service providers, and then placed clients' accounts in the name of the non-US shell companies which the clients controlled as part of a fiction to disguise this control. Such moves are illegal under US Controlled Foreign Corporation laws, specifically designed in the 1930s to invalidate such schemes. But effective enforcement of this law depends on being able to look through the foreign company to see the US beneficial owner. Huge fines have been levied against foreign banks, like the $780 million paid by UBS, while 10 other Swiss banks have also been targeted. The risk extends to individual bankers also, who have been taken aside in US airports and threatened with decades in prison, unless they hand over information on their clients and bear witness against their employers. Some of their colleagues are now effectively stuck in Switzerland for the indefinite future for fear of being arrested in third countries and then extradited to the United States.[2]

While it has been bankers in the firing line, there is no legal reason why those working for corporate service providers could not be targeted, as with the example of United Revenue Services discussed in the previous chapter, either by being cut off from international financial networks or by being criminally prosecuted. These possibilities are well known to some of the corporate service providers interviewed by the authors, who often regard US clients as more trouble than they are worth. As a result, some provider websites explicitly note that they do not do business with US clients. While some foreign banks have publicly ended their dealing with US clients, whether or not this extended to those in the shell company business more generally has until now been unknown.

Our US Origin treatment (which is simply the Placebo email with the Norstralians replaced by the American "Mark Brown") thus attempts to ascertain whether providers are any less likely to violate international standards when dealing with a citizen of the most powerful country. Relative to the Placebo condition, we expected the treatment to generate both a lower response rate and higher compliance rate. The hypothesis is that foreign providers would be wary of running afoul of extra-territorial US measures and would thus be more likely to either not respond or refuse service to US customers. We further expected that if providers were prepared to offer a shell company to a US client they would be more likely to follow Know Your Customer rules rather than later risk being caught having sold anonymous shell companies to Americans by the long arm of US extra-territorial law enforcement, especially to do with fiscal matters. The empirical implication from this hypothesis is that anonymous shell companies would be significantly less available to US customers relative to Norstralians.

However, while we would have liked to isolate the effects of US extra-territorial jurisdiction on the provision of anonymous shells, we could not conceive of an effective way to do so while preserving the

---

[2] Author interviews: Washington, DC, United States, March 22, 2011 and April 25, 2012; Bridgetown, Barbados, May 25–26, 2010.

essential believability of the email approaches. Thus, the US Origin treatment bundles together all of the factors that CSPs may associate with US customers. The technical term for this bundling in experimental research is "confounding." The US Origin treatment thus introduces many confounds to a clean assessment of the effects of US power, including the relatively high wealth of Americans, relatively low corruption rates, and relatively mobile financial capital, along with likely many others. Thus, the treatment is more appropriately labeled "US Origin" rather than US Power, and we interpret the results in the light that it includes many potential confounds.

US Origin results

Again we were surprised by the results (see Figure 6.1 and Table 6.1). We expected providers to be significantly less likely to respond to inquiries from the United States, but the non-response rate remained virtually unchanged from Placebo to the US Origin treatment, increasing only from 44.5 percent to 45.8 percent, a small bump that is not significant statistically in the basic difference comparisons. The non-compliance rate decreased from 8.7 percent in the Placebo to 7.5 percent for the US Origin treatment – a slight reduction that again is statistically insignificant – as is the difference in the Dodgy Shopping Count. Thus one Nigerian provider was notably untroubled by prospects of running afoul of extra-territorial US enforcement actions, providing rather similar advice to the Kenyan provider quoted above:

To enable your client incorporate in Nigeria, we would need a resolution of the parent company authorizing it to take shares in the proposed Nigerian subsidiary. We also need a copy of the Certificate of Incorporation of the parent company. If the company is to be set up by individuals, this requirement will not apply. 3. We need also the names of at least two persons over the age of 18 who would act as Directors of the new company.

The firm went on to note that total incorporation time was 2–3 weeks and the total fees would be approximately US$3,500. The refusal percentage for the US Origin condition increased slightly from 11.3 percent in the Placebo to 12.3 percent for the US customer, but the minor uptick once more failed significance tests. The upward change in the part-compliance rate from 16.5 percent in the Placebo to 20.3 percent for US Origin, however, did clear the 0.1 significance threshold. Running directly contrary to our expectations, there was a 4.9 percent decrease in the compliance rate, from 18.9 percent in the Placebo to 14.0 percent, for the US Origin treatment. This result is significant at the 0.05 level and reflects a drop in the base compliance rate of more than one quarter (looking at an exception, one especially fastidious provider from Macao required notarized identification not just of all shareholders, but also of their spouses too).

Once more we performed robustness checks to verify that the results held up to alternative statistical specifications. And the increase in non-response became statistically significant at the 0.05 level in the multinomial model, as shown in Appendix Table A6.1. The increase in part-compliance no longer proved statistically significant at conventional levels in the multinomial probit regression employing covariate controls for company and country type. However, the drop in the compliance rate for the US Origin treatment persisted at the 0.05 level of significance in the multinomial tests.

These results suggest that, rather than causing heightened caution and scrutiny on the part of CSPs globally, customer origin in the United States instead appears to induce statistically similar response rates, though this is somewhat dependent on model specification, but also significantly lower compliance rates. We expected the US Origin treatment to cause some of the strongest treatment effects given the well-publicized examples of extra-territorial enforcement by US government agencies, so the fact that US customers do not receive increased scrutiny suggests that this risk is not a major concern for international service providers. Or, at the very least, it indicates that any heightened skepticism is counterbalanced by the greater attractiveness of American customers compared to Norstralians.

Conclusion

The child-care example at the beginning of this chapter illustrates how experiments can confound prior expectations. A treatment designed to penalize non-compliance (a monetary penalty for tardy parents) actually caused an increase in non-compliance. A further parallel from this example is the question of to what extent behavior is motivated by calculations of individual gain and loss or by shared, social conceptions of appropriate behavior. In this case, the impact of a monetary penalty (in line with a rationalist logic of consequences) was overwhelmed by a logic of appropriateness whereby parents felt that paying the penalty legitimized their choice to leave the children at child-care longer than they otherwise would have. Of course just because this was the overall effect this is not to say that all parents felt the same way. Some might have been deterred from coming late by the penalty, while for others the new arrangement might not have made any difference either way.

We expected the Penalties, Norms, and US Origin treatments to have some effect in lowering the proportion of providers prepared to break international Know Your Customer rules by offering untraceable shell companies. It is a relatively easy matter to make more-or-less theoretical or policy-driven arguments as to why this should be the case. One does not have to be a dyed-in-the-wool exponent of rational choice scholarship to believe that signaling that a particular behavior is risky and may attract penalties will significantly reduce the incidence of that behavior. Similarly, one does not have to be a card-carrying constructivist to allow that appealing to widely shared community standards and notions of probity and esteem may influence some share of those receiving normative appeals to "do the right thing." With the recent publicity given to the US government's successful imposition of massive fines on foreign banks, the long prison terms threatened against these banks' employees, and the extra-territorial remit of measures like the USA PATRIOT Act and the Foreign Account Tax Compliance Act, unlike anything else imposed by any other government, it would seem reasonable to suppose some non-trivial share of corporate service providers would steer clear of US customers relative to low-risk Norstralians. Given the hegemonic status of the United States in the current international system, some strands of international relations theory would also support these expectations regarding the US Origins treatment.

As the findings have demonstrated, however, none of these treatments substantially increased compliance with international standards on beneficial ownership, and some actually seemed to undermine the enforcement of the standard. With regard to the Penalties treatment there was a significant decline in the number of providers refusing service. The multinomial model suggests that the level of compliance also dropped to a significant degree in the Penalties condition. These results might be explained if compliant providers were more likely to drop out when presented with this kind of approach, while their unscrupulous counterparts took the approach to be an invitation to collude in providing an anonymous shell company. With the Norms treatment there is some (non-robust) evidence of a drop in compliance. Once again, these contrasting effects may well be a result of a heterogeneous pool of providers. Finally, if the financial press is concerned about the long arm of US law enforcement, by and large providers are not. Once again, the notable change from this treatment was a lower compliance rate, rather than the higher one we expected.

In general, these three treatments underline the challenge of promoting compliance with international rules when the profit motive favors non-compliance. The experimental evidence here demonstrates that interventions which might have been expected to make rules more effective often have no impact, and sometimes actually make the rules less effective. Because more and more international rules seek to regulate non-state actors and transnational relations in pursuit of global public goods, such problems will only become more important to the practice and study of international relations. In the final chapter we take up this theme in reviewing the book's main conclusions and presenting a program for future research.

7 | Conclusion

Serious profit-driven crime depends on some measure of financial secrecy. Shell companies that cannot be traced back to their real owners have become one of the most important means by which criminals obtain this secrecy. Regulating shell companies thus poses a major challenge for many facets of global governance, but it also represents a point of entry from which we demonstrate the utility of a new approach to studying world politics: the experimental science of transnational relations. We premise this new approach on rigorous study of transnational relations and non-state actors through field experiments. Experiments have long been acknowledged as the most powerful way to accurately determine causal relationships. But conventional wisdom has presupposed experiments in international relations to be either impractical or unethical; we hope we have dispelled this myth through the extended example of our *Global Shell Games* experiments. We provide additional examples of Experimental TR in the pages to follow.

As would-be global governors seek to regulate a wider swath of human activity, the key agents of compliance are increasingly non-state actors such as firms and individuals rather than sovereign states. Global rules may depend on international agreements, but they both shape and are shaped by transnational relations.

The points raised above are thus relevant to scholars, policy-makers, and anyone else with an interest in facing the multitude of problems that require cooperation across borders. If getting international agreements on the environment and human rights to actually work depends more and more on non-state actors (as we argue it does), then the need to move away from state-centrism is not just an academic one. Similarly, our treatments to find out what causes corporate service providers to withhold or provide anonymous shell companies should be of interest to those in international organizations, national governments, and private financial firms. But we also hope that they provide international relations scholars with concrete illustrations of the practicality and potential of global field experiments.

In exploring the concerns raised so far, this concluding chapter has three main aims. We begin with a brief summary of the empirical results derived from the thousands of solicitations by our fictitious consultants. This includes the descriptive results of the varying performance between different categories of countries, but it mainly focuses on the experimental results from the ten different treatments. The next section looks at how our global field experiment can help resolve intersecting problems blocking progress both for scholars studying international compliance in general and for policy-makers tasked with developing better measures of the effectiveness of international rules. How might such experiments be performed in other realms of international relations research? The third section provides a thumbnail sketch of other IR field experiments currently in train to show the general applicability of this approach.

What have we learned about shell companies?

As we have documented throughout this book, shell companies are at the heart of many of the most serious crimes, especially corruption, money laundering, sanctions-busting, and the illegal trade in drugs, arms, and humans. Our experiment investigated the availability of untraceable shell companies in a systematic and rigorous way. The results are quite surprising and in many cases counter-intuitive. Sadly, they do not offer much optimism about global financial transparency.

First, overall just under half (48 percent) of all replies that we received did not request appropriate identification. Almost a quarter (22 percent) of replies made no requests for photo identification whatsoever. Taken together, this is troubling news about the efficacy of international standards. Untraceable shell companies are remarkably easy to obtain. Cast in terms of a Dodgy Shopping Count, on average an individual seeking to obtain an anonymous shell corporation internationally need only approach 12 providers before successfully obtaining such a company. Even less effort is needed if just searching within the United States, which has a Dodgy Shopping Count of just 10.9. Put differently, where we consider responses alone rather than replies as a share of inquiries, the proportion of providers in the United States that answered our inquiries *and* required no photo identity documents whatsoever was 41.5 percent, a staggering two-and-a-half times higher than the 16.4 percent average in the international sample.

Where are the easy pickings? Not the usual suspects, as it turns out. One of the most surprising results of the study is that the tax havens that have long been suspected to be weak links in the global financial system are among the most law-abiding countries anywhere in the world when it comes to beneficial ownership standards. The OECD countries – the states responsible for tightening up global financial rules – are the least compliant even when compared to poorer, developing countries. Incorporation service providers in the United States, especially in Delaware, Indiana, Wyoming, and Nevada, are among the worst in the world. Indeed, of the entire US sample only 9 of 1,722 providers required full, certified identity disclosure, and only 10 total fully compliant responses were received. But the country-by-country and state-by-state results are only descriptive and not experimental. What of the experimental results?

In the main, the findings from our treatments tell a story of dogs that did not bark, starkly illustrating the insensitivity of providers both to information regarding the rules they should be following, and in response to even obvious red flags about customer risk. One exception is our investigation of whether corporate service providers were more vigilant toward potential terrorist threats, which offers a glimmer of hope about the efficacy of the risk-based approach. When service providers received the Terrorism treatment – an alias from a citizen of a terror-prone country, residing in Saudi Arabia, and working for an Islamic charity – they responded significantly less relative to the Placebo condition. Crucially, when providers did respond, they were non-compliant significantly less often compared to the Placebo condition. This finding offers evidence that providers are at least potentially sensitive to different levels of customer risk.

Similarly, providers in the United States proved significantly less likely to reply – and when they did respond the rate of non-compliance dropped significantly – when told that the Internal Revenue Service enforces identity requirements. But the good news ends there. Partial compliance and compliance were not greater – and instead were probably worse – in the Terrorism condition relative to the Placebo, and the IRS treatment appeared to decrease the rate of refusals in the United States. This begins quite a collection of worrying results.

In terms of the magnitude of human suffering that stems from anonymous incorporation, controlling the misuse of shell companies in laundering the proceeds of serious corruption offenses is perhaps the single greatest priority. Alas, providers responding to the Corruption treatment in this study – an alias hailing from one of eight Guineastan countries claiming to work in government procurement – were less likely to demand certified identity documents. Some soft compliance likely occurred in that providers receiving the Corruption prompt were significantly less likely to respond relative to the Placebo, but a large non-response check suggests that soft compliance was not widespread. Providers seem to be indifferent to the damage they cause in aiding and abetting major corruption offenses, and they appear unafraid of the legal sanctions they may face for facilitating such activity. Alarmingly, simply offering providers more money to preserve anonymity decreases the compliance rate.

Among the most sobering discoveries in the experiment was that making corporate service providers aware of international standards rooted in both hard and soft international law motivates no more compliance than a Placebo condition with no mention of such standards. Unfortunately, there is not any evidence in this study supporting the idea that information about international law motivates greater compliance. The non-result persists even when considering the effect of notifying providers of private certification standards and when combining mention of the FATF with the private standards (the ACAMS and ACAMS + FATF treatments in Chapter 5).

Finally, we considered a set of observable implications from international relations theories regarding the threat of legal penalties, norms of appropriate business dealings, and origin within the United States. No clear pattern emerged from the results. The threat of legal penalties had little impact on response or compliance levels. Exceptions included lower refusal rates in the main analysis and, in statistical models with covariates, response rates, compliance, and non-compliance all decreased significantly, which offers mixed findings at best. The drop in response rates and non-compliance suggests that the threat of penalties may improve adherence with international law, but the decrease in compliance provides countervailing evidence of a possible collusion effect. Citing norms of appropriate behavior had almost no effect on response rates or compliance, save a marginally significant increase in non-response. Approaches hailing from a US alias resulted in lower compliance, and some evidence points to higher non-response and partial compliance rates.

As just reviewed, in most cases the results point to mixed conclusions. Sometimes a given treatment motivated higher non-response rates, which is what we expected, but then also lowered compliance (in the Corruption treatment, for example). Elsewhere, as in the Terrorism and IRS treatments, the treatment increased non-response as expected, decreased non-compliance as expected, but then also decreased part-compliance, compliance, or refusal, raising some questions about possible heterogeneous treatment effects that need to be explored in the future. And in other cases there are null findings – but important and telling null findings – that should not be ignored. As discussed, for example, despite large sums of money and extensive international coordination efforts, mention of international standards does not alter response or compliance behavior in any meaningful way. Clearly, there remains much more work to be done in the realm of financial transparency. One key step is to begin to think carefully and systematically about how experiments might further inform international policy initiatives.

Experiments as a solution to scholarly and policy problems

Having summarized the main findings, what are the more general implications of this study for global governance? Both policy-makers and scholars have long realized that the mere existence of formal international rules tells us very little as to whether those rules actually make any difference. At the same time as an impasse in the relevant international relations scholarship led us to use field experiments to test the effectiveness of international rules on corporate transparency, policy-makers have been wrestling with an analogous conundrum. However, both social scientists and those responsible for making and enforcing the relevant international rules have struggled to find a way to better understand whether, when, and how international rules are effective in changing actors' behavior. This section explores these parallels.

Accurately determining causal relationships in the social world is very difficult. The particular manifestations of this difficulty when it comes to studying global governance are the related problems of endogeneity and selection bias. Counter-intuitively, the multiplication of international rules and high rates of formal compliance might not tell us anything as to whether international politics is in fact becoming more rule-governed. As discussed at the beginning of this book, there is a key uncertainty over whether international treaties, conventions, and the like cause actors to be more law-abiding, or whether law-abiding actors are disproportionately more likely to sign up to such international legal instruments in the first place.

Similarly, when states and other actors commit to international rules, are these commitments only reflecting what these actors would have done anyway for reasons quite separate from the existence of the rule itself? These challenges add to the more familiar problem of leaders solemnly signing up to (for example) human rights conventions at various summits, and then going home and continuing to arbitrarily imprison, torture, or even execute their citizens regardless. Thus commitments to international rules may say nothing about what actually occurs on the ground, and even where commitments to rules and behavior do match up, we have not been able to tell whether the former causes the latter.

Though many circumstances and issue areas may not allow for field experiments, in many other instances randomized trials provide a way out of this intellectual dead end. Particularly in relation to the wide range of global governance domains where non-state actors are a – or perhaps even *the* – key locus of compliance, experiments can provide crucial insights on the extent to which and conditions under which rules are effective. We present several examples discussed in brief below. But how do these rarefied academic concerns relate to the world of policy, especially regarding the regulation of shell companies?

Twenty years after its founding and the release of the first version of its Recommendations, the FATF became fundamentally dissatisfied with the way it evaluated compliance. On paper the FATF has been an unqualified success. Its rules for countering money laundering and the financing of terrorism are unchallenged as the global gold standard in this area, to which almost every country has signed up. Though its country-by-country Mutual Evaluation Reports have regularly reported a long list of deficiencies, and a correspondingly long "to do" list for members and even more for non-members, these report cards indicate steady overall progress toward better compliance.

Yet for all this apparent success, there is very little evidence to show that there is any less financial crime now than there was before the FATF was created (Sharman 2011). A 2011 report from the United

Nations guesses that authorities capture only 0.2 percent of money laundered globally each year (United Nations Office on Drugs and Crime 2011: 7). The United States freezes and seizes more dirty money than the rest of the world put together, yet even here the proportion of funds intercepted seems to be only a small fraction of overall criminal flows (Reuter and Truman 2004; Levi and Reuter 2006.)[1] Just as those researching in the field of international relations worry that the superficial picture of a law-governed world overlays a far less ordered reality, so too those within the FATF have become afflicted with nagging doubts that their successes are only apparent, and that their rules may have much less impact than first impressions suggest.

In determining what might have gone wrong, the FATF and its regional satellite organizations have become increasingly worried that countries may pass the relevant legislation to incorporate the Recommendations within their national legislation, and even set up the necessary institutions, but then carry on as before, largely ignoring the complex regulatory edifice they have erected under foreign pressure.[2] Thus the FATF looks out and is confronted with a Potemkin village of facades and form that conceals a lack of substance and effectiveness. In response, it has settled on the need for a double-grading system of measuring compliance. For each Recommendation, countries will get two scores: one for "technical compliance," i.e. whether the right laws and regulations are in place, and the other for effectiveness. In many cases, field experiments provide the best way of achieving this second aim of measuring effectiveness.

Thus where observers often worry about a growing divide between scholars and policy-makers, or perhaps even scholars and society more generally, the kind of field experiments used in this book help to bridge this gap. Both social scientists and policy-makers are crucially concerned with knowledge of what causes what, of making accurate causal inferences. Those within the ivory tower may value this understanding for its own sake, whereas for those in the policy world such knowledge may be a means to an end of effecting change. But even in this rather caricatured portrayal, where policy-makers have no interest in knowledge outside its instrumental value, and scholars have no

---

[1] Author interview: Asia Pacific Group on Money Laundering, Brisbane, Australia, 2012.
[2] Author interview: Washington, DC, United States, April 24, 2012.

interest in promoting positive change in the wider world, field experiments enable both groups to achieve their aims in a complementary fashion.

Certainly, the chances that major progress will be made in better regulating shell companies – and thus diminishing the incidence of major crimes – are vanishingly small so long as we do not even know how well existing rules work, let alone why and under what conditions. It is our hope that this book can improve both scholarship and policy and act as a prompt and guide to how these seemingly conflicting aims can be productively reconciled. As scholars, of course, we hope to bring the academy closer to policy reality. And that, we argue, requires a new approach to international relations research.

Experimental transnational relations

As noted, a central goal of the book is to establish the value of experiments for scholars of international relations well beyond the particular focus of this book. In order to potentially spark creative research designs by other scholars, we provide some examples of field experiments we have undertaken (or are currently carrying out) at Brigham Young University's Political Economy and Development Lab and University of Texas at Austin's Innovations for Peace and Development to give a range of possibilities for low-cost, practical IR field experiments. We trust that future researchers will roam well beyond the boundaries of these examples as they perform innovative and informative research. We note also that none of the following experiments employed deception. We have found that in most topic areas beyond transnational incorporation – where inappropriate behavior is less systemic – methods can be developed that withhold only the purpose of the study but otherwise engage in no active deception.[3]

Crowdsourcing development information in Uganda. Working with UNICEF-Uganda, we randomly assigned various incentive

---

[3] Also, one interesting feature of experiments with organizations as subjects is that they do not qualify as human subjects under US Department of Health and Human Services regulations as stipulated in the Common Rule. They are thus exempt from conventional Institutional Review Board examination. With few exceptions, submission of the research design and a request for an exemption typically results in relatively rapid clearance. Several examples of Experimental TR research projects follow.

mechanisms to motivate citizens ($N = 27,000$) to use their cellphones to text-message development information about their neighborhoods and villages to UNICEF's UReport system. Material incentives promising to enter subjects in a lottery to potentially win a solar cellphone charger had the largest effects on subjects' likelihood of responding to inquiries and on the number of sent texts; direct feedback on texts from researchers, appeals to "make a difference," and contact with other subjects in thematic groups also significantly increased participation over the control condition.

NGO opportunism. As the Political Economy and Development Lab (PEDL) we approached 700 Ugandan NGOs in a first experiment and then 14,000 NGOs worldwide in a follow-up study with a tentative but sincere offer to consider a partnership for a research venture and asked them to provide an estimate on reimbursement costs for tasking employees to the project. We found that, in their estimates, NGOs inflated bids by four to eight times actual costs depending on the treatment. Mention of significant resources in past PEDL projects elicited the greatest opportunism (by more than 800 percent); paradoxically, invoking the possibility of competition with other NGOs also caused significant opportunism, whereas stipulating the promise of an audit or prior partnerships had no consistent significant effects.

Confirmation bias of microfinance institutions. As PEDL we contacted microcredit organizations ($N = 1,419$) around the world by email to offer more information on a possible partnership to perform a randomized evaluation on institutional effectiveness. In the control condition the offer was made without additional information; in one treatment arm a citation and summary was given to a study showing microcredit effectiveness; in another arm we provided information on research (by the same authors) indicating *in*effectiveness. The positive condition elicited twice as many responses as the negative condition, suggesting significant confirmation bias among microfinance institutions.

Uganda NGO scorecard. We visited 130 NGOs in Uganda to collect information on accountability and transparency, such as their written constitutions, personnel policies, budgets, and funding sources. We randomly assigned half of the NGOs to have their scores published in the first release of the scorecard in July 2012. In 2013 we will compare the transparency and accountability of treated to control NGOs to learn the effects of the published scorecard on organizational reform one year after publication of the scorecard.

Foreign aid endorsements. In collaboration with Helen Milner and her team at Princeton, we designed an experiment to probe behavioral support for actual foreign aid projects in Uganda (through in-person interviews). We used co-financed projects by major donors in order to randomly assign bilateral or multilateral funding sources and compared the donors with a control condition implying that the domestic government funded the project. We found that foreign donors induced significantly more citizens to sign a petition or send an SMS in support compared to the government. And multilateral donors also caused greater support for projects than bilateral agencies.

Municipal incentives for foreign direct investment. In collaboration with Nathan Jensen, we incorporated a consulting firm and represented an actual client in approaching roughly 4,000 cities in the United States. We provided the basic financial parameters of the possible investment by the client and then randomly assigned the projected timing of the investment announcement either one month before or one month after the next municipal election. We also randomly assigned the implied origin of the client between the United States, Japan, and China. Data from the experiment were still being collected at the time of this writing.

Online charitable contributions. In partnership with the NGO Sustain Haiti, we are probing actual online donors' susceptibility to different treatments involving emotional appeals, development buzzwords, and statistics. Subjects are recruited using Facebook ads targeting individuals interested in charitable causes and then randomly assigned to one of four websites where multiple outcomes are tracked (total time in visit, number of links clicked, and any donations made).

NGO coordination map. We probe the effects on communication and coordination of providing a Google mapping tool to NGOs in Uganda and India. NGOs were surveyed before the study began and then randomly assigned to the mapping condition or control. Treatment NGOs received the mapping tool and multiple reminders to use it to coordinate with other NGOs. Post-test surveys measure the degree of increased coordination with other NGOs between treatment and control subjects.

Foreign origin, status, and helping behavior. In the summer of 2012 PEDL researchers and a large team of Ugandan enumerators randomly stopped Ugandans at pre-assigned locations throughout urban Kampala and asked the subjects to buy airtime for the researchers' cellphones.

Systematically altering the identity and dress of the requester, the team randomly assigned conditions of status (businessperson, aid worker, student), nationality, and gender in a 3 × 2 × 2 full factorial design. The experiment identified causal effects of the three factors in subjects' willingness to provide help to a stranger in a developing country. We found that people with higher status, foreigners, and women were significantly more likely to receive assistance.

These are merely a sampling of the field experiments possible in international relations, providing a sense of the range of possibilities for Experimental TR. But again, we hope that researchers will roam well beyond the confines of these examples in their exploration of new domains and application of innovative field experiments.

In the end, we trust that this study has proven productive in introducing a new approach to international relations scholarship. It also tests key theoretical propositions experimentally and suggests ways forward in the study of transnational relations. Critically, it provides important results revealing patterns of behavior in worldwide financial transparency and the causes of compliance with global standards.

Good social science often creates more questions than it answers, and we hope that this study fits that description. Hence, we emphasize that much more work needs to be done as we continue to explore mechanisms that cause law-abiding behavior and the methods to measure it. Our aims in this book have thus targeted both normative and scientific concerns and have suggested new ways of addressing them. The study has produced provocative findings that we trust will stimulate discussion and productive action in both academic and policy circles. We look forward to participating in those discussions.

Appendices
Chapter 2 Appendix: Explaining the global shell game

General background

Data on the corporate service providers were collected from April 2010 to June 2011. Email communication with all of the service providers occurred between March 2011 and July 2012. As discussed below, we carried out the overall project in multiple stages and the results from each stage are pooled together.

We carried out the experiment with the help of a large group of research assistants (RAs) at Brigham Young University. The group's size fluctuated with up to seven RAs working on the project during the busiest times and as little as one working on it between waves of the experiment. A total of 25 RAs (11 women and 14 men) worked on the project over a period slightly longer than two years. One RA worked on the project for a year and a half, but RAs generally worked on the project for an average of four months before leaving the project to graduate, study abroad, accept other employment, or return home for the summer.

Dustin Homer and Brock Laney each led the research team at different times. Research team members included: Allyson Adams, Jessica Allred, Lauren Barden, Peter Carroll, Drew Chapman, Zach Christensen, Stephanie Dowdle, Madeleine Gleave, Dano Gunderson, Matt Hadley, Ben Haymond, James Juchau, Diana Kunakaeva, Robert Morello, Catie Nielson, Brian Reed, Wayne Sandholtz, Tara Simmons, Megan Spencer, Deborah Sutton, Brittany Thorley, Dane Thorley, and Danny Walker.

Registration, Institutional Review Board, and university clearance

Because registration of research is not common in political science, we were not aware of any formal mechanism for registering research when we began the experiment. But we wished to deposit our plans in some capacity. As such, we deposited a simple registration document on March 2, 2011 with the Institute for Social and Policy Studies (ISPS) at Yale University. The ISPS repository is not designed to be a registry as such, but it was the only forum of which we were aware at the time. In February 2013 we transferred the registration document to the EGAP registry (http://e-gap.org/design-registration/) with appropriate certification from the Yale ISPS group.

Standards for reporting on registered research are not established yet in political science. We therefore follow the general guidelines provided in a recent proposal on establishing a registry within political science (Findley et al. 2012a) by reporting on what we stated we planned to do in the original registration and also ways that we deviated from the original design.

First, all interventions that we originally identified upon registration are reported in this book. Thus, the substantive material we report in this book is fully consistent with all interventions we originally stated we would examine.

We note that we developed one additional intervention – the ACAMS treatment – after registration and include it in the book's results (Chapter 5). This newer intervention emerged based on an initiative of Duncan Snidal, Ken Abbott, Bernhard Zangl, and Philipp Genschel to understand how international organizations "orchestrate" private actors to accomplish international objectives. After receiving an invitation to their conference (in May 2011), we developed the ACAMS intervention. Because the invitation came early in the study, we note that the addition was not related to any analysis performed on previous interventions. In addition to the ACAMS-only treatment, we crossed the ACAMS and FATF treatments to learn about the joint effects of the two, one component of the orchestration idea.

In the main text we opted to report differences between Placebo and treatments for a set of multinomial outcomes (non-response, non-compliance, partial compliance, compliance, and refusal). This deviates from our registration wherein we anticipated coding responses dichotomously as compliant or non-compliant, given response. Thus we originally anticipated two separate outcome comparisons: (1) what encouraged response and (2) what encouraged compliance, where compliance included full compliance and refusal (in contrast to non-compliance and partial compliance, which we intended to lump together). But it became clear that the five categories were relatively distinct from one another and should accurately be treated as such. To remain consistent with the registration, we report in the appendices the analyses as we originally anticipated (see Table A2.7).

Also note that in the appendices we report the results of multinomial probit models that are designed to provide more demanding tests than the simpler difference in proportions tests. We also report selection models allowing an examination of how the intervention affected both response and compliance. We did not register the intention to report these additional results. We decided to report them, however, because they allow the inclusion of control variables, clustering across observations, and also provide a way of connecting the response and compliance stages explicitly rather than treating them separately. This seems to be a more appropriate modeling strategy than keeping the response/non-response and compliance/non-compliance stages separate, but we nonetheless report them only in the Appendices.

Institutional Review Board (IRB) clearance was received on July 7, 2010. Because organizations, as opposed to humans, were our subjects, we submitted an IRB application with request for exemption. The IRB consulted with the university administration and university legal counsel before granting exemption and clearance for the study. Before carrying out the experiment, we independently consulted with university legal counsel and made appropriate adjustments to the experiment including those described below about aliases as well as the particular email accounts used.

The study was funded primarily by the Australian Research Council with additional funds from the Department of Political Science, the College of Family, Home, and Social Sciences, and the David M. Kennedy Center for International Studies at Brigham Young University. None of the funders placed any restrictions on the reporting of the results and none have a stake in the outcome of the results that could bias the study design, reporting, or inferences. A spreadsheet containing a mapping of registration elements, deviations, and final results appears at http://michael-findley.com.

Sample

At the beginning of the study, there was no sampling frame that could serve as a basis for the selection of service providers. Some private companies and consultants have lists of providers, but they do not make them publicly available and the lists are not in any way comprehensive.

Some limited public lists exist through trade organizations, which we obtained wherever possible.

To gather data on service providers, we relied primarily on Google searches. For every country in the world, we searched based on a similar set of keywords – incorporation, company formation, corporate law, and business law – each coupled with the name of the target country.

We identified all possible companies that offer incorporation services. This list includes primarily exclusive corporate service providers (CSPs) as well as law firms that explicitly advertise incorporation services. We clearly do not have data on the universe of firms that provide incorporation services. But we nonetheless constructed a list that dwarfs any other social science or policy effort to understand incorporation services.

We identified 3,771 firms that provide incorporation services. Of these services, 1,376 are corporate service providers and 2,395 are law firms. In many analyses we pool the corporate service providers and law firms, but where appropriate we separate them or control for any differences. We were able to make 7,466 approaches to these firms, meaning that most providers were contacted at least twice.

In all, we obtained data on services in nearly every country of the world – 181 in all – as well as extensive data for every US state, including the District of Columbia. Because we had a substantially higher number of services in the United States, we kept the international and US samples separate, although we note that 63 services in the international sample were randomly selected from the US sample for comparison with the other countries.

In the data collection process, the most important piece of information was the contact information for each firm. In most cases we were able to obtain email addresses (72 percent in the international sample and 52 percent in the US sample) with the remaining requiring contact through web forms. Upon completion of the study all identifying information, including contact details, was securely purged.

Beyond the basic contact information, we collected as much data as possible from each firm. The data fields we attempted to populate include size, number of countries of operation, substantive areas of business, years in service, and company type. Unfortunately, there is considerable variability in the availability of data in many of these additional fields. Thus, we are not able to use most of them in the analysis. Because of the large sample size, we rely on randomization and blocking, as discussed below, to balance the possible confounding effects of these additional factors. We of course cannot be certain, but note that in expectation randomization should accomplish this.

What are the broader implications of the resultant sample? Although we were only able to construct a convenience sample, it is likely that we are capturing the biggest firms, which are the source of most of the new companies formed worldwide. In examining the final sample, it is clear that indeed some of the best-known providers in the world are represented. This does not preclude the possibility of bias, of course. We especially expect our sample not to be representative of smaller less well-known firms. Indeed, it is likely that some of the shadiest companies do not have a web presence precisely because they do not want to be detected by law enforcement. If this is the case, then the bias will result in overestimates of compliance, thus tempering any positive findings about the effects of international law. For additional details see Chapter 2.

Randomization strategy

In expectation, randomization balances the influence of possible con-founding factors. Blocking can improve balance even further and is often preferable to simple randomization (Gerber and Green 2012: 71–79). Fuller discussions of the benefits of randomization and block-ing appear in other places and are beyond the scope of this appendix. Instead, our purpose here is to detail the randomization strategy used in this experiment.

After collecting the data for our sample, we blocked as discussed below, and then randomized within the blocking strata. Within each blocking stratum, we assigned service providers to different conditions where each had an equal probability of assignment to Placebo or one of the treatments. To minimize possible multiple comparison prob-lems, we assigned a larger proportion of our sample to the control group than to treatment groups, with roughly 30 percent of all sub-jects being assigned to the control group.

Procedurally, we generated a list of random numbers for each block-ing stratum, ordered the subjects by the random number, and then allocated services using this random ordering to treatment or control groups using consistent proportions across blocking strata. For later iterations of the experiment, efforts to avoid detection necessitated randomly assigning each service with a treatment it had not previously received. We followed the same procedure as previously outlined, but

Table A2.1 *Countries' ease of doing business rating (World Bank 2011)*

Afghanistan	Low Bus. Friendliness
Albania	Med. Bus. Friendliness
Algeria	Low Bus. Friendliness
Andorra	Tax Haven
Angola	Low Bus. Friendliness
Anguilla	Tax Haven
Antigua & Barbuda	Tax Haven
Argentina	Med. Bus. Friendliness
Armenia	Low Bus. Friendliness
Aruba	Tax Haven
Australia	OECD
Austria	OECD
Azerbaijan	High Bus. Friendliness
Bahamas	Tax Haven
Bahrain	High Bus. Friendliness
Bangladesh	Low Bus. Friendliness
Barbados	Tax Haven
Belarus	High Bus. Friendliness
Belgium	OECD
Belize	Tax Haven
Bermuda	Tax Haven
Bolivia	Low Bus. Friendliness
Bosnia and Herzegovina	Med. Bus. Friendliness
Botswana	High Bus. Friendliness
Brazil	Med. Bus. Friendliness
British Virgin Islands	Tax Haven
Brunei Darussalam	Med. Bus. Friendliness
Bulgaria	High Bus. Friendliness
Burkina Faso	Low Bus. Friendliness
Cambodia	Low Bus. Friendliness
Cameroon	Low Bus. Friendliness
Canada	OECD
Cayman Islands	Tax Haven
Chile	OECD
China	High Bus. Friendliness
Colombia	High Bus. Friendliness
Cook Islands	Tax Haven
Costa Rica	Med. Bus. Friendliness
Cote d'Ivoire	Low Bus. Friendliness
Croatia	Med. Bus. Friendliness

Table A2.1 (*cont.*)

Cuba	Low Bus. Friendliness
Cyprus	Tax Haven
Czech Republic	OECD
D.R. Congo	Low Bus. Friendliness
Denmark	OECD
Djibouti	Low Bus. Friendliness
Dominica	Tax Haven
Dominican Republic	Med. Bus. Friendliness
Ecuador	Low Bus. Friendliness
Egypt	Low Bus. Friendliness
El Salvador	Low Bus. Friendliness
Estonia	High Bus. Friendliness
Faroe Islands	Low Bus. Friendliness
Fiji	High Bus. Friendliness
Finland	OECD
France	OECD
Gambia	Low Bus. Friendliness
Georgia	Low Bus. Friendliness
Germany	OECD
Ghana	High Bus. Friendliness
Gibraltar	Tax Haven
Greece	OECD
Grenada	Tax Haven
Guam	Low Bus. Friendliness
Guatemala	Med. Bus. Friendliness
Guernsey	Tax Haven
Guyana	Med. Bus. Friendliness
Honduras	Low Bus. Friendliness
Hong Kong	High Bus. Friendliness
Hungary	OECD
Iceland	OECD
India	Low Bus. Friendliness
Indonesia	Med. Bus. Friendliness
Iran	Low Bus. Friendliness
Iraq	Low Bus. Friendliness
Ireland	OECD
Isle of Man	Tax Haven
Israel	High Bus. Friendliness
Italy	OECD
Jamaica	Med. Bus. Friendliness

Table A2.1 (*cont.*)

Japan	OECD
Jersey	Tax Haven
Jordan	Low Bus. Friendliness
Kazakhstan	High Bus. Friendliness
Kenya	Med. Bus. Friendliness
Korea	OECD
Kosovo	Med. Bus. Friendliness
Kuwait	High Bus. Friendliness
Kyrgyzstan	High Bus. Friendliness
Latvia	High Bus. Friendliness
Lebanon	Med. Bus. Friendliness
Libya	Low Bus. Friendliness
Liechtenstein	Tax Haven
Lithuania	High Bus. Friendliness
Luxembourg	OECD
Macao	Low Bus. Friendliness
Macedonia	High Bus. Friendliness
Madagascar	Low Bus. Friendliness
Malawi	Low Bus. Friendliness
Malaysia	High Bus. Friendliness
Maldives	Med. Bus. Friendliness
Mali	Low Bus. Friendliness
Malta	Tax Haven
Marshall Islands	Tax Haven
Mauritius	Tax Haven
Mexico	OECD
Moldova	Med. Bus. Friendliness
Monaco	Tax Haven
Mongolia	High Bus. Friendliness
Montenegro	High Bus. Friendliness
Morocco	Med. Bus. Friendliness
Mozambique	Med. Bus. Friendliness
Namibia	High Bus. Friendliness
Nauru	Tax Haven
Netherlands	OECD
Netherlands Antilles	Tax Haven
New Zealand	OECD
Nicaragua	Low Bus. Friendliness
Nigeria	Low Bus. Friendliness
Norway	OECD
Oman	High Bus. Friendliness

Table A2.1 *(cont.)*

Pakistan	Low Bus. Friendliness
Panama	Tax Haven
Papua New Guinea	Med. Bus. Friendliness
Paraguay	Med. Bus. Friendliness
Peru	High Bus. Friendliness
Philippines	Low Bus. Friendliness
Poland	OECD
Portugal	OECD
Puerto Rico	High Bus. Friendliness
Qatar	High Bus. Friendliness
Romania	High Bus. Friendliness
Russia	Med. Bus. Friendliness
Rwanda	High Bus. Friendliness
Samoa	Tax Haven
San Marino	Tax Haven
São Tomé and Príncipe	Low Bus. Friendliness
Saudi Arabia	High Bus. Friendliness
Senegal	Low Bus. Friendliness
Serbia	Med. Bus. Friendliness
Seychelles	Tax Haven
Sierra Leone	Low Bus. Friendliness
Singapore	High Bus. Friendliness
Slovak Republic	OECD
Slovenia	OECD
Solomon Islands	Med. Bus. Friendliness
South Africa	High Bus. Friendliness
Spain	OECD
Spain (Canary Islands)	OECD
Sri Lanka	Med. Bus. Friendliness
St. Kitts and Nevis	Tax Haven
St. Lucia	Tax Haven
St. Vincent and Grenadines	Tax Haven
Sudan	Low Bus. Friendliness
Suriname	Low Bus. Friendliness
Swaziland	Med. Bus. Friendliness
Sweden	OECD
Switzerland	OECD
Syrian Arab Republic	Low Bus. Friendliness
Taiwan	High Bus. Friendliness
Tajikistan	Low Bus. Friendliness
Tanzania	Low Bus. Friendliness

Table A2.1 (*cont.*)

Thailand	High Bus. Friendliness
Togo	Low Bus. Friendliness
Trinidad and Tobago	Med. Bus. Friendliness
Tunisia	High Bus. Friendliness
Turkey	OECD
Turks and Caicos	Tax Haven
Uganda	Med. Bus. Friendliness
UK	OECD
Ukraine	Low Bus. Friendliness
United Arab Emirates	High Bus. Friendliness
Uruguay	Med. Bus. Friendliness
United States	OECD
US Virgin Islands	Tax Haven
Uzbekistan	Low Bus. Friendliness
Vanuatu	High Bus. Friendliness
Venezuela	Low Bus. Friendliness
Vietnam	High Bus. Friendliness
West Bank and Gaza	Low Bus. Friendliness
Yemen	Med. Bus. Friendliness
Zimbabwe	Low Bus. Friendliness

added the stipulation that a subject be reassigned a new treatment if it was assigned to one it had previously received.

The blocks were formed using information on company type, CSP or law firm, as well as country grouping where the firm is located. For the international sample, we stratified countries by tax havens, OECD countries, and developing countries. Because the developing country category is so large and varied, we further stratified developing countries by ease of doing business: high, medium, and low business friendliness (World Bank 2011). Table A2.1 displays all countries along with their associated business friendliness status.

In the US sample, we first blocked by putting states with the most firms (California and Nevada) and with reputations for ease of incorporation (Delaware and Wyoming) into their own strata. We created strata for all remaining states according to their ease of setting up a business code (Beacon Hill Institute's 2010 State Competitiveness Report). Finally, and like the international sample, we also blocked on law firm versus CSP status. Table A2.2 displays all states along with their associated ease of setting up business status.

Table A2.2 *States' ease of setting up business rating (Beacon Hill Institute 2010)*

State	Ranking	State	Ranking
North Dakota	1	Maryland	26
Colorado	2	Alaska	27
Massachusetts	3	Connecticut	28
Wyoming	4	California	29
Minnesota	5	Missouri	30
Nebraska	6	New York	31
Utah	7	Maine	32
South Dakota	8	Michigan	33
Iowa	9	Illinois	34
New Hampshire	10	Pennsylvania	35
Virginia	11	New Jersey	36
Florida	12	Indiana	37
Kansas	13	Arkansas	38
Washington	14	Louisiana	39
Oregon	15	Hawaii	40
Nevada	16	Kentucky	41
Montana	17	South Carolina	42
Idaho	18	Ohio	43
Vermont	19	Tennessee	44
Rhode Island	20	Oklahoma	45
North Carolina	21	Georgia	46
Delaware	22	New Mexico	47
Wisconsin	23	Alabama	48
Arizona	24	West Virginia	49
Texas	25	Mississippi	50

Although we (Findley, Nielson, Sharman) designed the randomization strategy, none of us actually carried out the randomization procedure. Instead, two of the team members with no stake in the outcome of the research (Dustin Homer and Brock Laney) performed the actual randomization. After the randomization strategy was developed, randomization occurred once with no "redraws."

Randomization sensitivity

Although randomization should theoretically balance the effects of observable and unobservable characteristics, we checked the success of the randomization to the extent possible. Using all available covariates, we conducted randomization checks to determine whether any factors were correlated with assignment to any given treatment. We do not include randomization check tables here, because we estimated a large number of possible models. The data and Stata code for analysis can be found in the replication information available at http://michael-findley.com.

For the international sample, when regressing assignment to treatment on company and economic grouping variables, not a single variable is statistically related to treatment when using the 0.05 threshold. In a few cases, results are significant at the 0.1 level, but more generally nearly all of them are unrelated. For the US sample, none of the covariates are statistically related to treatment assignment, regardless of significance threshold used.

To supplement the randomization checks, we also estimated the results in a variety of ways to address possible bias. Below we discuss our analysis strategy, which is based primarily on simple difference of proportions tests, which are appropriate given the large sample size and the implementation of blocked randomization. Despite following a basic differences setup, we conducted a set of sensitivity tests using covariates to control for other possible confounding factors. The results of these additional tests are reported in the appendices for Chapter 3–6.

Interventions and procedures

We primarily contacted service providers by email. In cases where firms did not provide an email we used their web forms. Getting the email or web approach right was absolutely critical. Chief among our concerns was making the approach letter credible and, related, minimizing detection.

We designed the letters based on an extensive set of interviews with CSPs in the United States, Britain, Switzerland, Australia, Austria, Norway, the Netherlands, Hong Kong, Singapore, Panama, Cayman Islands, and other financial centers. This background research led to several different conclusions, which formed the basis for our approaches. Chapter 2 contains a discussion of these considerations and we elaborate on a few points below.

Letter content

Thirty-three emails were drafted and each included (1) a polite salutation, (2) brief background information on the alias, (3) telling the subject the alias is interested in incorporation, and (4) asking the service what was necessary to move forward with the process of incorporation. The vast majority, though not all, of the emails included a request for the subject's pricing as well as a list of their required identifying documents. Treatments, alias names, company names, and alias countries of origin were inserted into the text of the email at predetermined and standardized locations indicated as outlined in the examples below. Corruption and Terrorism treatments were pasted into the CORRUPTIONORTERROr designated area, while all other treatments were pasted into the area marked by the word TREATMENt.

For all but eight of the email texts, standardized and minor grammatical and spelling errors were added to the emails to increase the authenticity of the messages originating from non-English speaking countries. The eight emails without errors were assigned to aliases who told subjects they lived in an English-speaking country (i.e. Australia, New Zealand, or the United States). The other aliases sent any of the other 25 emails with the standardized errors.

We conducted robustness checks including fixed effects for letter type and report those results in the online appendix (http://michael-findley.com). The main results reported in the text are in most cases qualitatively similar when including the letter fixed effects. Like the letter types, we also conducted robustness checks including fixed effects for alias (reported below) and report those results in the online appendix. Similarly, the main results reported in the text are in most cases qualitatively similar when including the alias fixed effects. Below we include two example approaches. All 33 letters are available upon request.

English as official language email sample (free of obvious errors)

Dear NAMECOMPANY,

I am an international consultant living in **COUNTRy**. My associates and I have been based in **COUNTRy** for some time and we have done extensive international work, especially in your area. After looking at the specific needs of our growing company, we were feeling that it would make sense for us to expand and to set up an international company. We would like to form a new company in your area as private individuals. We especially hope to limit taxes and reduce liability.

We were wondering what you require us to give in order to do this. We would like to form this corporation as privately as possible. **TREATMENt** What identifying documents will you need from us? We would also like to know what your usual prices are. We appreciate the help.

I travel a lot for my work, so I communicate best via email. I hope to hear from you soon.

Yours,

ALIAs

Non-English email example (with standardized misspelling)

Dear **NAMECOMPANY**,

I am writing to aks about the possibility of creating an international company. I live in **COUNTRy** and I do consulting work with some colleagues here. **CORRUPTIONORTERROr** We have started doing quite a bit of foreign work, including in your area, and we have reached point where it makes sense for us to open up a corporation, both to decrease tax obligations and limit liability. We would like to form a new company in your area as private individuals.

We want to ask you what you need from us to set up such a corporation. What are your rates? Also, we want to know what identifying documents will be required. Privacy is very important to us, and we would like to set this up in a way that will keep this as confidential as possible, in case of any complications down the road. **TREATMENt** We travel a lot, so it makes most sense to continue our communication through email. Your timely response would very much be appreciated.

Sincerely,

ALIAs

In addition to altering each letter, we also randomly selected one of ten different subject headings for the email. Each subject line signals the same general idea but with different words. The ten subject lines used in the study appear below:

1. Incorporation Question
2. Assistance with Incorporation
3. Forming an international corporation
4. International corporation help

5. International Incorporation Query
6. International Corporation
7. Forming a corporation internationally
8. Incorporating internationally
9. International Formation of a Corporation
10. International incorporation assistance

And we furthermore selected from among a set of fictitious identities, which we discuss below.

Treatments

Each of the interventions is discussed at length in the text itself. We briefly summarize each of the treatments here to be comprehensive. In all conditions, the emails requested confidential incorporation in addition to providing the following information.

Placebo: in the control or Placebo condition, the email approach originates in one of eight minor-power countries. Those countries are Australia, Austria, Denmark, Finland, the Netherlands, New Zealand, Norway, and Sweden ("Norstralia" for short). Each of these countries is rated very well on Transparency International's (2010) corruption scale. Those scores are listed below in the section describing the origin countries. Besides the language of the emails themselves, no additional text was added to the Placebo emails.

FATF/Managerial: in this condition, the email makes reference to the Financial Action Task Force and its requirements to establish the identity of the customer for whom the company is being formed. Like the Placebo, the email comes from an alias associated with one of the eight Norstralia countries.

My internet searches show that the international Financial Action Task Force requires disclosure of identifying information when forming a company. But I would like to avoid providing any detailed personal information if possible.

US Origin: like the Placebo, the email asked for anonymous incorporation without additional language, but the alias originates from the United States rather than one of the Norstralia countries. This condition is used in the international sample only.

Penalties: this condition is a combination of the FATF/Managerial treatment and additional information about the legal penalties that providers could face for failing to comply with international standards. It would not make sense to discuss the legal penalties without making reference to the FATF standards, thus we only investigated the combination of the two.

My internet searches show that the international Financial Action Task Force requires disclosure of identifying information when forming a company. I also understand that legal penalties may follow violation of these standards. But I would like to avoid providing any detailed personal information if possible.

Norms: like the Penalties treatment, this condition is a combination of the FATF/Managerial treatment and additional information about the shared norms related to abiding by FATF standards. It would not make sense to discuss the shared norms without making reference to the FATF standards, which are the basis of those norms.

My internet searches show that the international Financial Action Task Force requires disclosure of identifying information when forming a company and most countries have signed on to these standards. As reputable businessmen, I am sure we both want to do the right thing by international rules. But I would like to avoid providing any detailed personal information if possible.

Premium: in the emails for the Premium treatment, we offered to pay a premium for confidential incorporation, which directly contravenes FATF recommendations.

I am willing to pay a premium to maintain confidentiality.

Corruption: the corruption email originates from a consultant working in "government procurement" and hailing from one of the eight corrupt "Guineastan" countries as discussed below. This treatment attempts to understand whether FATF cautions against possible corruption are effective. We focus specifically on public-sector consulting for government procurement.

Terrorism: this terrorism email originates from a citizen of Lebanon, Pakistan, Palestine, or Yemen living in Saudi Arabia and consulting for a Muslim charity. The Terrorism treatment accounts for the efficacy of two of the FATF risk factors: perceived high-risk terrorism countries and charities.

We consult for a number of Muslim aid organizations.

ACAMS: this condition makes reference to identification standards, but attributes the standards to the Association of Certified Anti-Money Laundering Specialists rather than the Financial Action Task Force.

My internet searches show that the Association of Certified Anti-Money Laundering Specialists requires disclosure of identifying information when forming a company. But I would like to avoid providing any detailed personal information if possible.

ACAMS + FATF: this treatment makes reference to identification standards of the private ACAMS group as well as the public FATF organization together.

My internet searches show that international Financial Action Task Force requirements and Association of Certified Anti-Money Laundering Specialists standards mandate disclosure of identifying information when forming a company. But I would like to avoid providing any detailed personal information if possible.

IRS (for the US treatment): this treatment indicates that the IRS enforces the requirement to disclose a customer identification when incorporating. This condition is used in the US sample only.

My internet searches show that United States law, enforced by the Internal Revenue Service, requires disclosure of identifying information when forming a company. But I would like to avoid providing any detailed personal information if possible.

No Documents: this condition was designed as a check on the Placebo. In it, we did not ask which identity documents they required. Instead, it simply indicates that we would prefer to preserve anonymity.

Origin countries

Each email request was signed with an alias, which means that the name potentially signaled information about an origin country. We opted, however, to explicitly state country of origin in the email to avoid any confusion. As such, we faced important questions about which countries to use as the associated origins. Ultimately, we decided to use a basket of countries for the Placebo and several of the treatments, which we discuss more in Chapter 2.

For the Placebo emails, we included eight different origin countries all of which are minor-power OECD countries ("Norstralia" for short). As discussed in the Treatments section above, these countries should all signal low-risk potential clients because they are ranked high on Transparency International's (2010) Corruption Perceptions Index, where higher scores indicate greater transparency and, thus, lower corruption risk. The countries in the Placebo condition with their associated score are:

Australia	8.7
Austria	7.9
Denmark	9.3
Finland	9.2
Netherlands	8.8
New Zealand	9.3
Norway	8.6
Sweden	9.2

In most of the treatments, the origin countries remained the same. Exceptions include the US Origin, Corruption, and Terrorism treatments. To understand the possible impact of originating in the United States, the US Origin treatment included a corresponding US alias. In the Corruption and Terrorism conditions we used completely different sets of origin countries.

For the Corruption treatment, we chose a basket of eight relatively unknown countries that are nearly identical on their corruption scores ("Guineastan" for short). Those countries are included below along with their corruption ranking according to Transparency International (2010).

Equatorial Guinea	1.9
Guinea	2.0
Guinea-Bissau	2.1
Kyrgyzstan	2.0
Papua New Guinea	2.1
Tajikistan	2.1
Turkmenistan	1.6
Uzbekistan	1.6

As discussed in the Terrorism treatment, we chose four countries that have experienced significant levels of terrorism or otherwise have a reputation for experiencing terrorist violence. Moreover, we deliberately avoided picking countries that were under sanctions, which is why a country like Iran is not a possible origin.

Lebanon
Pakistan
Palestine
Yemen

Aliases and deception

Each email was associated with one of 21 unique and fictitious identities. We created 21 fictitious names that were common enough to ensure authenticity. The names were well vetted to avoid association of the name with prominent individuals in that country. Because potential consultants from many of these countries were most likely to be male, we held gender constant by assigning male names to all aliases.

In the design of the project we debated at length whether to recruit confederates from the different countries represented in the study or rather to use fictitious aliases. The decision was complicated and one not to be taken lightly given standards and practices that caution against the use of deception. Indeed we consulted with other academics, university legal counsel, and others in arriving at the decision to use aliases.

Two of the key reasons we opted to use aliases included protection of research staff and a sounder experimental design. In consulting with university legal counsel, they advised us to use aliases because recruiting confederate research staff from other countries and having them use their own names could create liability issues for them in their home countries both from their domestic legal environment as well as from any problems that could possibly arise in the experiment.

Aliases also allow for a sounder experimental design especially through control and minimizing detection. The set of countries from which the emails and aliases hail is rather mixed. On the one hand, we would have needed staff from minor-power OECD countries, which we could have recruited easily. On the other hand, recruiting subjects from the "Guineastan" countries would have been complicated. Indeed, we sent out a "pre-call" for applications to gauge which nationalities we could get representation from. Nobody from any of the Guineastan countries expressed any interest. Thus, had we continued with recruitment of confederates we might have needed to change the set of countries.

Working with confederates would have also increased the chances of detection. We would have needed to screen online and other material from confederates to avoid any ties back to the project. Such screening would need to occur at the outset of the study, but also throughout in the event that the confederates posted information about the project using their own identities.

Finally, as a more general comment we note that deception is not prohibited in scientific research. Indeed, there are valid justifications for using deception. In our case, we could not have carried out the research in any other way. Informing subjects they would be part of a study would have compromised the research in fatal ways (Levitt and List 2007; Singleton et al. 1988). We discuss issues of deception in the text in Chapter 1.

Minimizing detection risks

Detection represented our greatest concern for the study. As such, we researched the best alternatives for email accounts, including consulting with professionals working in IT security. We found one particular internet email provider that best met our needs. Because the internet email accounts required phone numbers to be set up, and we did not want those numbers traced back to a university or university town, we purchased SIM cards for Ugandan cellphones (while in Uganda for other research). We downloaded and entered proxy servers (discussed below) from a coffee shop in Kampala, Uganda and only then set up the internet email accounts. All further communications took place from within the proxy server networks.

The majority of emails sent to firms worldwide were sent from proxy servers on or near Brigham Young University's campus in Provo, Utah. Several emails were also sent by RAs who worked while traveling including in Boise, Idaho; Fair Oaks, California; Williamsburg, Virginia; Kampala, Uganda; and Seoul, South Korea. RAs used proxy servers (as outlined in the Protocol for Sending Email instructions) to send the emails in the interest of protecting their anonymity. Proxy server browsers were downloaded free of charge from the proxy server website.

The proxy server operates by threading a user's actual IP address through a number of randomly selected IP addresses on the proxy network before finally arriving at an IP address that is used as the browsing address for any given session. Thus, when an RA accesses the internet using the proxy server, he or she can browse using a random IP address from anywhere in the world where the proxy network exists. The fact that the proxy server funnels the original IP address through several others before finally assigning a browsing address prevents webmasters and others from tracing the assumed IP address to its origin.

To create this network of IP addresses, proxy server users can choose to volunteer their IP address to the network with an allotment of bandwidth to be used by others. Because the proxy server is accessible throughout the world, proxy users often browse with IP addresses from other countries. Common hosts are in Europe, Asia, and North America, where internet penetration and usage is also high.

There were a total of 113 errors committed throughout the course of the experiment (out of more than 7,400 total email approaches and countless follow-ups). Errors are defined as any deviation from the protocol that could potentially bias the subjects' response. Significant errors were dropped from the sample completely because we cut off communication before any outcomes could be received. These errors included leaving treatment language in the email, signing the email with an incorrect name, or addressing an email to the incorrect firm. These three errors were the most common of any type of error and the latter two are unlikely to pose major threats to detection, in any case.

Small errors, such as minor misspellings, were left in the sample, but coded with an error code of 1 in our final dataset. The response rate appears to have decreased slightly, but we have not noticed any other differences. Specifically, in the international sample the non-response rate for error-free services is 48 percent, while the services receiving defective emails were 41 percent non-responsive. Responses to the emails with errors offered no evidence that they picked up on the error.

Protocol for sending emails

Each of our research assistants was trained extensively before sending any emails to service providers. We do not reproduce all training materials in this appendix, but instead include the procedures that research assistants followed each time they sent an email. Despite extensive training, some errors did occur as just discussed.

Instructions for each email initiation:

- Open a standard browser window.
- Open appropriate US or International database.
- Open "Treatments" Google document.
- Open "Guineastan Aliases" Google spreadsheet.
- Open "Guineastan Emails."
- Open "Subject lines" Google document.
- Locate your assigned alias code. You will be assigned one of 21 specific alias email accounts (these have been randomized across treatment and control conditions). The spreadsheet will be sorted by alias. You will send all emails that are designated for your assigned alias. All login information can be obtained from the "Guineastan Aliases" document.
- Open the R: drive, select the "PLAID2" folder, then the "Guineastan Experiment" folder.
- Within "Guineastan Experiment" folder, open the "[proxy server] Files" and select your [proxy server] program folder and run the program by clicking "Start [proxy server] Browser.exe" icon.
- It should bring up an internet browser (always use Mozilla) with the [proxy server] button already installed and enabled, but if not, see directions below about downloading the [proxy server] button add-on.
- *For information*: "[proxy server] button is a 1-click way for Firefox users to enable or disable the browser's use of [proxy server]. It adds a panel to the status bar that says '[proxy server] Enabled' (in green) or '[proxy server] Disabled' (in red). The user may click on the panel to toggle the status." The button is located in the bottom-right corner of the browser window.

- In the [proxy server] browser, go to Internet email account; sign into your designated alias email account (according to information provided by "Guineastan Aliases" Google document).
- Select the first incorporation service under your alias designation (in column "G" – sort by column "G" so you can see all observations assigned to your alias).
- Click "Compose mail" in the email account.
- Draft the email:
- Add appropriate email address from column E of spreadsheet.
- Copy the appropriate subject line (see column H for code) from the "Subject lines" document and paste into subject box (simply take the code number from column H, find the corresponding numbered subject in the document, and copy that subject into the email. Follow the same pattern for each email field below).
- Copy the appropriate email text (see column I) from the "Guineastan Emails" document and paste in the body of the email. **Also, make sure to remove all of the bolded indicators from each email.**
- Make the salutation "Dear [Company Name]" (see column B for company name). Leave off any unnecessary phrases or initials at the end of the name – e.g. "LLC".
- Make alias-specific changes to the email text (Country and Alias name – the areas in need of change will be bolded).
- Ensure that the name used to close the email is consistent with the alias account.
- Copy the appropriate treatment text (see column J for code) from the Treatments document and paste in the designated area in the text of the email (as necessary).
- Click the "plain text" option to standardize fonts.
- Review the email very carefully to ensure that each step is completed adequately.
- Click "send."

Note: Some services will not have an email address listed; instead, they require you to use an online email form to initiate contact. Go to the designated form and enter [all of the information in the checklist above] as appropriate in the comment box; proofread and send as normal. If the form requires a phone number, address, or other identifier, simply add "0000" as necessary to complete the boxes you do not have information for.

This is the crux of the experiment. Triple-check the email to make sure everything is accurate before sending it. Remove any distractions that might

keep you from being 100% accurate. A mistake in an email could significantly increase the probability of detection and may have ramifications for
the entire study.

The outcomes

Most importantly, we were interested in whether firms offering
incorporation services complied or not with international law. Such
dichotomization is clean in theory, but difficult in practice. In some
cases, providers would not even respond, making it impossible to
decide whether they were compliant or not. In other cases, providers responded but refused service due to lack of fit or interest. In still
other cases, the providers would be agreeable, but provide mixed signals about whether they were complying or not. Thus, we realized
that we needed to expand the set of possible outcomes from comply/
no comply to five different outcomes: non-response, non-compliance,
part-compliance, compliance, and refusal, which we discuss below and
also in Chapter 2 along with the associated international legal requirements. In Chapter 2, we also discuss the possibility that responses to
emails were not meaningful and that providers would possibly switch
their strategy at a later stage.

Operational coding of outcomes

Research assistants coded the outcomes of all responses. Because the
experiment involved email communication with organizational representatives, the team members could not always be blind to the treatment administered when they were coding the outcomes. That said,
independent members of the research team double-coded (blind to
each other's codes) and arbitrated every observation in the study as
the study progressed. Then when the study was completed, separate
team members double-coded and arbitrated the entire sample again,
blind to previously assigned codes. Any differences in the two arbitra-
tion rounds were then reconciled by the team project lead.

Non-response

Subjects were coded as non-responsive if they did not respond to our
original email solicitation or to a follow-up email sent five business
days after the initial contact.

Table A2.3 *Code sheet for outcome categories*

Level of compliance	Code	Documents
Non-compliant	101	No identifying documentation required
	102	Require certified or non-certified non-photo documents
Partially compliant	201	Require non-certified copy/scan of photo ID
	202	Require non-certified photo ID with other non-certified documents
	203	Require non-certified copy/scan of photo ID with other certified documents
Compliant	301	Require certified copy or scan of photo ID
	302	Require certified photo ID with any other combination of certified or non-certified documents
	303	Require certified photo ID with certified proof of address
	304	Require certified photo ID with certified proof of address and other documents
	305	Require a personal visit
Service refusal	401	Outright refusal
	402	Qualified refusal – they cite a reason/concern for refusing service.
Non-response	501	Non-response
	502	Previously non-responsive subjects that respond to the innocuous email checks sent out in the final response checks sample
	503	Previously non-responsive subjects from which we receive an automated response in the final non-response checks sample
Non-codable	601	Outcome of interest cannot yet be determined
	602	Subject stops responding to email prompts
	603	Subject requires information that we cannot provide
	604	Subject requires payment before proceeding with communication

Table A2.4 *Code sheet to assign specific document code requests*

Specific document	Code	Notes
Photo ID (passport, driver's license, identification card)	1.1	Anything that establishes identity and has a photo
Certified photo ID	1.2	Notarized, certified, apostilled, verified
Identification documents	1.3	Other documents that verify identity but do not have a photo (birth certificates, social security cards)
Proof of address	2.1	Utility bill, bank statement, or other document used to verify address. In this case, they usually ask for a "copy" or "scan"
Certified proof of address	2.2	An "original" utility bill counts as "certified." May also be "notarized," "verified," etc.
Bank reference letter	3.1	Document from bank that proves good financial standing and supports identification
Professional reference letter	3.2	Document from business associate or other that supports character/business practices
Résumé or CV	4.1	Or similar if it helps to establish occupation or current employer
Criminal/police record	4.2	
Signature form	5.1	Specialized form usually supplied by the company
Certified signature form	5.2	Supplied by company but you get it notarized
Documentation related to business activity	6.1	This could be a detailed business plan or company records
Documentation related to source of funds	6.2	Old bank receipts or just a detailed description
Personal visit	7.1	Not a document, but worth noting specifically

Note: These were the only documents considered when coding subject responses. Many subjects asked for non-identifying documents and a varying array of other documents and forms of varying relevance. Any document not included in this table was not, however, considered when coding subject responses.

Non-compliance

Subjects were coded as non-compliant if they did not require any identifying documentation or if they asked for personal documents that do not have a photograph.

Part-compliance

Subjects were coded as partially compliant if they required some form of non-certified identification bearing a photograph (e.g. a photocopy of a passport or driver's license). These subjects may or may not have also required any other combination of documents to be included in this category.

Compliance

Subjects were coded as compliant if they required some form of certified identification bearing a photograph (e.g. a certified copy of a passport). These subjects may or may not have also required any other combination of documents to be included in this category.

Refusal

Subjects were coded as refusing service if they responded saying that they could/would not help us with the incorporation for any reason. Subject responses were also coded as refusals if they referred us to another company without attempting to answer our questions.

Tables A2.3 and A2.4 illustrate the code sheets we used to account for all possible types of documents that providers could request.

Following up and ending communication

If the information in a response was overly vague, we followed up with the providers using a simple and mostly scripted response. An example of a follow-up prompt appears below.

Thank you for your response. Our work involves assisting global clients with integration strategies, mostly dealing with IT consulting. While I do operate a business here in Guinea-Bissau, I would like to create the new corporation as a private individual in your region. Perhaps you inform us specifically the kind of information you require about our business to get things moving? Also, if convenient, please let us know what identifying documents you require, so that we may move forward quickly. See our prior correspondence for more information about our situation.

Once we obtained sufficient information from a subject, we closed out communication with a very simple statement thanking them for their time and noting that "our needs have been met" or that our "circumstances had changed." After this, we did not engage in any further communication until another round of the study in which they would receive a different approach – treatment, letter content, subject line, origin country, and alias.

Example replies

To provide some sense of the types of replies received, we include several below for each type of outcome excluding, of course, a non-response. Additional examples appear throughout the text in conjunction with specific treatments.

Non-compliant

Thank you for your email. We typically suggest that you incorporate in the state in which you will be transacting business in. We do not provide legal advice. We would need the following information in order to proceed with the formation of a corporation: Company Name: Company Address: Directors: Officers: Shareholders: Principal Activity of Business: Credit Card information (credit card number, exp. date, security code, billing zip code).

Part-compliant

Dear Sir, Thank you for your enquiries. The Seychelles jurisdiction does not require disclosure of any documents and particulars of clients to any authority whatsoever save upon a Court Order for purposes of criminal investigation and money laundering. Your type of transactions that you wish to use the proposed company is ideal for a Seychelles International Business Company. This kind of company pays zero tax, does not require annual return of accounts, does not disclose the Directors and Shareholders. You can open a bank account in its name and make use of a credit card to access your funds as you wish. As your Registered Agent, we are required by Law to maintain details of our clients for our own protection. To incorporate the company we require scanned copies of your passport, proof of your residential address (not post office box address) by way of a utility bill drawn on your name and if it is in a non English language, it needs to be translated and notarized before a Notary in your country. Given the nature of your proposed business transactions, we are willing to offer our services for the sum of Euro 600 per year. This will include the following services:- 1. Incorporation 2. Registered Office 3. Registered Agent 4. Opening of Bank Accounts as a separate service at Euro 200 per account We trust you will find our quote reasonable and we look forward to hearing from you. Yours faithfully,

Compliant

Herewith, the requisite forms for your to complete. The identifying documents you must send are as follows: 1. Certified copies of the information pages of your passport or of your driver's licence 2. Certified copies of two utility bills or other, showing your usual place or residence 3. Two reference letters, one from a bank and the other form a business or other associate. Have these sent directly to us from the persons giving the same. Please remit half of the fee at this time (see wire instructions below).

Refusal

Sorry, we cannot help. Best regards,

Waves

We completed the study in multiple waves contacting each of the providers twice on average with long separations in between. In the initial wave, we contacted 2,050 providers in the international sample and 1,455 providers in the US sample. The results reported in this book report include the first round pooled with the later rounds. In the logit and multinomial probit regression analysis reported in the main text and the appendix for each corresponding chapter, we account for the non-independence of observations by clustering standard errors.

Between the first and second full rounds, we explored two additional conditions on a subset of the subjects. In this intermediate round, which occurred almost two months after the first round, we investigated how the ACAMS and No Documents conditions affected response and compliance rates (551 and 1,299 subjects, respectively). We also sent emails with the Placebo condition again, but with a much larger number of emails (691 total).

We conducted the second full wave of the experiment nine months after the first round ended and immediately after the intermediate round. In the second wave we investigated all of the conditions used in the first round. We did not return to the ACAMS or No Documents conditions.

Importantly, when we conducted follow-up rounds, we did not ever repeat the same treatment, origin country, alias, or letter content with the same individual. Even variations of a subject's first treatment were ruled out in follow-up rounds. If a subject received the FATF treatment in the first round, for example, they were not allowed to receive the FATF treatment in the second round; nor were they allowed to receive the Penalties or Norms treatment afterwards because both of those treatments include language about the FATF. Additionally, we ensured that follow-up emails and subject lines were not repeated. Once the basic set of restrictions was in place, we randomly assigned subjects to one of the remaining conditions.

Over the course of the study, many questions arose about what the non-response outcome represents. We suspected non-response could represent a form of soft compliance in which providers chose not to respond to an email requesting anonymous incorporation rather than declining in an explicit response. It is also possible that non-response was simply capturing emails routed to a spam folder or were otherwise deemed not worthy of response.

We thus sent a completely innocuous email to all providers who had not previously responded. In the email we simply signaled that we hoped to find out whether they were in business and possibly accepting customers.[1] An example non-response email appears below:

Good afternoon,
I am an international consultant living in **COUNTRy**. After looking at the specific needs of our growing company, we were feeling that it would make sense for us to expand and to set up an international company. We were wondering if you will be able to help us with the incorporation.

---

[1] We are grateful to Don Green, Jeremy Weinstein, and Mike Tomz who each suggested this approach.

I travel a lot for my work, so I communicate best via email. I hope to hear from you soon.

Yours,
ALIAs

If we received a high proportion of responses to the innocuous email then this should provide evidence for the soft compliance conjecture. A low response rate would suggest soft compliance is not at work, but does not necessarily resolve other possibilities. As it turned out, we received very few responses to this non-response check. Of those that had not previously responded, only 16 percent in the international sample and 5.6 percent in the US sample switched and responded to the follow-up; we received automatic or out-of-office replies from an additional 2 percent of the providers.

The final stage of the study involved a survey questionnaire to our subjects. In the survey we did not make mention that we had previously sent fictitious emails. Instead, we simply noted that we were researchers (and provided our names and affiliations) interested in understanding the incorporation industry. We asked some basic questions and then "piped" in information about one of the treatments they had received previously but which we now asked in survey format. The content of the survey is still in progress and will be reported elsewhere, but we note here that the response rate was drastically lower in the survey (only roughly 9 percent completed the survey), vindicating our decision to conduct an experiment anonymously, even though mild deception was required.

Analysis strategy

Conceptually, the primary outcome of interest in our study is compliance or lack thereof. And yet as discussed above, dichotomizing poses serious challenges and risks to accurate inference. Instead, we needed to separate the outcome into all possible categories, which then created a multinomial outcome measure consisting of five possibilities.

We thus based all analysis decisions on the expanded set of possible outcomes. At the most basic level, we compare each of the treatments against the Placebo along each possible outcome in a simple difference of proportions setup, which is appropriate given the blocked randomized design we employ. For instance, we compared the Terrorism treatment against the Placebo along each of the possible outcomes (e.g., non-response in Terrorism vs. non-response in Placebo, compliance in Terrorism vs. compliance in Placebo). We report all of the differences in proportions in the main text.

To provide an intuitive interpretation, we also recast the results in terms of a "Dodgy Shopping Count" (DSC). Throughout the text we rely on the DSC measure to provide a better sense of the practical implications of the different treatments on the non-compliance rate. The essence of the DSC is to capture how many firms one could select randomly and then approach before finding one that would form a corporation without requiring identifying information.

Note that the DSC could be conceptualized in different ways, all of which return qualitatively similar results. Any quantitative differences between the different approaches are trivial. We thus opt for the simplest version, which – using p as notation for "the probability of" – is simply: $1/p$ (finding fully non-compliant provider). Depending on the assumptions one makes about sampling – with or without replacement as well as the size of the overall population from which one samples – the DSC calculation is more complicated, but yields a result that is only slightly different than $1/p$ (finding fully non-compliant provider). And the relative distinctions across conditions are unchanged. Because the purpose of the DSC is to facilitate comparison and general interpretation, we opt for $1/p$ (finding fully non-compliant provider), which is simply the expected value if one assumes that sampling occurs with replacement, or that sampling without replacement occurs from an infinitely large underlying population.

In addition to the difference in proportions tests and the DSC, we also conducted a series of robustness checks using different estimators and assumptions. First, we employ multinomial probit models, which account for the difference between treatment and control while also using information about the other possible outcomes. Moreover, the multinomial probit model allows us to include additional covariates that could have an impact on the results. Note that in the US sample, we had so few cases of compliance (10 in total) that we could not obtain statistical estimates. As such, we collapsed the compliance and refusal categories together for multinomial models.

In reporting the multinomial regression models, we note that we include covariates for company type as well as economic grouping, but we do not report the results of the covariates. See Appendix Tables A3.1, A4.1, A4.3, A5.1, A5.3, and A6.1 for reports that contain the predicted probabilities. The online appendix (http://michael-findley.com) contains all of the basic multinomial estimates. We also check the multinomial results rotating the base outcomes and dividing the outcomes into nine instead of five outcomes (four additional outcomes for when we needed to provide a follow-up prompt and then received one of the four outcomes). See the online appendix for these results.

Although the most appropriate measurement and estimation strategies involve the multinomial interpretation, we still wanted to understand whether dichotomizing the results led to substantially different conclusions. We thus report additional results in the appendix where the dichotomized measures are included. See Table A2.7. We also report the results as such because this is what we indicated when we originally registered the study, as discussed in the registration section of this appendix.

We report the dichotomized results in two ways. First, we compare simple difference in proportions on response (respond vs. not respond) and then on compliance (comply vs. not comply, given response). There is a tension in the response/compliance dimensions: in order to assess compliance, one must first receive a response. Thus, this suggests the possible need for a selection model. Standard selection models require an instrument to identify the model, but because of the limited data we had, we could not follow that strategy. Instead, we rely on a separate selection model (Sartori 2003), which does not depend on an instrument. See Tables A4.2, A4.4, A5.2, A5.4, and A6.2.

Companion survey

Service providers

At the completion of the experiment, we emailed service providers revealing our identity as researchers, but in no way signaling that we had conducted an experiment previously. We invited them to take a survey in which, among other things, we presented hypothetical situations and asked them how they would respond. Crucially, we piped in information about the actual experimental treatments that they received earlier. Thus, this will allow us to compare service providers' behavioral responses in the field experiment when they did not know they were being studied with survey responses when they did know they were under study. The survey results have not yet been completed, but we provide the text of the survey below.

Corporate service provider survey

Intro

Thank you for your willingness to take this survey. Please complete all of the questions on the screen before moving on to the next page. Once you have moved onto the next page, you will not be able to go back to the previous page. Attempting to go back using your browser could invalidate your survey results.

Q1: What are the primary activities of your company? Please select all that apply.
❑ Banking Management (1)
❑ Corporate Litigation (2)
❑ Estate Planning (3)
❑ General Legal Practice (4)
❑ Incorporation (5)
❑ Insurance (6)
❑ Tax Law (7)
❑ Other (8)

Q1a: You selected "Other" in the question above. Please indicate the other primary activities of your company by typing them in the space below.

Q2: How many employees does your company have? If you have more than 35 employees, please slide the bar to the rightmost position.
❑ Number of employees (Please move the slider to your answer)

Q3: In how many different countries does your company work? If the number is greater than 15, please slide the bar to the rightmost position.
❑ Number of countries (Please move the slider to your answer)

Q4: Does your company provide incorporation services?
❑ Yes (1)
❑ No (2)
❑ Yes, but rarely (3)
If "Yes, but rarely" is selected: What are the primary activities of your company? If "Yes" is selected: Please select all that apply.

Q4a: How many corporations per year does your company incorporate? If you incorporate more than 1,000 companies per year, please slide the bar to the rightmost position.

Number of companies (Please move the slider to your answer)

Q4b: What percentage of companies you incorporate are foreign companies (companies based in a country other than yours)?

Percentage (Please move the slider to your answer)

Q4c: In general, how much do you charge for incorporation services? Please indicate the total amount in US Dollars in the space provided below.

In the following section you will be presented with three hypothetical situations and asked questions regarding those situations.

Hypothetical Situation 1: The international community is trying to create laws that prevent individuals from forming companies for illegal purposes while still allowing all others to use companies for legitimate purposes without unnecessary regulation.

Q5: How many documents from the list below do you feel should be required by law to achieve the balance described above? Please select the number below. (Example, if you feel that four of the documents below should be required, please select the number 4.) A, Photo ID. B, Certified copy of passport. C, Proof of address. D, Bank reference letter. E, Professional reference letter. F, Certified signature form. G, Personal visit. H, Source of funds documentation. I, Personal résumé (curriculum vitae).

❑ 0
❑ 1
❑ 2
❑ 3
❑ 4
❑ 5
❑ 6
❑ 7
❑ 8
❑ 9

Q6: How many documents from the list below do you feel should be required by law to achieve the balance described above? Please select the number below. (Example, if you feel that four of the documents below should be required, please select the number 4.) A, Photo ID. B, Copy of passport. C, Proof of address. D, Bank reference letter. E, Professional reference letter. F,

Certified signature form. G, Personal visit. H, Source of funds documentation. I, Personal résumé (curriculum vitae).

❑ 0
❑ 1
❑ 2
❑ 3
❑ 4
❑ 5
❑ 6
❑ 7
❑ 8
❑ 9

Q7: Hypothetical Situation 2: You have received an email from the owners of a company in [Hypothetical Country]. These individuals are planning to incorporate their business in your country and would like to procure the help of your firm. They indicate that they want to get things started as quickly and anonymously as possible. [Additional Treatment Language]

Q8: If these individuals were unable to meet with you in person, would you require any identifying documents before incorporating their company in your country?
❑ Yes (1)
❑ No (2)
Answer If Q10: (treatment text). If these individuals were unable to meet with you in person, would you require any identifying documents before incorporating their company in your country? If Yes Is Selected.

Q8a: What identifying documents would you require from these individuals? Please list below.

Q8b: List Experiment Condition 1: How many of the following factors played a role in deciding which documents (if any) you required from the clients in the previous hypothetical situation. Please select the number below. (Example, if you feel that four of the reasons played a role, please select the number 4.) A, Personal belief that these documents are important. B, My country's laws require them. C, Firm policy requires them. D, The manner in which the client contacted you. E, The race of the prospective client. F, The country in which the prospective client works. G, The nature of the prospective client's business.

❑ 0
❑ 1

❑ 2
❑ 3
❑ 4
❑ 5
❑ 6
❑ 7

Q8c: List Experiment Condition 2: How many of the following factors played a role in deciding which documents (if any) you required from the clients in the previous hypothetical situation. Please select the number below. (Example, if you feel that four of the reasons played a role, please select the number 4.) A, International law requires them. B, My country's laws require them. C, Firm policy requires them. D, The manner in which the client contacted you. E, The race of the prospective client. F, The country in which the prospective client works. G, The nature of the prospective client's business.

❑ 0
❑ 1
❑ 2
❑ 3
❑ 4
❑ 5
❑ 6
❑ 7

Q9: Hypothetical Situation 3: The Financial Action Task Force (FATF) has recently passed a set of regulations concerning international incorporation. These new regulations stipulate that incorporation firms must meet with individuals in person before they can incorporate those individuals' companies. The regulations were unanimously accepted by all the FATF-member nations as proper guidelines for incorporation. Your country supports the regulations, but has not created any laws in your country to enforce the requirements.

Q10: Assuming the hypothetical circumstances above are real, would you be likely to require an in-person meeting with all prospective clients wanting incorporation assistance?

❑ Yes (1)
❑ No (2)

Q10a: Why did you answer yes to the previous question? Please select all that apply.

❑ My firm already requires in-person meetings with prospective clients wanting incorporation assistance. (1)

❏ I believe the benefits of meeting with prospective clients outweigh the costs. (2)

❏ I believe that international law should be followed, even if it is not enforced domestically. (3)

Q10b: Why did you answer no to the previous question? Please select all that apply.

❏ I see no benefit in meeting with prospective clients wanting incorporation assistance. (1)

❏ International law has little influence on my decisions. (2)

❏ The costs of requiring in-person meetings are too high. (3)

Q11: The remaining questions are not related to any hypothetical situation. Please answer as honestly as possible based on your past experience and current circumstances.

Q12: Are you more willing to incorporate a company for an individual working in Iceland than one from Burundi?

❏ Yes (1)

❏ No (2)

Q12a: Please explain why you answered yes to the question above.

Q12b: Please explain why you answered no to the question above.

Q13: Have you ever read or been briefed on FATF (Financial Action Task Force) recommendations or policy?

❏ Yes (1)

❏ No (2)

Q14a: Condition 1 of List Experiment: Below is a selection of four recommendations from the FATF regarding incorporation services: A, Companies or firms should identify high risk countries and make specific laws in regards to incorporating in those countries. B, Countries should make money laundering illegal. C, Companies should conduct ongoing due diligence in business relationships. D, Companies should be required to maintain, for at least five years, all necessary records on transactions, both domestic and international. How many of the FATF recommendations above do you feel are necessary? Please select the number below. (Example, if you feel that two of the recommendations are necessary, please select the number 2.)

❏ 0

❏ 1

❏ 2

❑ 3
❑ 4

Q14b: Condition 2 of List Experiment: Below is a selection of four recommendations from the FATF regarding incorporation services: A, Companies or firms should identify high risk countries and make specific laws in regards to incorporating in those countries. B, Countries should make money laundering illegal. C, Companies should not allow anonymous accounts. D, Companies should be required to maintain, for at least five years, all necessary records on transactions, both domestic and international. How many of the FATF recommendations above do you feel are necessary? Please select the number below. (Example, if you feel that two of the recommendations are necessary, please select the number 2.)

❑ 0
❑ 1
❑ 2
❑ 3
❑ 4

Q15: Which of the following activities do you find suspicious? Please select all that apply.

❑ Individuals who are trying to incorporate from Middle Eastern countries (1)
❑ Companies that do not have any type of website (2)
❑ Individuals who contact you through email (3)
❑ Prospective clients who mention that they want to maintain anonymity (4)
❑ Individuals who contact you through public email servers (gmail, yahoo, etc.) (5)
❑ Prospective clients who indicate they need to incorporate as quickly as possible (6)
❑ International clients (7)
❑ Individuals who take more than five business days to respond to emails (8)
❑ None of the above (9)

Q16: What ideas or suggestions do you have to improve international efforts against the misuse of incorporation?

Overall results by treatment, international/US

To summarize the results from each of the chapters, we provide an overview table for the international and US samples here (Tables A2.5

Table A2.5 *International sample overall summary results*

Condition	N	No response	Non-compliant	Part-compliant	Compliant	Refusal
Placebo	1,112	495	97	184	210	126
Proportion		44.5%	8.7%	16.5%	18.9%	11.3%
Premium	385	191*	24	66	56*	48
Proportion		49.6%	6.2%	17.1%	14.5%	12.5%
Corruption	428	225***	38	61	64*	40
Proportion		52.6%	8.9%	14.3%	15.0%	9.3%
Terrorism	424	247***	24**	46***	64*	43
Proportion		58.3%	5.7%	10.8%	15.1%	10.1%
FATF	390	190	35	62	66	37
Proportion		48.7%	9.0%	15.9%	16.9%	9.5%
ACAMS	109	50	9	19	27	4**
Proportion		45.9%	8.3%	17.4%	24.8%	3.7%
ACAMS + FATF	114	59	13	16	18	8*
Proportion		51.8%	11.4%	14.0%	15.8%	7.0%
US Origin	413	189	31	84*	58**	51
Proportion		45.8%	7.5%	20.3%	14.0%	12.3%
Penalties	379	187	28	75	60	29**
Proportion		49.3%	7.4%	19.8%	15.8%	7.7%
Norms	391	192	41	58	61	39
Proportion		49.1%	10.5%	14.8%	15.6%	10.0%

***$p < 0.01$, **$p < 0.05$, *$p < 0.1$.

and A2.6). Each separate chapter shows the results grouped with the associated content.

As outlined in the registration document, in Table A2.7 we report response and compliance separately. In this table, we collapse non-compliant and part-compliant into a single category of non-compliant. Further, we collapse compliant and refusal into a single category of compliant. As such, Table A2.7 shows response rates and then the combined compliance category as a percentage of response.

Table A2.6 *US sample overall summary results*

Condition	N	No response	Non-compliant	Part-compliant	Compliant	Refusal
Placebo	816	602	92	13	3	106
Proportion		73.8%	11.3%	1.6%	0.4%	13.0%
Corruption	532	417*	54	8	1	52*
Proportion		78.4%	10.2%	1.5%	0.2%	9.8%
Terrorism	550	458***	32***	8	2	50**
Proportion		83.3%	5.8%	1.5%	0.4%	9.1%
FATF	546	417	54	11	2	62
Proportion		76.4%	9.9%	2.0%	0.4%	11.4%
IRS	552	442***	42**	12	2	54*
Proportion		80.0%	7.6%	2.2%	0.4%	9.8%

***$p < 0.01$, **$p < 0.05$, *$p < 0.1$.

Table A2.7 *International and US sample results dichotomized as based on research registration*

Condition	N	Responses	Response rate	Sig.	Compliant	Compliance rate as percent of responses	Sig.
International							
Placebo	1,112	617	55.5%		336	54.5%	
Premium	385	194	50.4%	*	104	53.6%	
Corrupt	428	203	47.4%	***	104	51.2%	
Terror	424	177	41.7%	***	107	60.5%	
FATF	390	200	51.3%		103	51.5%	
ACAMS	109	59	54.1%		31	52.5%	
ACAMS + FATF	114	55	48.2%		26	47.3%	
US Origin	413	224	54.2%		109	48.7%	
Penalties	379	192	50.7%		89	46.4%	**
Norms	391	199	50.9%		100	50.3%	
US sample							
Placebo	816	214	26.2%		109	50.9%	
Corrupt	532	115	21.6%	*	53	46.1%	
Terror	550	92	16.7%	***	52	56.5%	
FATF	546	129	23.6%		64	49.6%	
IRS	552	110	19.9%	***	56	50.9%	

***$p < 0.01$, **$p < 0.05$, *$p < 0.1$.

Chapter 3 Appendix: Overall compliance and country groupings

Table A3.1 *Chapter 3 predicted probabilities multinomial probit (international sample)*

Conditions	No response	Non-compliant	Part-compliant	Compliant	Refusal
OECD versus tax haven					
OECD	54.0%	13.1%	13.1%	11.9%	8.2%
Tax haven	36.5%	3.9%	18.8%	34.9%	5.9%
Change	−17.5%***	−9.2%***	5.7%***	23.0%***	−2.3%
OECD versus developing country					
OECD	54.0%	13.1%	13.1%	11.9%	8.2%
Developing	59.4%	8.3%	16.2%	9.3%	6.9%
Change	5.4%**	−4.8%***	3.1%	−2.6%**	−1.3%*

***$p < 0.01$, **$p < 0.05$, *$p < 0.1$.

Chapter 4 Appendix: Terrorism, Corruption, Premium

Table A4.1 *Chapter 4 predicted probabilities multinomial probit (international sample)*

Conditions	No response	Non-compliant	Part-compliant	Compliant	Refusal
Premium					
Placebo	43.1%	9.6%	23.2%	14.8%	9.3%
Treatment	49.0%	7.1%	22.8%	12.9%	8.3%
Change	5.9%	–2.5%**	–0.4%	–1.9%	–1.0%
Corruption					
Placebo	43.7%	10.0%	21.8%	14.9%	9.6%
Treatment	50.4%	10.6%	18.1%	12.2%	8.8%
Change	6.7%**	0.6%	–3.7%**	–2.7%**	–0.8%
Terrorism					
Placebo	43.6%	9.6%	22.8%	15.3%	8.8%
Treatment	59.9%	6.8%	14.0%	11.7%	7.6%
Change	16.3%***	–2.3%***	–8.8%***	3.6%***	–1.2%**

*** $p < 0.01$, ** $p < 0.05$, * $p < 0.1$.

Table A4.2 *Chapter 4 selection model (international sample)*

Treatments	Response	Compliance	Selection constant	Outcome constant	N
Premium	–0.105	–0.064	0.240**	–0.567***	1,497
	(0.075)	(0.080)	(0.066)	(0.070)	
Corruption	–0.187***	–0.187**	0.241***	–0.529***	1,540
	(0.072)	(0.078)	(0.065)	(0.070)	
Terror	–0.364***	–0.168**	0.231***	–0.554***	1,536
	(0.073)	(0.078)	(0.065)	(0.069)	

Standard errors in parentheses.

*** $p < 0.01$, ** $p < 0.05$, * $p < 0.1$.

Table A4.3 *Chapter 4 predicted probabilities multinomial probit (US sample)*

Conditions	No response	Non-compliant	Part-compliant	Comply/ Refuse
Corruption				
Placebo	84.5%	3.7%	0.8%	11.1%
Treatment	88.9%	3.0%	0.8%	7.3%
Change	4.4%**	−0.7%	0.0%	−3.8%**
Terrorism				
Placebo	83.8%	3.9%	0.5%	11.8%
Treatment	92.1%	1.3%	0.3%	6.3%
Change	8.2%***	−2.6%***	−0.2%	−5.5%***

*** $p < 0.01$, ** $p < 0.05$, * $p < 0.1$.

Table A4.4 *Chapter 4 selection model (US sample)*

Treatments	Response	Compliance	Selection constant	Outcome constant	N
Corruption	−0.171**	−0.179**	0.076	−1.049***	1,348
	(0.079)	(0.090)	(0.131)	(0.155)	
Terror	−0.365***	−0.225**	0.200	−0.816***	1,366
	(0.082)	(0.090)	(0.131)	(0.150)	

Standard errors in parentheses.
*** $p < 0.01$, ** $p < 0.05$, * $p < 0.1$.

Chapter 5 Appendix: FATF and ACAMS

Table A5.1 *Chapter 5 predicted probabilities multinomial probit (international sample)*

Conditions	No response	Non-compliant	Part-compliant	Compliant	Refusal
FATF					
Placebo	46.6%	9.7%	21.2%	14.0%	8.5%
Treatment	50.7%	10.3%	19.6%	12.4%	7.0%
Change	4.1%	0.6%	−1.6%	−1.6%	−1.5%
ACAMS					
Placebo	42.5%	9.6%	24.6%	14.7%	8.5%
Treatment	43.2%	10.0%	26.6%	19.2%	1.1%
Change	0.7%	0.4%	2.0%	4.5%	−7.4%**
ACAMS + FATF					
Placebo	42.0%	10.5%	24.1%	14.7%	8.7%
Treatment	47.0%	15.4%	20.7%	11.7%	5.1%
Change	5.0%	4.9%	−3.4%	−3.0%	−3.6%

***$p < 0.01$, **$p < 0.05$, *$p < 0.1$.

Table A5.2 *Chapter 5 selection model (international sample)*

Treatments	Response	Compliance	Selection constant	Outcome constant	N
FATF	−0.114	−0.139*	0.144**	−0.630***	1,502
	(0.075)	(0.080)	(0.066)	(0.070)	
ACAMS	−0.061	−0.088	0.243***	−0.595***	1,221
	(0.129)	(0.136)	(0.072)	(0.076)	
ACAMS + FATF	−0.163	−0.249*	0.254***	−0.586***	1,226
	(0.126)	(0.139)	(0.072)	(0.076)	

Standard errors in parentheses.
***$p < 0.01$, **$p < 0.05$, *$p < 0.1$.

Table A5.3 *Chapter 5 predicted probabilities multinomial probit (US sample)*

Conditions	No response	Non-compliant	Part-compliant	Comply/Refuse
FATF				
Placebo	84.4%	2.9%	0.3%	12.5%
Treatment	87.2%	2.1%	0.3%	10.3%
Change	2.8%	−0.8%	0.0%	−2.2%**
IRS				
Placebo	85.6%	3.6%	0.5%	10.3%
Treatment	90.6%	1.8%	0.6%	6.9%
Change	5.0%**	−1.8%***	0.1%	−3.4%**

***$p < 0.01$, **$p < 0.05$, *$p < 0.1$.

Table A5.4 *Chapter 5 selection model (US sample)*

Treatments	Response	Compliance	Selection constant	Outcome constant	N
FATF	−0.102	−0.077	0.246*	−0.786***	1,362
	(0.078)	(0.087)	(0.131)	(0.149)	
IRS	−0.210***	−0.156*	0.193	−0.890***	1,368
	(0.080)	(0.090)	(0.133)	(0.151)	

Standard errors in parentheses.
***$p < 0.01$, **$p < 0.05$, *$p < 0.1$.

Chapter 6 Appendix: Penalties, Norms, US Origin

Table A6.1 *Chapter 6 predicted probabilities multinomial probit (international)*

Conditions	No response	Non-compliant	Part-compliant	Compliant	Refusal
US Origin					
Placebo	45.9%	10.2%	21.4%	14.8%	7.7%
Treatment	48.6%	8.5%	24.8%	10.3%	7.9%
Change	2.7%**	–1.7%	3.4%	–4.5%**	0.2%
Penalties					
Placebo	43.0%	8.9%	23.1%	16.1%	9.0%
Treatment	48.8%	7.0%	25.9%	12.8%	5.5%
Change	5.8%*	–1.9%*	2.8%	–3.3%*	–3.5%**
Norms					
Placebo	46.2%	9.7%	22.3%	14.8%	7.1%
Treatment	50.2%	10.8%	19.7%	13.5%	5.9%
Change	4.0%	1.1%	–2.6%	–1.3%	–1.2%

$***p < 0.01, **p < 0.05, *p < 0.1.$

Table A6.2 *Chapter 6 selection model (international)*

Treatments	Response	Compliance	Selection constant	Outcome constant	N
US Origin	–0.034	–0.131*	0.170***	–0.635***	1,525
	(0.073)	(0.078)	(0.065)	(0.069)	
Penalties	–0.135*	–0.226***	0.235***	–0.558***	1,491
	(0.075)	(0.082)	(0.066)	(0.070)	
Norms	–0.099	–0.137*	0.159**	–0.652***	1,503
	(0.075)	(0.080)	(0.066)	(0.070)	

Standard errors in parentheses.
$***p < 0.01, **p < 0.05, *p < 0.1.$

References

Abbott, Kenneth W., Robert O. Keohane, Andrew Moravcsik, Anne-Marie Slaughter, and Duncan Snidal. 2000. "The Concept of Legalization." *International Organization* 54: 401–419.

Abdelal, Rawi, Mark Blyth, and Craig Parsons. 2010. "Introduction: Constructing the International Economy." In *Constructing the International Economy*, edited by Rawi Abdelal, Mark Blyth, and Craig Parsons. Ithaca, NY: Cornell University Press.

Adelaja, Tai. 2012. "Vladimir Putin Aims to Boost Russia's Investment Climate." *The Telegraph* June 15, 2012. Accessed January 9, 2013 at www.telegraph.co.uk/sponsored/russianow/business/9333604/vladimir-putin-russia-investment.html.

Al Jazeera. 2012. "How to Rob Africa." November 8, 2012. Accessed December 2012 at www.aljazeera.com/programmes/peopleandpower/2012/11/201211714649852604.html.

Alpert, Bill. 2011. "Crime and Punishment in Putin's Russia." *Barron's Online* April 16, 2011. Accessed May 30, 2012 at http://online.barrons.com/article/SB50001424052970204569604576259313266852054.html#articleTabs_panel_article%3D1.

Andersson, Staffan and Paul M. Heywood. 2009. "The Politics of Perception: Use and Abuse of Transparency International's Approach to Measuring Corruption." *Political Studies* 57, no. 4: 746–767.

Andreas, Peter. 2010. "The Politics of Measuring Illicit Flows and Policy Effectiveness." In *Sex, Drugs, and Body Counts: The Politics of Numbers in Global Crime and Punishment*, edited by Peter Andreas and Kelly M. Greenhill. Ithaca, NY: Cornell University Press, pp. 23–45.

Andreas, Peter and Kelly M. Greenhill, eds. 2010. *Sex, Drugs, and Body Counts: The Politics of Numbers in Global Crime and Punishment*. Ithaca, NY: Cornell University Press.

Andreas, Peter and Ethan Nadelmann. 2006. *Policing the Globe: Criminalization and Crime Control in International Relations*. Oxford University Press.

Association for Accountancy and Business Affairs. 2002. "No Accounting for Tax Havens." Prepared by Austin Mitchell, Prem Sikka, John Christensen, Philip Morris, and Steven Filling. London.

Association of Certified Fraud Examiners. 2012. www.acfe.com. Accessed December 2012.

Atkinson, Michael M. 2011. "Discrepancies in Perceptions of Corruption, Or Why is Canada So Corrupt?" *Political Studies Quarterly* 126, no. 3: 445–464.

Avant, Deborah D., Martha Finnemore, and Susan K. Sell, eds. 2010. *Who Governs the Globe?* Cambridge University Press.

Axelrod, Robert M. 1984. *The Evolution of Cooperation*. New York: Basic Books.

Banerjee, Abhijit, Shawn Cole, Esther Duflo, and Leigh Linden. 2007. "Remedying Education: Evidence from Two Randomized Experiments in India." *Quarterly Journal of Economics* 122, no. 3: 1235–1264.

Baradaran, Shima, Michael Findley, Daniel Nielson, and J. C. Sharman. 2013. "Does International Law Matter?" *Minnesota Law Review* 97, no. 1: 845–937.

2014. "Funding Terror." *University of Pennsylvania Law Review* 162 no. 1 (forthcoming).

Barnett, Michael and Martha Finnemore. 2004. *Rules for the World: International Organizations in Global Politics*. Ithaca, NY: Cornell University Press.

Barnett, Michael and Raymond Duvall. 2005. "Power in International Politics." *International Organization* 59, no. 1: 39–75.

Bartley, Tim. 2007. "Institutional Emergence in an Era of Globalization: Transnational Private Regulation of Labor and Environmental Conditions." *American Journal of Sociology* 113, no. 2: 297–351.

BBC News. 2004. " 'Zarqawi' beheaded US man in Iraq." May 13, 2004. Accessed May 17, 2012 at http://news.bbc.co.uk/2/hi/middle_east/3712421.stm.

Beacon Hill Institute. 2010. "Tenth Annual State Competitiveness Report." Accessed March 1, 2011 at www.beaconhill.org/Compete10/Compete2010State.pdf.

Becker, Joe. 2010. "Web of Shell Companies Veils Trade by Iran's Ships." *New York Times* June 7, 2010. Accessed May 30, 2012 at www.nytimes.com/2010/06/08/world/middleeast/08sanctions.html?pagewanted=all.

Bertrand, Marianne and Sendhil Mullainathan. 2004. "Are Emily and Greg more Employable than Lakisha and Jamal? A Field Experiment on Labor Market Discrimination." *American Economic Review* 94, no. 4: 991–1013.

Best, Jacqueline. 2005. *The Limits of Transparency: Ambiguity and the History of International Finance*. Ithaca, NY: Cornell University Press.

Biersteker, Thomas J. and Rodney Bruce Hall, eds. 2002. *The Emergence of Private Authority in Global Governance*. Cambridge University Press.

Biersteker, Thomas J. and Sue E. Eckert, eds. 2007. *Countering the Finance of Terrorism*. London: Routledge.

Blyth, Mark. 2002. *Great Transformations: Economic Ideas and Institutional Change in the Twentieth Century*. Cambridge University Press.

Bohnet, Iris and Bruno S. Frey. 1999. "Social Distance and Other-Regarding Behavior in Dictator Games." *American Economic Review* 89, no. 1: 335–339.

Burns, John F. 2006. "U.S. Strike Hits Insurgent at Safehouse." *New York Times* June 8, 2006. Accessed May 17, 2012 at www.nytimes.com/2006/06/08/world/middleeast/08cnd-iraq.html?pagewanted=all.

Burns, Michael J. and James McConvill. 2011. "An Unstoppable Force: The Offshore World in a Modern Global Economy." *Hastings Business Law Journal* 205: 7.

Büthe, Tim. 2010. "Private Regulation in the Global Economy: A (P)Review." *Business and Politics* 12, no. 3: 1–38.

Büthe, Tim and Walter Mattli. 2011. *New Global Rulers: The Privatization of Regulation in the World Economy*. Princeton University Press.

Butler, Daniel M. and David E. Broockman. 2011. "Do Politicians Racially Discriminate Against Constituents? A Field Experiment on State Legislators." *American Journal of Political Science* 55, no. 3: 463–477.

Carr, Kelly and Brian Grow. 2011. "Special Report: A Little House of Secrets on the Great Plains." *Reuters* June 28, 2011. Accessed August 2012 at www.reuters.com/article/2011/06/28/us-usa-shell-companies-idUSTRE75R20Z20110628.

Chattopadhyay, Raghabendra and Esther Duflo. 2004. "Women as Policy Makers: Evidence from a Randomized Policy Experiment in India." *Econometrica* 72, no. 5: 1409–1443.

Chayes, Abram and Antonia Chayes. 1995. *The New Sovereignty: Compliance with International Regulatory Agreements*. Cambridge, MA: Harvard University Press.

Chayes, Abram and Antonia Handler Chayes. 1993. "On Compliance." *International Organization* 47, no. 2: 175–205.

Checkel, Jeffrey T. 2001. "Why Comply? Social Learning and European Identity Change." *International Organization* 55, no. 3: 553–588.

Christian Aid. 2008. *Death and Taxes: The True Toll of Tax Dodging*. London.

Chwieroth, Jeffrey M. 2010. *Capital Ideas: The IMF and the Rise of Financial Liberalization*. Princeton University Press.

Cockburn, Patrick. 1993. "Farmer's Son who Bribed and Murdered his way into Drugs: Neither Government Forces nor other Drug Traffickers were Interested in Taking Pablo Escobar Alive." *The Independent* December 3,

1993. Accessed December 5, 2012 at www.independent.co.uk/news/world/farmers-son-who-bribed-and-murdered-his-way-into-drugs-neither-government-forces-nor-other-drug-traffickers-were-interested-in-taking-pablo-escobar-alive-patrick-cockburn-reports-1465001.html.

Council on Foreign Relations. 2002. "Terrorist Financing." Prepared by Maurice E. Greenberg, William F. Wechsler, and Lee S. Wolosky. Washington, DC.

2004. "Update on the Global Campaign Against Terrorist Funding." Prepared by Maurice E. Greenberg, Mallory Factor, William F. Wechsler, and Lee S. Wolosky. Washington, DC.

Crawford, Neta C. 2002. *Argument and Change in World Politics: Ethics, Decolonization, and Humanitarian Intervention.* Cambridge University Press.

Cutler, A. Claire. 2003. *Private Power and Global Authority: Transnational Merchant Law in the Global Political Economy.* Cambridge University Press.

Cutler, A. Claire, Virginia Haufler, and Tony Porter, eds. 1999. *Private Authority and International Affairs.* Albany NY: SUNY Press.

Dai, Xinyuan. 2006. "The Conditional Nature of Democratic Compliance." *Journal of Conflict Resolution* 50, no. 5: 639–662.

2007. *International Institutions and National Policies.* Cambridge University Press.

de Soto, Hernando. 1989/2002. *The Other Path: The Invisible Revolution in the Third World.* New York: Harper Collins.

2000. *The Mystery of Capital: Why Capitalism Triumphs in the West and Fails Everywhere Else.* New York: Basic Books.

Deaton, Angus. 2007. "Evidence-Based Aid must not become the Latest in a Long String of Development Fads." In *Making Aid Work*, edited by Abhijit Vinayak Banerjee. Cambridge MA: MIT Press.

Decoster, Jamie and Heather M. Claypool. 2004. "A Meta-Analysis of Priming Effects on Impression Formation Supporting a General Model of Informational Biases." *Personality and Social Psychology Review* 8, no. 1: 2–27.

Department of Justice. 2011. Indictment: United States District Court Southern District of New York. United States of America versus Wegelin Bank. S1 12 Cr.02.

2012. "Three Tax Return Preparers Charged with Helping Clients Evade Taxes by Hiding Millions in Secret Accounts in Two Israeli Banks." Press release June 15, 2012. Accessed August 28, 2013 at www.justice.gov/opa/pr/2012/June/12-tax-762.html.

Dollar, Rachel. 2006. "FBI Joint Terrorism Task Force Makes Arrests in Fraud and Money Laundering Cases." *Mortgage Fraud Blog*, May 8, 2006. Accessed May 17, 2012 at http://mortgagefraudblog.com/perp-walk/item/10716-fbi_joint_terrorism_task_force_makes_arrests_in_fraud_and_money_laundering.

Downs, George, David Rocke, and Peter Barsoom. 1996. "Is the Good News about Compliance Good News about Cooperation?" *International Organization* 50, no. 3: 379–406.

Drezner Daniel, W. 2007. *All Politics is Global: Explaining International Regulatory Regimes*. Princeton University Press.

Druckman, Daniel. 1993. "The Situational Levers of Negotiating Flexibility." *Journal of Conflict Resolution* 37, no. 2: 236–276.

Druckman, Daniel, Benjamin J. Broome, and Susan H. Korper. 1988. "Value differences and Conflict Resolution: Facilitation or Delinking?" *Journal of Conflict Resolution* 32, no. 3: 489–510.

Eckert, Sue E. and Thomas J. Biersteker. 2010. "(Mis)Measuring Success in the Fight Against the Financing of Terrorism." In *Sex, Drugs, and Body Counts: The Politics of Numbers in Global Crime and Conflict*, edited by Peter Andreas and Kelly M. Greenhill. Ithaca, NY: Cornell University Press, pp. 247–263.

Economist Intelligence Unit. 2002. *Tax Havens and their Uses*, 10th edn. Prepared by Caroline Doggart. London.

Eccleston, Richard. 2013. *The Dynamics of Global Economic Governance: The Finance Crisis, the OECD and the Politics of International Tax Co-operation*. Cheltenham: Edward Elgar.

Ehrenfeld, Rachel. 2003. *Funding Evil: How Terrorism is Financed and How to Stop It*. New York: Taylor.

Elkins, Zachary, Andrew T. Guzman, and Beth A. Simmons. 2006. "Competing for Capital: The Diffusion of Bilateral Investment Treaties, 1960–2000." *International Organization* 60, no. 4: 811–846.

Elster, Jon. 1986. *Rational Choice*. New York University Press.
    1989. *Nuts and Bolts for the Social Sciences*. Cambridge University Press.

Etheredge, Lloyd S. 1978. *A World of Men: The Private Sources of American Foreign Policy*. Cambridge, MA: The MIT Press.

FATF. 1996. "The Forty Recommendations." Paris.
    2000a. "Report on Non-Co-operative Countries and Territories." Paris.
    2000b. "Review to Identify Non-Co-operative Countries or Territories: Increasing the Worldwide Effectiveness of Anti-Money Laundering Measures." Paris.
    2002. "Combating the Abuse of Non-Profit Organizations." Paris.
    2006a. "The Misuse of Corporate Vehicles, Including Trust and Corporate Service Providers." Paris.

2006b. *Mutual Evaluation Report on the United States of America.* Paris.

2008. "Terrorist Financing." Paris.

2011. "Laundering the Proceeds of Corruption." Paris. Accessed May 30, 2012 at www.fatf-gafi.org/media/fatf/documents/reports/Laundering%20the%20Proceeds%20of%20Corruption.pdf.

2012. "The FATF Recommendations: International Standards on Combating Money Laundering and the Financing of Terrorism and Proliferation." Paris.

FATF Expert Working Group on Evaluation and Implementation. 2009. "Securing Timely Access to Beneficial Ownership Information (Legal Persons)." Expert Group A. Washington, DC.

Fearon, James D. 1998. "Bargaining Enforcement and International Cooperation." *International Organization* 52, no. 2: 269–305.

Ferran, Lee and Jason Ryan. 2011. "Smooth Criminal? DOJ Wants Michael Jackson's Glove." *ABC News* October 25, 2011. Accessed May 30, 2012 at http://abcnews.go.com/Blotter/doj-seeks-jackson-glove-dictators-son/story?id=14812081#.T8agme3lPoE.

Ferwerda, Joras. 2009. "The Economics of Crime and Money Laundering: Does Anti-Money Laundering Policy Reduce Crime?" *Review of Law and Economics* 5: 903–929.

Field, Michael. 2011. "Web of Intrigue." *Fairfax NZ News* May 29, 2011. Accessed April 30, 2012 at www.stuff.co.nz/national/crime/5070730/Web-of-intrigue.

Financial Crimes Enforcement Network. 2006. *The Role of Domestic Shell Companies in Financial Crime and Money Laundering.* Washington, DC.

Financial Stability Forum. 2000. "Report of the Group on Offshore Centres." Basel.

"Find Your Own Offshore Wealth Haven." Accessed November 10, 2012 at www.quatloos.com/wealth-haven.pdf.

Findley, Michael, Macartan Humphreys, and Jeremy Weinstein. 2012a. "Draft proposal for a Pilot Registry for Political Science (PREPS)." Presented at the 8th Experiments in Governance and Politics Network Meeting, Stanford University, November 2–3.

Findley, Michael G., Daniel L. Nielson, and J. C. Sharman. 2014, forthcoming. "Orchestrating the Fight Against Anonymous Incorporation: A Field Experiment." In Kenneth W. Abbott, Philipp Genschel, Duncan Snidal, and Bernhard Zangl, eds. *International Organizations as Orchestrators.* Cambridge, UK: Cambridge University Press.

2013. "Using Field Experiments in International Relations: A Randomized Study of Anonymous Incorporation." *International Organization* 67, no. 3: 657–93.

Finkelstein, Ken H. 1998. *The Tax Haven Guidebook: How to Safeguard Your Money, Your Privacy, Your Paradise!* Big Island Media.

Francis, Clio. 2010. "Mystery 'Arms Firm' Director Revealed." *Fairfax NZ News* March 3, 2010. Accessed April 30, 2012 at www.stuff.co.nz/national/4090241/Mystery-arms-firm-director-revealed.

Friman, H. Richard, ed. 2009. *Crime and the Global Political Economy.* Boulder, CO: Lynne Reiner Publishers.

GAO. 2000. *Suspicious Banking Activities: Possible Money Laundering by US Corporations formed for Russian Entities.* Washington, DC: US Government Accountability Office.

2006. *Company Formations: Minimal Ownership Information is Collected and Available.* Washington, DC: US Government Accountability Office.

Gerber, Alan S. and Donald P. Green. 2003. "The Underprovision of Experiments in Political Science." *Annals of the American Academy of Political and Social Science* 589, no. 3: 94–112.

2012. *Field Experiments: Design, Analysis, and Interpretation.* New York: W.W. Norton.

Gerber, Alan S., Donald P. Green, and Edward H. Kaplan. 2004. "The Illusion of Learning from Observational Research." In *Problems and Methods in the Study of Politics*, edited by Ian Shapiro, Rogers Smith, and Tarek Massoud. Cambridge University Press.

Gilmore, William C. 1995. *Dirty Money: The Evolution of Money Laundering Counter-Measures.* Strasbourg: Council of Europe.

2011. *Dirty Money: The Evolution of Money Laundering Countermeasures*, 4th edn. Strasbourg: Council of Europe.

Gilpin, Robert. 1981. *War and Change in World Politics.* Cambridge University Press.

1987. *The Political Economy of International Relations.* Princeton University Press.

Global Financial Integrity. 2012. *Illicit Financial Flows from Developing Countries 2001–2010.* Washington, DC.

Global Witness. 2009. *Undue Diligence: How Banks do Business with Corrupt Regimes.* London.

2012. *Grave Secrecy: How a Dead Man can Own a UK Company and other Hair Raising Stories about Hidden Company Ownership from Kyrgyzstan and Beyond.* London.

Gneezy, Uri and Aldo Rustichini. 2000. "A Fine is a Price." *Journal of Legal Studies* 29, no. 1: 1–18.

Gordon. Richard K. 2008. "Trysts or Terrorists? Financial Institutions and the Search for Bad Guys." *Wake Forrest Law Review* 43: 699–738.

2009. "Laundering the Proceeds of Public Sector Corruption: A Preliminary Report." Washington, DC: World Bank.

2010. "International Organizations and the Regulation of Offshore Financial Centers: The IMF and the Imposition of Standards." In *Offshore Financial Centers and Regulatory Competition*, edited by Andrew P. Morriss. Washington, DC: American Enterprise Institute.

2011. "Losing the War Against Dirty Money: Rethinking Global Standards on Preventing Money Laundering and Terrorist Financing." *Duke Journal of Comparative and International Law* 21: 503–565.

Green, Donald P. and Ian Shapiro. 1995. *Pathologies of Rational Choice Theory: A Critique of Applications in Political Science*. New Haven, CT: Yale University Press.

Guzman, Andrew T. 2008. *How International Law Works: A Rational Choice Theory*. Oxford University Press.

Hafner-Burton, Emilie. 2009. *Forced to be Good: Why Trade Agreements Boost Human Rights*. Ithaca, NY: Cornell University Press.

Haufler, Virginia. 2001. *A Public Role for the Private Sector: Industry Self-Regulation in a Global Economy*. Washington, DC: Carnegie Endowment for International Peace.

2010. "Corporations in Zones of Conflict: Institutions, Issues, and Actors." In *Who Governs the Globe?*, edited by Deborah D. Avant, Martha Finnemore, and Susan K. Sell. Cambridge University Press.

Heng, Yee-Kuang and Ken McDonagh. 2008. "The Other War on Terror Revealed: Global Governmentality and the Financial Action Task Force's Campaign against Terrorist Financing." *Review of International Studies* 34, no. 4: 553–573.

Henkin, Louis. 1979. *How Nations Behave: Law and Foreign Policy*, 2nd edn. New York: Council on Foreign Relations Press.

Henry, James S. 2012. "The Price of Offshore Revisited: New Estimates for 'Missing' Global Wealth, Income, Inequality, and Lost Taxes." London: Tax Justice Network.

Hyde, Susan D. 2007. "The Observer Effect In International Politics: Evidence from a Natural Experiment." *World Politics* 60, no. 1: 37–63.

2010. "Experimenting in Democracy Promotion: International Observers and the 2004 Presidential Elections in Indonesia." *Perspectives on Politics* 8: 511–527.

2011. *The Pseudo-Democrat's Dilemma: Why Election Monitoring Became an International Norm*. Ithaca, NY: Cornell University Press.

Ikenberry, G. John. 2011. *Liberal Leviathan: The Origins, Crisis, and Transformation of American World Order*. Princeton University Press.

Internal Revenue Service. 1981. "Tax Havens and their Use by United States Tax-Payers." Prepared by Richard Gordon. Washington, DC. Accessed

August 14, 2013 at www.archive.org/stream/taxhavenstheirus01gord/taxhavenstheirus01gord_djvu.txt.

2012a. "Criminal Investigation Responds to Terrorism." Accessed December 15, 2012 at www.irs.gov/uac/Criminal-Investigation-Responds-to-Terrorism.

2012b. "International Investigations – Criminal Investigation (CI)." Accessed December 15, 2012 at www.irs.gov/uac/International-Investigations-Criminal-Investigation-(CI).

Jensen, Nathan M. 2003. "Democratic Governance and Multinational Corporations: Political Regimes and Inflows of Foreign Direct Investment." *International Organization* 57, no. 3: 587–616.

Kahneman, Daniel and Amos Tversky. 1979. "Prospect Theory: An Analysis of Decision under Risk." *Econometrica* 47, no. 2: 263–292.

Kantz, Carola. 2007. The Power of Socialization: Engaging the Diamond Industry in the Kimberley Process. *Business and Politics* 9, no. 3: 1–20.

Kaplan, Morton A. 1966. "The New Great Debate: Traditionalism versus Science in International Relations." *World Politics* 19, no. 1: 1–20.

Katzenstein, Peter, ed. 1996. *The Culture of National Security.* Ithaca, NY: Cornell University Press.

Keck, Margaret and Kathryn Sikkink. 1998. *Activists Beyond Borders: Advocacy Networks in International Politics.* Ithaca, NY: Cornell University Press.

Keene, Edward C. 2007. "A Case Study of the Construction of International Hierarchy: British Treaty-Making Against the Slave Trade in the Early Nineteenth Century." *International Organization* 61, no. 2: 311–339.

Kelley, Judith. 2008. "Assessing the Complex Evolution of Norms: The Rise of International Election Monitoring." *International Organization* 62, no. 2: 221–255.

Keohane, Robert O. 1997. "International Relations and International Law: Two Optics." *Harvard International Law Journal* 38, no. 2: 487–502.

Keohane, Robert O. and Joseph S. Nye, Jr., eds 1972. *Transnational Relations and World Politics.* Cambridge, MA: Harvard University Press.

Keohane, Robert O, Peter M. Haas, and Marc A. Levy, eds 1993. "Effectiveness of International Environmental Standards." In *Institutions for the Earth: Sources of Effective International Environmental Protection*, edited by Peter M. Haas, Robert Keohane, and Marc A. Levy. Cambridge, MA: MIT Press.

Kern, Holger Lutz and Jens Hainmueller. 2009. "Opium for the Masses: How Foreign Media Can Stabilize Authoritarian Regimes." *Political Analysis* 17, no. 4: 377–399.

Kerry, John. 1997. *The New War: The Web of Crime that Threatens America's Security*. New York: Simon and Schuster.

KPMG. 2004. *Global Anti-Money Laundering Survey 2004: How Banks are Facing up to the Challenge*.

2007. *Global Anti-Money Laundering Survey 2007: How Banks are Facing up to the Challenge*.

2011. *Global Anti-Money Laundering Survey 2011: How Banks are Facing up to the Challenge*.

Kindleberger, Charles P. 1973. *The World in Depression, 1929–1939*. Berkeley: University of California Press.

Kirshner, Jonathan. 2009. "Realist Political Economy: Traditional Themes and Contemporary Challenges." In *Handbook of International Political Economy: IPE as a Global Conversation*, edited by Mark Blyth. London: Routledge, pp.36–47.

Krasner, Stephen D. 1991. "Global Communications and National Power: Life on the Pareto Frontier." *World Politics* 43, no. 3: 336–366.

Lake, David A. 1993. "Leadership, Hegemony, and the International Economy: Naked Emperor or Tattered Monarch with Potential?" *International Studies Quarterly* 37, no. 4: 459–489.

Larmour. Peter. 2006. "Civilizing Techniques: Transparency International and the Spread of Anti-Corruption." In *Global Standards of Market Civilization*, edited by Brett Bowdon and Leonard Seabrooke. London: Routledge.

Lebovic, James and Erik Voeten. 2009. "The Cost of Shame: International Organizations and Foreign Aid in the Punishing of Human Rights Violators." *Journal of Peace Research* 46, no. 1: 79–97.

Leebron, David W. 2002. "Linkages." *American Journal of International Law* 96, no. 1: 5–27.

Levi, Michael and Peter Reuter. 2006. "Money Laundering." In *Crime and Justice: A Review of Research*, edited by M. Tonry. Chicago University Press.

Levin, Carl. 2006. "Statement of Senator Carl Levin at the Permanent Subcommittee on Investigations Hearing: Failure to Identify Company Owners Impedes Law Enforcement." US Senate, November 14, 2006. Accessed May 2012 at www.levin.senate.gov/newsroom/press/release/?id=db331b9d-7ac6–4143–943b-8119b0270ba7.

Levitt, Stephen D. and John A. List. 2007. "What do Laboratory Experiments Measuring Social Preferences Reveal about the Real World?" *Journal of Economic Perspectives* 21, no. 2: 153–174.

Lichtblau, Eric, David Rohde, and James Risen. 2011. "Shady Dealings Helped Qaddafi Build Fortune and Regime." *New York Times* March 24, 2011. Accessed May 30, 2012 at www.nytimes.com/2011/03/24/world/africa/24qaddafi.html?pagewanted=all.

Lipschutz, Ronnie D. and James K. Rowe. 2005. *Globalization, Governmentality, and Global Politics: Regulation for the Rest of Us?* London: Routledge.

Long, Andrew G., Timothy Nordstrom, and Kyeonghi Baek. 2007. "Allying for Peace: Treaty Obligations and Conflict between Allies." *Journal of Politics* 69, no. 4: 1103–1117.

Maliniak, Daniel, Susan Peterson, and Michael J. Tierney. 2012. "TRIP Around the World: Teaching, Research, and Policy Views of International Relations Faculty in 20 Countries." Report prepared by the Institute for the Theory and Practice of International Relations, May.

March, James G. and Johan P. Olsen. 1989. *Rediscovering Institutions: The Organizational Basis of Politics.* New York: Free Press.

  1998. "The Institutional Dynamics of International Political Orders." *International Organization* 52, no. 4: 943–969.

Mastanduno, Michael. 1998. "Economics and Security in Scholarship and Statecraft." *International Organization* 53, no. 4: 825–854.

Mattli, Walter and Tim Büthe. 2003. "Setting International Standards: Technological Rationality or Primacy of Power?" *World Politics* 56, no. 1: 1–42.

  2011. *The New Global Rulers: The Privatization of Regulation in the World Economy.* Princeton University Press.

Mayhew, David. 1974. *Congress: The Electoral Connection.* New Haven, CT: Yale University Press.

McDermott, Rose, Dustin Tingley, Jonathan Cowden, Giovanni Frazzetto, and Dominic Johnson. 2009. "Monoamine Oxidase A Gene (MAOA) Predicts Behavioral Aggression Following Provocation." *Proceedings of the National Academy of Sciences* 106, no. 7: 2118–2123.

Mearsheimer, John J. 1994/95. "The False Promise of International Institutions." *International Security* 19, no. 3: 5–49.

  2001. *The Tragedy of Great Power Politics.* New York: W.W. Norton.

Mercer, Jonathan. 1996. *Reputation in International Politics.* Ithaca, NY: Cornell University Press.

Michaels, Daniel and Margaret Coker. 2009. "Arms Seized by Thailand Were Iran-Bound." *Wall Street Journal* December 21, 2009. Accessed April 30, 2012 at http://online.wsj.com/article/SB126134401523799287.html.

Miklaszewski, Jim. 2004. "Avoiding Attacking Suspected Terrorist Mastermind." *NBC News* March 2, 2004. Accessed May 17, 2012 at www.msnbc.msn.com/id/4431601/ns/nbcnightlynews/t/avoiding-attacking-suspected-terrorist-mastermind/#.T7S0E-1jXXc.

Milner, Helen. 1988. *Resisting Protectionism: Global Industries and the Politics of International Trade.* Princeton University Press.

Mintz, Alex and Nehemia Geva. 1993. "Why Don't Democracies Fight Each Other? An Experimental Study." *Journal of Conflict Resolution* 37, no. 3: 484–503.

Mintz, Alex, Nehemia Geva, Steven B. Redd, and Amy Carnes. 1997. "The Effect of Dynamic and Static Choice Sets on Political Decision Making: An Analysis Using the Decision Board Platform." *American Political Science Review* 91, no. 3: 553–566.

Mistry, Percy S. 2009. "Making Mumbai an International Financial Centre." Report of the High-Powered Expert Commission for the Government of India. New Delhi.

Morrow, James D. 2007. "When Do States Follow the Laws of War?" *American Political Science Review* 101, no. 3: 559–572.

Moseley, J. Bruce, Kimberly O'Malley, Nancy J. Petersen, Terri J. Menke, Baruch Brody, David H. Kuykendall, John C. Hollingsworth, Carol M. Ashton, and Nelda P. Wray. 2002. "A Controlled Trial of Arthroscopic Surgery for Osteoarthritis of the Knee." *New England Journal of Medicine* 347: 81–88.

Mosley, Layna. 2009. "Private Governance for the Public Good? Exploring Private Sector Participation in Global Financial Regulation." In *Power, Interdependence and Non-State Actors in World Politics*, edited by Helen Milner and Andrew Moravcsik. Princeton University Press.

MSNBC. 2006. "Five Relatives of Terrorism Suspect Arrested." April 27, 2006. Accessed May 17, 2012 at www.msnbc.msn.com/id/12523560/ ns/us_news-security/t/five-relatives-terrorism-suspect-arrested/#. T7TNFu1jXXc.

Mueller, John and Mark G. Stewart. 2012. "The Terrorism Delusion: America's Overwrought Response to September 11." *International Security* 37, no. 1: 81–110.

Naim, Moises. 2006. *Illicit: How Smugglers, Traffickers, and Copycats are Hijacking the Global Economy*. New York: Anchor.

Naylor, R. T. 2004. *Wages of Crime: Black Markets, Illegal Finance, and the Underworld Economy*. Ithaca, NY: Cornell University Press.

NBC News. 2006. "Kin of American Held in Iraq Fight Back." February 13, 2006. Accessed May 17, 2012 at www.msnbc.msn.com/id/11225752/ ns/world_news-terrorism/t/nbc-kin-american-held-iraq-fight-back/#. T7SuiO1jXXc.

Nocera, Joe. 2012. "Turning the Tables on Russia." *New York Times* April 4, 2012. Accessed May 30, 2012 at www.nytimes.com/2012/04/17/ opinion/nocera-turning-the-tables-on-russia.html.

Nolan, Erika and Shannon Crouch. 2009. *Offshore Investments that Safeguard your Cash: Learn How Savvy Investors Grow and Protect their Wealth*. New York: McGraw Hill.

North, Douglass C. 1990. *Institutions, Institutional Change and Economic Performance*. Cambridge University Press.

Nye, Joseph S. Jr. and Robert O. Keohane. 1971. "Transnational Relations and World Politics: An Introduction." *International Organization* 25, no. 3: 329–349.

OECD. 1998. *Harmful Tax Competition – An Emerging Global Issue*. Paris.

2000. *Towards Global Tax Co-operation*. Paris.

2001. *Behind the Corporate Veil: Using Corporate Entities for Illicit Purposes*. Paris.

2007. *Integrity in Public Procurement: Good Practice from A to Z*. Paris.

Onuf, Nicholas. 1989. *A World of Our Making: Rules and Rule in Social Theory and International Relations*. Columbia: University of South Carolina Press.

Orlov, Mykola. 2004. "The Concept of Tax Haven: A Legal Analysis." *Intertax* 32: 95–111.

Oxfam. 2000. "Tax Havens: Releasing the Hidden Billions for Poverty Eradication." London.

Palan, Ronen. 2003. *The Offshore World: Sovereign Markets, Virtual Places, and Nomad Millionaires*. Ithaca, NY: Cornell University Press.

Palan, Ronen, Richard Murphy, and Christian Chavagneux. 2010. *Tax Havens: How Globalization Really Works*. Ithaca, NY: Cornell University Press.

Picciotto, Sol. 2011. *Regulating Global Corporate Capitalism*. Cambridge University Press.

Pieth, Mark. 2002. "Financing of Terrorism: Following the Money." *European Journal of Law Reform* 4: 115–126.

Preasca, Ion, Mihai Munteanu, and Matt Sarnecki. "Taylor Network Back in Business." *Organized Crime and Corruption Reporting Project*. July 15, 2012. Accessed August 13, 2012 at www.reportingproject.net/occrp/index.php/en/ccwatch/cc-watch-indepth/1592-taylor-network-back-in-business.

Price, Richard. 1998. "Reversing the Gun Sights: Transnational Civil Society and Land Mines." *International Organization* 52, no. 3: 613–644.

Putnam, Robert D. 1988. "Diplomacy and Domestic Politics: The Logic of Two-Level Games." *International Organization* 42, no. 3: 427–460.

Raustiala, Kal and Anne-Marie Slaughter. 2002. "International Law, International Relations and Compliance." In *Handbook of International Relations*, edited by Walter Carlsnaes, Thomas Risse, and Beth A. Simmons. Thousand Oaks, CA: Sage.

Redd, Steven. 2002. "The Influence of Advisers on Foreign Policy Decision Making: An Experimental Study." *Journal of Conflict Resolution* 46, no. 3: 335–364.

Reuter, Peter. 2012. "Introduction and Overview: The Dynamics of Illicit Flows." In *Draining Development: Controlling Flows of Illicit Finance from Developing Countries*, edited by Peter Reuter. Washington, DC: World Bank.

Reuter, Peter and Edwin M. Truman. 2004. *Chasing Dirty Money: The Fight Against Money Laundering*. Washington, DC: International Institute of Economics.

Rider, Barry A. K. 2004. "Law: The War on Terror and Crime and the Offshore Centres: The 'New' Perspective?" In *Global Financial Crime: Terrorism, Money Laundering, and Offshore Centres*, edited by Donato Masciandaro. Aldershot: Ashgate.

Risse-Kappen, Thomas, ed. 1995. *Bringing Transnational Relations Back In: Non-State Actors, Domestic Structures and International Institutions*. Cambridge University Press.

Rodrik, Dani. 2008. "The New Development Economics: We Shall Experiment, but How Shall We Learn?" Harvard Kennedy School Working Paper RWP08–055.

Rosenau, James N. and Ernst-Otto Czempiel, eds. 1992. *Governance without Government: Order and Change in World Politics*. Cambridge University Press.

Ruggie, John Gerard. 1998. *Constructing the World Polity: The Institutionalization of World Politics*. London: Routledge.

Russian Untouchables. 2012. "The Torture and Murder of Sergei Magnitsky and the Cover Up by the Russian Government." Accessed May 30, 2012 at http://russian-untouchables.com/eng/cover-up-presentation/.

Ryle, Gerard. 2011. "Inside the Shell: Drugs, Arms and Tax Scams." *Sydney Morning Herald* May 15, 2011. Accessed May 1, 2012 at www.smh.com.au/national/inside-the-shell-drugs-arms-and-tax-scams-20110514–1enkz.html.

Sahara Reporters. 2008. "How Bhadresh Gohil, a UK Lawyer Collaborated with James Ibori in Looting Delta State Treasury." September 26, 2008. Accessed January 4, 2013 at http://saharareporters.com/news-page/how-bhadresh-gohil-uk-lawyer-collaborated-james-ibori-looting-delta-state-treasury.

2011. "V-Mobile $37Million Shares Fraud-Bhadresh Gohil, Ibori's UK Lawyer Sentenced To 7 Years In Prison." March 8, 2011. Accessed January 4, 2013 at http://saharareporters.com/news-page/v-mobile-37million-shares-fraud-bhadresh-gohil-ibori's-uk-lawyer-sentenced-7-years-prison.

2012. "Ibori: The Chronicle of the Dramatic Trial and Guilty Verdict of a Thief. April 20, 2012." Accessed January 4, 2013 at http://saharareporters.com/report/ibori-chronicle-dramatic-trial-and-guilty-verdict-thief.

Saigol, Lina. 2012. "Iran Helps Syria Defy Oil Embargo." *Financial Times* May 18, 2012. Accessed May 30, 2012 at www.ft.com/intl/cms/s/0/9704c760–9abe-11e1–9c98–00144feabdc0.html#axzz1wOGjCtCW.

Sartori, Anne E. 2003. "An Estimator for Some Binary-Outcome Selection Models without Exclusion Restrictions." *Political Analysis* 11, no. 2: 111–138.

Saunders, Laura. 2012. "Israeli Tax Preparers Snared." *Wall Street Journal* June 17, 2012. Accessed January 9, 2013 at http://online.wsj.com/article/SB10001424052702303410404577468901036376714.html.

Schachter, Oscar. 1991. *International Law in Theory and Practice*. Leiden, Netherlands: Brill Academic Publishers.

Schäfferhoff, Marco, Sabine Campe, and Christopher Khan. 2009. "Transnational Public-Private Partnerships in International Relations – Making Sense of Concepts, Research Frameworks and Results." *International Studies Review* 11, no. 3: 451–474.

Schimmelfennig, Frank. 2001. "The Community Trap: Liberal Norms, Rhetorical Action, and the Eastwards Expansion of the European Union." *International Organization* 55, no. 1: 47–80.

Seabrooke, Leonard. 2006. *The Social Sources of Financial Power: Domestic Legitimacy and International Financial Orders*. Ithaca, NY: Cornell University Press.

Sharman, J. C. 2006. *Havens in a Storm: The Struggle for Global Tax Regulation*. Ithaca, NY: Cornell University Press.

2007. "Rationalist and Constructivist Perspectives on Reputation." *Political Studies* 55, no. 1: 20–37.

2011. *The Money Laundry: Regulating Criminal Finance in the Global Economy*. Ithaca, NY: Cornell University Press.

2012. "Chinese Capital Flows and Offshore Financial Centres." *Pacific Review* 25, no. 3: 317–337.

Shaxson, Nicholas. 2011. *Treasure Islands: Tax Havens and the Men who Stole the World*. London: The Bodley Head.

Shapiro, Jacob N. and David A. Siegel. 2007. "Underfunding in Terrorism Organizations." *International Studies Quarterly* 52, no. 2: 405–429.

Sheppard, Lee A. 2009. "Dear Former Tax Evasion Services Customer." *Tax Notes International* 56: 92.

Sikkink, Kathryn. 2011. *The Justice Cascade: How Human Rights Prosecutions are Changing World Politics*. New York: W.W. Norton.

Simmons, Beth A. 1998. "Compliance with International Agreements." *Annual Review of Political Science* 1: 75–93.

2000. "International Law and State Behavior: Commitment and Compliance in International Monetary Affairs." *American Political Science Review* 99, no. 4: 623–631.

2009. *Mobilizing for Human Rights: International Law in Domestic Politics*. Cambridge University Press.

2010. "Treaty Compliance and Violation." *Annual Review of Political Science* 13: 273–296.

Simmons, Beth A. and Allison Danner. 2010. "Credible Commitments and the International Criminal Court." *International Organization* 64, no. 2: 225–256.

Sinclair, Timothy J. 2005. *The New Masters of Capital: American Bond Ratings Agencies and the Politics of Credit-Worthiness*. Ithaca, NY: Cornell University Press.

Singleton, Royce Jr., Bruce C. Straits, Margaret M. Straits, and Ronal J. McAllister. 1988. *Approaches to Social Research*. New York: Oxford University Press.

Slaughter, Anne-Marie. 1995. "International Law in a World of Liberal States." *European Journal of International Law* 6, no. 1: 503–538.

Slovic, P. 1987. "Perception of Risk." *Science* 236: 280–285.

Snidal, Duncan. 2002. "Rational Choice and International Relations." In *Handbook of IR*, edited by Walter Carlsnaes, Thomas Risse, and Beth A. Simmons. Thousand Oaks, CA: Sage.

Sowore, Omoyele. 2007. "How James Ibori bought a Bombardier Challenger Jet." October 21, 2007. Accessed January 4, 2013 at www.nigeriavillagesquare.com/articles/omoyele-sowore/how-james-ibori-bought-a-bombardier-challenger-jet.html.

StAR (Stolen Asset Recovery) Initiative. 2011. *The Puppet Masters: How the Corrupt Use Legal Structures to Hide their Stolen Assets and What to do About It*. Prepared by, Emile van der Does de Willebois, Emily Halter, Robert A. Harrison, Ji Won Park, and J. C. Sharman. Washington, DC: World Bank.

Strasser, Stephen, ed. 2004. *The 9/11 Investigations: Staff Reports of the 9/11 Commission*. New York: Public Affairs.

Sullivan, Jeremiah John. 2011. "You Blow My Mind. Hey, Mickey!" *The New York Times Magazine* June 8, 2011. Accessed May 30, 2012 at www.nytimes.com/2011/06/12/magazine/a-rough-guide-to-disney-world.html?pagewanted=all.

Tannenwald, Nina. 1999. "The Nuclear Taboo: The United States and the Normative Basis of Nuclear Non-Use." *International Organization* 53, no. 3: 433–468.

Tax Justice Network. 2011. *Financial Secrecy Index*. Accessed October 17, 2012 at www.financialsecrecyindex.com/.

Tolbert, Pamela S. and Lynne G. Zucker. 1996. "The Institutionalization of Institutional Theory." In *Handbook of Organization Studies*, edited by Stewart R. Clegg, Cynthia Hardy, and Walter R. Nord. London: Sage, pp. 175–190.

Tomz, Michael. 2007. "Domestic Audience Costs in International Relations: An Experimental Approach." *International Organization* 61 no. 4: 821–840.

Transparency International. 2010. *Corruption Perceptions Index 2010.* Accessed 7 March 2010 at www.transparency.org/cpi2010/results.

United Nations Office for Drug Control and Crime Prevention. 1998. "Financial Havens, Banking Secrecy, and Money Laundering." Prepared by Jack Blum, Michael Levi, R. Thomas Naylor, and Phil Williams. Vienna.

United Nations Office on Drugs and Crime. 2011. "Estimating Illicit Financial Flows Resulting from Drug Trafficking and Other Transnational Organized Crime." Vienna.

United Nations Office on Drugs and Crime/World Bank. 2007. *Stolen Asset Recovery (StAR) Initiative: Challenges, Opportunities, and Action Plan.* Washington, DC.

United Nations. 1999. "International Convention for the Suppression of the Financing of Terrorism" Accessed August 14, 2013 at www.un.org/law/cod/finterr.htm.

United States District Court Southern District of New York. 2009. United States of America vs. Viktor Bout. Case 1:09-cr-01002-WHP, Document 5, filed November 3, 2009. Accessed August 14, 2013 at www.scribd.com/doc/71319832/Viktor-Bout-Indictment-Case-No-09-CR-1002.

US Senate Permanent Subcommittee on Investigations. 2004. "Money Laundering and Foreign Corruption: Enforcement and Effectiveness of the PATRIOT Act: Case Study Involving Riggs Bank." Washington, DC.

2005. "Money Laundering and Foreign Corruption: Enforcement and Effectiveness of the PATRIOT Act: A Supplemental Staff Report on US Accounts used by Augusto Pinochet." Washington, DC.

2006. *Tax Haven Abuses: The Enablers, The Tools, and Secrecy.* Washington, DC.

2010. *Keeping Foreign Corruption out of the United States: Four Case Histories.* Washington, DC.

Verret, J. W. 2010. "Terrorism Finance, Business Associations, and the 'Incorporation Transparency Act.'" *Louisiana Law Review* 70, no. 3: 857–910.

Vogel, David. 2008. "Private Global Business Regulation." *Annual Review of Political Science* 11: 262–281.

Von Stein, Jana. 2005. "Do Treaties Constrain or Screen? Selection Bias and Treaty Compliance." *American Political Science Review* 99, no. 4: 611–622.

2012. "The Engines of Compliance." In *Synthesizing Insights from International Law and International Relations*, edited by Jeffrey Dunoff and Mark Pollack. Cambridge University Press.

Walker, John and Brigitte Unger. 2009. "Measuring Global Money Laundering: The 'Walker Gravity Model.'" *Review of Law and Economics* 5, no. 4: 821–853.

Waltz, Kenneth. 1959. *Man, the State and War: A Theoretical Analysis*. New York: Columbia University Press.

1979. *Theory of International Politics*. New York: Addison Wesley Longman.

Weaver, Catherine E. 2008. *Hypocrisy Trap: The World Bank and the Poverty of Reform*. Princeton University Press.

Wechsler, William. 2001. "Follow the Money." *Foreign Affairs* 80: 40–57.

Wendt, Alexander. 1992. "Anarchy is what States Make of It: The Social Construction of Power Politics." *International Organization* 46, no. 2: 391–425.

1999. *Social Theory of International Politics*. Cambridge University Press.

World Bank. 2011. "Doing Business 2012: Doing Business in a More Transparent World." Washington, DC.

2012. "Measuring Financial Inclusion Unbanked: The Global Findex Database." Prepared by Asli Demirgur-Kunt and Leora Klapper. Washington, DC.

2013. *Doing Business*. Washington, DC.

Young, Oran. 1979. *Compliance and Public Authority*. Baltimore, MD: Johns Hopkins University Press.

Zill, Oriana and Lowell Bergman. 2000. "Frontline: The Black Peso Money Laundering System." *Frontline* 2000. Accessed December 8, 2012 at www.pbs.org/wgbh/pages/frontline/shows/drugs/special/blackpeso.html.

Zoromé, Ahmed. 2007. "The Concept of Offshore Financial Centers: In Search of an Operational Definition." International Monetary Fund Working Paper WP/07/87. Washington, DC.

Index

Cambridge Studies in International Relations

Made in United States
Orlando, FL
21 May 2022

18044031R00150